Children Exploring
Their World

Children Exploring Their World

Theme Teaching in Elementary School

Sean A. Walmsley

Associate Professor
Department of Reading
State University of New York at Albany

Heinemann
Portsmouth, NH

HEINEMANN
A division of Reed Elsevier Inc.
361 Hanover Street   Portsmouth, NH 03801-3912
Offices and agents throughout the world

Every effort has been made to contact the copyright holders for permission to reprint borrowed material where necessary. We regret any oversights that may have occurred and would be happy to rectify them in future printings of this work.

The author and publisher are grateful to the following for permission to reprint previously published material:

Excerpt from *Wordstruck* by Robert MacNeil. Copyright © 1989 by Neely Productions, Ltd. Used by permission of Viking Penguin, a division of Penguin Books USA Inc.

Figure 2-4 and Figure 2-5 from *The Warren County Fish Hatchery Self Guided Tour*. Reprinted with permission from the Warren County Dept. of Public Works, Warrensburg, N.Y.

Figure 3 from "Webbing and historical fiction," Donna E. Norton. *The Reading Teacher*, February 1993, p. 435. Reprinted with permission of Donna E. Norton and the International Reading Association.

Figure 5 from *Engaging Children's Minds* by Katz & Chard, 1989. Reprinted with permission of Ablex Publishing Corporation.

Library of Congress Cataloging-in-Publication Data
Children exploring their world /theme teaching in elementary school/
    by Sean A. Walmsley.
        p.   cm.
        "June 1993."
        Includes bibliographical references and index.
        ISBN 0–435–08804–1
        1. Education, Elementary—United States—Curricula. 2. Elementary
school teaching—United States. 3. Interdisciplinary approach in
education—United States. 4. Education, Elementary—United States—
Activity programs. I. Walmsley, Sean A.
LB1570.C487 1994   93–31221
372.13—dc20   CIP

Editor: Philippa Stratton
Production: J. B. Tranchemontagne
Design: Catherine Hawkes
Cover Illustration: Lois Leonard Stock

Printed in the United Sates of America on acid-free paper
99 98 97 96 95 94 CP 7 6 5 4 3 2 1

This book is dedicated to Bonnie, Katharine, and Jonathan and to theme-a-holics everywhere.

Contents

vii

Acknowledgments

This book is based on theme work done in three settings over the past ten years—in my graduate class *ERDG615: Reading & Writing* at SUNY-Albany, in the North Warren Central School District, and in a research project carried out in 1988 by the author under the auspices of the CRC Institute of SUNY-Albany.

I am grateful to Len Smith, who first taught me about theme-based instruction at Millfield School in Somerset, U.K., during the 1960s; to Trudy Walp, Director of Reading at North Warren Central Schools, New York, from whom I have learned so much over the years and who was particularly helpful with final drafts of the manuscript; to the hundreds of graduate students in my reading and writing courses who have tempered my theory with reality and whose class projects have taught me about so many topics; to the teachers and students of North Warren Central School District, who have demonstrated the long-term benefits of a theme-based curriculum; and to Sandra Ray, CRC Director, and the teachers who participated in the CRC Research Project program in 1988.

Louise Walmsley (no relation) helped to research background material for the book, and her assistance is gratefully acknowledged.

I am especially indebted to Philippa Stratton for her support, gentle and wise advice, and good humor. More than anyone, Philippa has helped me rediscover my writing voice. We also share a British passion for gardening.

Once a manuscript has been accepted, there's a lot of work still to be done to get it ready for publication. My thanks to Joanne Tranchemontagne, production editor; Robin Hogan, copy editor; Lois Leonard Stock, illustrator; and Catherine Hawkes, designer. Without their expertise, commitment, and care, this book would not now be in your hands. The assistance (and forbearance) of the production staff was especially appreciated because this book was typeset by the author (on a Macintosh Quadra 700, using Microsoft Word and Aldus PageMaker). I am grateful to Renee LeVerrier and Matt Schaepe at Heinemann, and to Fred Doyle and his colleagues in the University at Albany's Educational Communications Center, for their technical support and advice. I also learned a lot from Olav Kvern and Stephen Roth's *Real World PageMaker* (Bantam, 1990).

Finally, I want to thank the teachers whose themes are described in Part 2 of this book. We worked together on writing each of the chapters, and the process of transforming classroom practice into a written description and explanation was lengthy and usually done after a long day's teaching. I'm not sure I'd want my own teaching to be examined in such detail, and I appreciate even more their willingness to share their experiences in print.

Contributors

DONNA BEAUDRY

Martin Van Buren Elementary School, Kinderhook, New York

Donna Beaudry received her B.A. from Rhode Island College and her M.S. in Reading from State University of New York at Albany. She has taught in the Ichabod Crane Central School District for the past ten years. Her hobbies include tennis, the ocean, and picture books.

PAM BRUMBAUGH

Elmer Avenue School, Schenectady, New York

Pam Brumbaugh earned her B.A. in Elementary Education from the College of St. Rose in Albany, New York, and her M.S. in Reading from State University of New York at Albany. She is now in her sixth year at Elmer Avenue Elementary School in the Schenectady City School District, where she has taught third grade and a third-fourth combination.

ANNE-MARIE CAMP

Arongen Elementary School, Clifton Park, New York

Anne-Marie Camp received her B.A. in Early Childhood Education from State University of New York at Brockport and her M.S. in Elementary Education at State University of New York at New Paltz. Anne-Marie has taught kindergarten and has been director of a day-care center. She currently teaches kindergarten in Arongen School, Shenendehowa Central School District, Clifton Park, New York. She is coauthor of *Teaching Kindergarten: A Developmentally-Appropriate Approach* and *Teaching Kindergarten: A Theme-Centered Curriculum.*

MARY CAPOBIANCO

Glenmont Elementary School, Glenmont, New York

Mary Capobianco received her B.A. in English, her M.A. in English Education, and her M.S. in Reading from State University of New York at Albany. She has taught ninth and tenth grade English, fifth grade reading, and study skills at the community college level. Since 1985, she has been teaching fourth grade and a multi-age fourth-fifth combination class.

DEBBY FABIAN

North Warren Elementary School, Brant Lake, New York

Debby Fabian graduated from State University of New York at Geneseo in 1973 and has been teaching in the North Warren School District since then. She has taught second grade and kindergarten and is now in her tenth year as a first grade teacher at North Warren Elementary School. Debby lives in Chestertown with her husband, Robert. They have two children: Allison, a sophomore at North Warren High School, and John, currently in the fifth grade.

JANICE FINGAR

Martin Van Buren Elementary School, Kinderhook, New York

Janice Fingar received her bachelor's degree from State University of New York at Potsdam and her master's from North Adams State College, North Adams, MA. She has taught in Ichabod Crane Central Schools for the past twelve years. Janice loves to travel and play tennis. She's also active in the Columbia County 4-H program.

MARY ELLEN GADDY

North Warren Elementary School, Brant Lake, New York

Mary Ellen (Mel) Gaddy graduated from State University of New York at Plattsburgh in 1975. She has taught second, fourth, and fifth grades in North Warren Central Schools and is now in her twelfth year as a first grade teacher in North Warren Elementary School. Mel and her husband, David, live in Brant Lake with their two children, Erin and Daniel.

COLLEEN McNALL

Hamagrael Elementary School, Delmar, New York

Colleen McNall has her B.A. in Elementary Education from the College of St. Rose in Albany, New York, and her M.S. in Reading from State University of New York at Albany. She taught fourth grade for two years at St. Augustine's, Lansingburg, New York. For the past four years she has taught remedial math, and now second grade, in the Bethlehem Central School District, Delmar, New York.

JOANNE KELLY PAULSON

North Warren Middle School, Pottersville, New York

Joanne Kelly Paulson is currently teaching fifth grade in North Warren Middle School, Pottersville, New York. She earned her B.A. in Sociology from the College of St. Rose in Albany, New York, and her M.S. in Reading from

State University of New York at Albany. She enjoys traveling through the western states and the western provinces of Canada, and has spent several summers fishing for salmon in Alaska. Her hobbies include crafts, photography, and music.

BONNIE BROWN WALMSLEY

Arongen Elementary School, Clifton Park, New York

Bonnie Brown Walmsley received her B.A. in Early Childhood Education from Kent State University and her M.S. in Reading at Harvard Graduate School of Education. She teaches kindergarten in Arongen School, Shenendehowa Central School District, Clifton Park, New York. Bonnie is coauthor of *Teaching Kindergarten: A Developmentally-Appropriate Approach* and *Teaching Kindergarten: A Theme-Centered Curriculum*, both published by Heinemann in 1992. Bonnie has taught Headstart, first grade, second grade, and kindergarten.

MARGARET WERTIME

North Warren Elementary School, Brant Lake, New York

Margaret Wertime graduated from State University of New York at Plattsburgh in 1971 and has been teaching at North Warren Central Schools ever since. She taught third grade for five years and has been teaching first grade for the past seventeen years in North Warren Elementary School. Margaret and her husband, George, live in Chestertown, New York. They have two daughters: Elizabeth, a freshman at SUNY-Geneseo, and Laurie, an eighth grader at North Warren.

TANYA WILLCOX-SCHNABL

Farnsworth Middle School, Guilderland, New York

Tanya Willcox-Schnabl attended State University of New York at Albany and graduated with a B.A. in English Education and an M.S. in Reading. She has taught eleventh and twelfth grade English and for the past five years has been teaching sixth grade language arts and social studies at Farnsworth Middle School in Guilderland, New York. Tanya and her husband, Eric, live in the country with their new daughter Kaitlyn and their dog, Jake. She enjoys hiking, camping, and cooking.

Introduction

This book is about theme teaching and its role in helping children develop their literacy abilities and enlarge their knowledge of the world.

The primary mission of elementary schools has always been to teach basic literacy skills. Over the years, especially since the Second World War, this mission became more and more focused on the teaching and learning of reading skills. Donald Graves's pioneering studies in the mid-1970s showed the extent to which reading skills instruction had overwhelmed the elementary curriculum, and he argued that composing—not just editing skills—should occupy more of the curriculum and more of the teacher's attention. More recently, studies of children's knowledge of literature and the place of literature in the language arts curriculum (Ravitch & Finn, 1987; Walmsley & Walp, 1989; Walmsley, 1992) have raised questions about the somewhat peripheral role of literature in the elementary curriculum. Some have argued that children's experiences with literature are too narrowly focused on fiction and ignore nonfiction literature (Venezky, 1987; Wray, 1985). Studies of children's knowledge of history (Ravitch, 1985), geography (Grosvenor, 1985), and science (Mullis & Jenkins, 1988) have also lamented children's historical, geographic, and scientific understanding of their world.

Anyone who reads these studies or has observed closely in elementary schools might conclude, as I have, that the elementary curriculum has become rather unbalanced. With the exception of mathematics, which has its sacrosanct position in the daily schedule, the content areas (especially history, geography, and science) have been systematically given less attention than language arts, and it's tempting to argue that disappointing performance on content area assessments is simply a result of too little time devoted to these subjects. At particular risk are music and art. In many elementary schools, budget cuts have eliminated or seriously threatened these two areas.

But things are changing. Donald Graves's work in the 1970s has spawned two generations of classroom teachers and teacher-trainers committed to increasing the presence of composing in the writing curriculum and increasing writing in language arts and subject areas. Literature is enjoying a revival again, too, vindicating children's literature authorities like Charlotte Huck, who had been saying all along that literature should play a central role in the literacy curriculum. The newly formed National Council on History Education has not only reminded elementary schools of their obligation to teach history as history (rather than as a basal reader), but it now provides teachers with a new framework for designing history curricula. Similar efforts are being made in geography and in science.

These new pressures to do a better job of teaching content areas in elementary school come at a time when teachers are already being blamed for declining (or at least the appearance of declining) basic literacy test scores. A teacher might despair, therefore, that there really isn't enough time to restore these subjects to a curriculum that isn't able to keep up with the demands of even basic literacy. And there's always the feeling among some teachers that these new demands are simply evidence of a swinging pendulum, and interest in such things as science and history will surely pass.

As I have argued elsewhere (see Walmsley, 1991), I think these criticisms of elementary school curricula shouldn't be dismissed lightly. The problem is that many of the criticisms come from politicians and academics with a conservative political agenda (e.g., Finn, 1991; Hirsch, 1987), and sometimes teachers are prone to disregard their arguments or their logic simply on the basis of politics. For example, I would take issue with Hirsch's analysis of the current state of literacy among young children, and the reasons for it. I agree with Bracey (1991) that the situation isn't nearly as bad as Hirsch makes it out to be, but I think Hirsch is right when he says that we have created a largely contentless elementary curriculum. We *have* made reading and writing skills the be-all and end-all of the elementary curriculum, and we've forgotten what it was that we learned reading and writing for—namely, to gain access to something else, be it knowledge, pleasure, or satisfaction. Elementary schools do spend too much time preparing children for, but not engaging them sufficiently in, knowledge about the world. However, Hirsch's proposal for reforming the elementary curriculum, and the elementary curriculum he has subsequently offered, seems too narrowly focused on traditional knowledge and values.

The challenge, it seems to me, is to rethink the elementary curriculum so that it better balances reading and writing within language arts and better balances language arts with other subject areas. One way to do this is to simply reapportion the time we devote to each so that the subject areas are properly attended to and not simply relegated to the afternoon or excluded altogether. This would be a good first step, but it doesn't really address the problem of a fragmented curriculum in which all the areas are treated as separate aspects of the curriculum. I think a more satisfactory approach is to think of reading and writing (as well as speaking, listening, and drama) as processes that are best learned within the context of exploring knowledge of the world, rather than as subject areas in their own right. So, instead of a language arts block, a math block, a science block, and a history block, we think instead of the subject areas with reading, writing, speaking, listening, and drama as vehicles for accessing, exploring, and communicating content knowledge. Thus, we read in order to gain access to history, to geography, to science, and so on; we write, also to gain access to knowledge—Emig's (1977) notion of writing as a mode of learning; Graves's (1983) and Murray's (1989) notion of writing to find out what you know—and to communicate what we've found out. We talk formally and informally about what we know and what others know (Moffett & Wagner,

1992); we listen to and learn from each other's knowledge. In other words, we can tuck language arts inside the content areas, and teach them both together. As we do so, children acquire, extend, and deepen their knowledge of the world, while at the same time they develop their language abilities.

An important element of this approach is that children will come into contact with real knowledge as represented in real books and other materials (e.g., newspapers, magazines, documents, documentaries, paintings, photographs), as opposed to what is largely fabricated, second-hand knowledge—the watered-down, conflict-free, vocabulary-controlled, abstracted versions typically found in traditional elementary textbooks. Until fairly recently, there really wasn't an abundance of nonfiction materials suitable for younger children (in grades K–4), and so it was quite a challenge for an elementary teacher to assemble a collection of good nonfiction literature. But in the last ten years, there's been an explosion of interest in nonfiction children's literature, and while some topics are not well represented—try finding good nonfiction material on any of the U.S. presidents other than Washington and Lincoln—the quantity of nonfiction material continues to increase, and its quality steadily improves.

I should also say that when I talk about "knowledge," I'm not referring to the rote memorization and regurgitation of largely factual information that characterized my own school days in England in the 1950s and 1960s. I use the term *knowledge* in its broadest sense to mean that children will come into contact with the history, geography, science, and literature of a broad spectrum of people and events, present and past, from Western and other cultures, and representing different points of view. One's understanding of the world accumulates across an entire lifetime, so it may be rather artificial to assign a particular body of knowledge to elementary school, but there is so much knowledge and so much new knowledge each year (quite apart from the ever growing number of books in which that knowledge is represented), that only a small fraction can be accessed in a given year or even across the elementary years. Thus it makes sense to think carefully about the topics we want students to encounter in a given year, or across the grades, so that we don't inadvertently overdo certain topics at the expense of others and so that children's exposure is indeed both broad and deep. We don't need to agree on a specific set of topics for elementary students, especially not a standardized curriculum, because what's important is that children come into contact with substantive knowledge, not that they come into contact with a particular set of knowledge. For example, it really doesn't matter if children study whales or penguins or sharks because studying any animal in any depth will bring to the surface knowledge about animals' roles in nature, their relationship with humans, and our responsibilities to them. Not every country can be studied (although it would be useful for children to have more than a passing knowledge about the countries in different regions of the world), but in studying even a small number of countries, useful knowledge about their history, cultures, literature, geography, economics, and people will be gained that eventually gets linked to other information picked up during the course of a lifetime. There is literally not enough time to cover even a fraction of what might be appropriate for an elementary school child to know about history, geography, science, and literature. All the more reason, then, to ensure that the topics we do cover are substantive and worthwhile.

Exploring knowledge through themes offers the elementary teacher unique opportunities for studying content while at the same time nurturing children's language abilities without adding to an already overcrowded curriculum. Themes allow teachers and students to explore meaningful topics in science, history, geography, and other subjects in sufficient depth and breadth so that children's learning goes well beyond the surface. Themes encourage integration not only of content but also of language arts so that children see how things are connected by actually connecting them.

For brief periods in educational history, approaches bearing a strong resemblance to the approach advocated in this book are proposed, flourish for a while, and then disappear. While the particulars vary, what these approaches all have in common is that they encourage students to study topics of interest to them, explore books and other media to acquire new knowledge, and share their new knowledge with others.

In the 1870s, Francis Parker (1894) proposed, and for a few years carried out, a project in which children pursued field-based studies in such subjects as geography and geology as their entire curriculum. Some older teachers will probably recall "unit" teaching approaches, popular in teacher training institutions in the 1940s and 1950s; units were essentially what we now call themes. In the 1960s, the theme approach was again revived, partly as an antidote to depersonalized skills curricula and partly because of the popularity of British infant school programs where theme work had always been a prominent feature of the curriculum. In the late 1980s, the approach again became popular, especially among early childhood educators, mostly because of its fit with the philosophy of developmentally appropriate education (Bredekamp, 1987; Katz & Chard, 1989; Strickland, 1989; Strickland & Morrow, 1990) but partly, too, because it had been endorsed by the whole language movement (Goodman, 1986; Edelsky et al., 1991). Nevertheless, the theme approach has never become "institutionalized" in American elementary schools; it has yet to become part of the mainstream activities typically found in elementary school classrooms.

The purpose of this book is to further the cause of institutionalizing theme work in elementary school, not only by addressing the many issues that surround theme-based instruction, but also by laying out principles and practical procedures for use in the regular classroom and providing a number of case studies showing different kinds of themes in real K–6 classrooms.

The book is divided into two major parts. In Part 1, I address the theory and practice of teaching through themes in elementary school. The purpose of this discussion is to place the theme approach into the broader context of elementary school learning and curriculum. I also describe the principles and a range of practical techniques for creating and carrying out themes in the classroom. Part 2 is entirely devoted to descriptions of themes drawn from kindergarten to grade six. These projects are varied in their topics and in their activities, but they all exemplify in one way or another the principles described in Part 1. I have deliberately drawn examples across the grades from kindergarten to grade six and across different content areas (science, social studies, and so on) so as to illustrate the practicability of the approach in a variety of settings and content areas.

Part One

Theory and Practice of Teaching Through Themes

Sean A. Walmsley

In this first part, I want to explore some of the underlying theory surrounding teaching through themes. There isn't a single definition of "theme"—for some, the terms *theme* and *unit* are synonymous; for others, a theme simply involves coordinating different kinds of activities—and there are many different approaches to theme teaching, including ones that differ quite substantially from the approach taken in this book. In the next few pages, I'd like to explain the range of definitions and approaches, and consider a number of issues that teachers need to think about as they embark on—or deepen their understanding of—theme teaching. I'll start with definitions, and then move on to some of the issues. Following that, I will devote a considerable amount of time to the practical business of designing, carrying out, and assessing themes in the classroom.

WHAT IS A THEME?

A simple definition of a theme is that it's a "central idea" (Haggitt, 1975) and an organizing framework for teaching and learning. A theme is something substantive and worth exploring; it provides teachers and students with a focus for their teaching and learning. A theme is composed of appropriate activities that explore topics that make up, relate to, or stem from the central idea. Thus, a theme comprises both meaning (the central idea) and structure (the way in which the central idea is explored).

Primarily, I think of themes as being focused on meaning or content (Greece and Rome, survival, the post office, or Martin Luther King, Jr.). But a theme can also focus on form (the alphabet, poetry, mysteries, humor, or personification). Typically, specific skills (reading skills such as getting the main idea, word identification, letter knowledge, detecting the author's mood, tone, or purpose; writing skills such as paragraphing, spelling, handwriting, or grammar) aren't really appropriate for themes; these should be taught within the context of a theme or outside of it.

3

Different Definitions of Themes

Like the term *whole language*, people define the terms *theme* and *theme-based instruction* in very different ways. In recent articles and books, I have encountered "themes," "thematic units," "theme cycles," "theme explorations," and "theme immersions," not to mention the notion of "theme" as in the "underlying theme of a novel." Do they all mean the same thing? For example, if you ask a kindergarten teacher who organizes her curriculum around a letter of the week, she'll probably tell you that she teaches through themes. Teachers who use basal reading series will often claim their program is "theme-based." One of the problems in defining themes is that a theme can mean a central idea (meaning), but it also can be used to denote an organizing framework (structure). While we might take the kindergarten teacher to task for having no central idea in terms of pursuing meaning for her letter of the week, she certainly has a structure for her instruction. Themes need to have an organizing framework, but without a central idea (whether focused on content or form), I don't think they can legitimately be called themes. In fact, these contentless themes ought to be called "units."

One way of defining themes is according to their focus or purpose: is it to enlarge children's knowledge of content, skills, or both? Another is according to the nature and extent of integration: are themes supposed to integrate language arts, integrate language arts with content areas, or integrate content areas? Another definition relates to who puts the theme together: is it created ahead of time by the teacher, constructed as it goes along by teacher and students, or is it entirely a student-run project? A fourth dimension is how substantive the theme is: does it pursue important concepts, or is it simply a set of enjoyable but intellectually trivial activities?

Content vs. Skills

Most of the people who have written about theme-based instruction (for example, Edelsky et al., 1991; Gamberg et al., 1988; Katz & Chard, 1989; Pappas et al., 1990; Walmsley et al., 1992a; Walmsley & Walp, 1990; Weaver et al., 1993; Wilson et al., 1993) say that *the primary purpose of themes is to explore content, with skills development as a secondary goal.* Edelsky et al. (1991, p. 65) put it succinctly: "Symbolic skills and tools serve content, not the other way around." Even though they don't call their approach "theme-based," Pigdon and Woolley's (1993) integrated approach to children's learning provides good examples of themes that integrate substantive content learning with skills development; Walmsley and Walp (1990) describe a theme-based curriculum for third and fourth grade that tucks skills within the themes; Walmsley et al. (1992b) describe the same for kindergarten. However, Wray (1985) argues for an equal balance between content and skills, and Moss (1984) appears to have literary skills as the primary purpose of her "focus units." (Her approach is widely used and respected; and, to be fair, she calls them units, not themes.)

I have already suggested that a theme can legitimately focus on either content or form, and so a theme on personification isn't any less a theme than one on courage. I do have a problem, however, with themes that focus primarily or exclusively on skills. Many units in basal reading series come under this heading. Although the unit might be called "Courage," with several extracts from books relating to courage, the exercises and activities are primarily designed to teach comprehension, vocabulary, and word study techniques (and frequently the skills instruction isn't even related to the theme readings). What's missing from these themes is any sustained effort to focus the children's attention on the dimensions of courage or to have them enlarge their understanding of the concept. "Courage" is simply an organizing framework for gathering a number of pieces of literature; it isn't the conceptual focus of the instruction.

A wholly skills-based approach is represented by the letter of the week themes typically found in kindergartens. The purpose of these themes is to introduce children to each of the letters and to ensure that through repeated exposure children will learn the names and sounds of the letters—a major goal of the traditional kindergarten. Thus, during the "L" week, children will be read books by authors whose names begin with an L (Arnold Lobel, Leo Leonni, and so on); they will identify items in the environment that begin with or contain L; they'll write the letter L in their journals, and so on. The only thing that holds these letter themes together are the letters themselves, and so these themes are without content, unless by accident content learning takes place within an activity that is organized around the letter L—for example, doing a mini-theme on letters (i.e., mail).

In this book, the approach I take is that a theme should focus on content or form (whether drawn from subject areas or not), and that skills should be subsumed within the exploration of content. This doesn't diminish the importance of skills, but it puts them where they belong and teaches them within a meaningful context.

Themes and Integration

To what extent is a theme defined in terms of how it integrates language arts, other processes (e.g., math, music, art), or content areas? Lipson et al. (1993) suggest two broad types of themes: *intradisciplinary* themes (integrating elements of language arts, usually with literature as the central focus) and *interdisciplinary* themes (involving other subject areas). Jacobs (1989) goes one step further by categorizing themes as *interdisciplinary* (viewing a topic from more than one discipline), *crossdisciplinary* (viewing one discipline from the perspective of another), *multidisciplinary* (juxtaposing several disciplines randomly), *pluridisciplinary* (juxtaposing several related disciplines), and *transdisciplinary* (beyond the disciplines). I cannot imagine a theme that does not meaningfully integrate elements of language arts (reading, writing, speaking, listening). How could one genuinely explore a substantive topic without reading about it, writing about it, and discussing it? And so integration of language arts is an essential feature of a theme. On the other hand, I can easily imagine themes—and I propose some later—that don't integrate math, music, or art and that don't cross subject area or discipline boundaries. I like Jacobs's idea of themes that weave in and out of disciplines (these work especially well in secondary school), but I don't think a theme has to do this, and therefore one that doesn't is no less of a theme for staying within the confines of a single discipline. Although themes will frequently integrate processes (such as math, music, and art) and content areas, integration of processes other than language arts and of subject areas or disciplines is not a defining characteristic of a theme. What's critical is that whatever integration occurs does so because it fits the purpose and nature of the theme and helps children more effectively explore the "central idea."

Teacher-Generated vs. Student-Generated Themes

Most of those who have written about themes propose or describe *teacher-generated themes* (Gamberg et al., 1988; Haggitt, 1975; Katz & Chard, 1989; Kostelnik, 1991; Pappas et al., 1990; Pigdon & Woolley, 1993; Thompson, 1991; Walmsley et al., 1992a). Recently, however, Bess Altwerger and others have proposed and described *student-generated themes* (Altwerger & Flores, 1991; Altwerger & Flores, 1994; Byrum & Pierce, 1993; Edelsky et al., 1991; Harste et al., 1987; Manning et al., 1994; Strube, 1993), and this has led others (Weaver et al., 1993) to worry about the appropriateness of teacher-generated themes.

Bess Altwerger differentiates between "thematic units" (topics used to teach subjects or skills), and what she calls "theme cycles" (subjects and skills used to explore topics). The former are teacher-oriented, predetermined, and based on the teacher's learning goals, while theme cycles are student-oriented, have negotiated topics, share responsibility between teacher and student, and are based on students' and teacher's knowledge, questions, and interests. Manning et al. (1994) similarly differentiate between "traditional theme units" (selected by teachers, dictated by the curriculum, and consisting of a behavioristic theoretical framework), and "theme immersion" (topics that are negotiated between teacher and student, focused on broad issues, and have a constructivist theoretical framework).

There is no doubt that Altwerger & Flores and Manning, et al. challenge not only skills-based themes but also teacher-generated themes, and Altwerger's notion of a theme cycle represents a unique contribution to the theme literature. On the other hand, I see little evidence in the work of the authors cited above (with the possible exception of Wray, 1985) that the primary mission of themes is to learn subject areas and literacy skills—in a narrow sense—nor do I see that their philosophical orientation is behavioristic. In fact, most of them reject narrow subject area learning and specific literacy skills as their primary purpose, and they either implicitly or explicitly embrace constructivist approaches to learning (see Katz & Chard, 1989; Walmsley et al., 1992a). What really sets Altwerger's approach apart from all others is that she sees themes as negotiated topics for collaborative exploration that lead to further questions and further topics. It's an open-ended approach that is truly child-centered. Its practicability within the existing curricular framework of American public schools aside, it nonetheless faithfully represents the whole language philosophy from which it is drawn.

In defining what counts as themes, I think there's room for both teacher-generated and student-generated themes, and provided that teachers are sensitive to children's needs and interests, they shouldn't feel guilty about playing a major role in developing and carrying out themes. On the other hand, if I were teaching in an elementary school this year, I probably couldn't resist trying a theme cycle alongside the themes I had created for the year.

Substantive vs. Trivial Themes

There seems to be agreement among those who have written about themes that too many themes in elementary school lack substance. What's meant by this is that the theme purports to be about some content (say, bears) but it treats it in a trivial fashion by merely doing activities that have only a surface relationship to the topic or by using the theme as an excuse to teach literacy skills. Routman (1991) calls such themes "correlational": they may draw activities from the various disciplines (art, math, science, etc.), but they fail to integrate them in any meaningful way; rather, teachers are more interested in having students do "fun type" activities around a topic. What's missing from these themes, according to Routman, is "the development of important concepts and skills" (p. 277). These are the themes that Edelsky et al. (1991) criticize for exploiting "music, art, and literature for nonmusical, nonart, nonliterary ends" (p. 65), and for "Disneyfying" important topics.

In the books and articles I have read on themes, I have found very few examples of trivial themes, but in elementary classrooms I have visited over the years, I've observed many themes that lacked substance. The notion that themes should be defined in terms of substantive explorations of important ideas isn't practiced as widely as it should be, despite a plethora of books that show how substantive themes can be created and carried out.

Different Kinds of Themes

Over the many years I have been exploring theme-based instruction, I have found it helpful to categorize themes according to their source rather than on the basis of whether they are content or skills driven, whose themes they are, or the nature of their integration. From my perspective, it seems that there are six major sources for themes: content area, calendar-related, conceptual, biographical, current events, and form. All of these themes integrate language arts, and most of them integrate subject areas with language arts.

Content area themes are drawn from science (life cycle of the butterfly), social studies (westward movement), math (measurement), health (food and nutrition), music (musical instruments, Bach, jazz), art (Picasso, impressionists), architecture (colonial houses, Native American homes), and business (global economy).

Calendar-related themes, popular in elementary school, include those drawn from seasons, those that celebrate national holidays (Martin Luther King, Jr., President's Day, Veterans Day), those that celebrate "folk" events (Valentine's Day, Groundhog Day), and those that celebrate religious events (Easter, Hanukkah, Chinese New Year).

Conceptual themes involve studying aspects of an abstract concept such as growing and changing relationships, or survival.

Biographical themes focus on specific individual people, their lives, and their contributions (poets, painters, musicians, politicians, inventors, sports players, authors and illustrators, and so on).

Current events themes focus on specific political, natural, geographical, religious and other events (international, national, or local) that are, by definition, in the news.

Form themes focus on form rather than content (genres such as humor or mystery, aspects of language such as personification or characterization).

These different kinds of themes are explained in more detail on pages 11–18.

Primary Ingredients of Theme Teaching

In a theme, teachers and children work through a topic in a number of ways. At the very least they *read* about the topic with the teacher reading aloud, children reading independently, and/or teachers and children reading together; *write* about the topic to learn more about it, to pursue a specific subtopic, or to communicate to others what has been found out; *talk* about the topic informally and formally with the teacher and other children; *do some activities or a project* on the topic; and *present or share* what has been explored. A teacher might incorporate mathematics, music, or art, depending on the nature of the theme and the suitability of these processes in helping children work it through. As teachers and children engage in a theme, opportunities will inevitably arise for both direct and indirect teaching of the strategies and skills needed by the children to accomplish the tasks they have undertaken. But these skills should not be the focus of the theme.

Relationship of Themes to the Regular Curriculum

At one extreme, themes could define the entire elementary curriculum; at the other, they could represent "special" projects that supplement the traditional curriculum. Or, the curriculum could alternate between themes and regular instruction. One way of thinking about themes is to see them as "intensive" studies of particular topics, while the regular curriculum covers topics more rapidly, and more "extensively." Thus, a teacher who uses a traditional textbook for the subject areas could cover the science curriculum broadly with a textbook, but create several themes that explore a few science topics in-depth and alternate between the textbook and the themes.

If the regular curriculum is heavily skills-based, then themes could be introduced as a means of balancing content with skills instruction. One way of doing this would be to alternate between themes and skills instruction; another would be to create themes for the entire year but weave skills instruction into each theme, using the literature and the writing as the major sources for reading and writing skills instruction.

A question I am often asked by elementary teachers is how themes and basal reading series can coexist. If the basal is not organized around themes, or if the basal's themes are simply labels for a collection of loosely related activities, then it probably makes sense to develop themes independently of the basal and alternate between the basal and the themes. If the basal does have themes, they most likely will be "correlational" (Routman, 1991) and thus will need some modification to make them substantive. This isn't all that difficult to do if you follow the techniques suggested in this book. Sometimes it's easier to modify an existing theme than to start one from scratch.

The Unique Contribution of Theme Teaching

The traditional elementary curriculum focuses primarily on literacy skills, and it does so in a highly fragmented fashion where reading is largely kept separate from writing, reading skills from reading literature, composing from editing, and language arts from content areas. Literary, historical, scientific, aesthetic, and cultural knowledge is a primary focus of secondary school but a secondary focus of the elementary school, if it's a focus at all. Themes restore content as the primary focus; they also integrate knowledge and skills, and they coordinate and combine aspects of the curriculum that are presently fragmented. While the major purpose of themes is to acquire and communicate genuine knowledge about worthwhile topics, learning how to gain access to this knowledge is, of course, important (you need the tools to do the job); but the skills themselves aren't the primary goal of a theme any more than learning how to use a saw is the primary goal of making a cabinet. One of the benefits of making genuine knowledge the primary object of a theme is that it not only increases children's knowledge of the world, but also helps develop many of their language abilities (e.g., reading, research skills, comprehension, writing, etc.). Wray (1985) makes the point that teachers are more concerned about teaching skills, while children are more interested in the content; I'd like to think that content and skills are equally important to teachers and children. Integration of knowledge and skills also has particular benefits for at-risk children because it allows and encourages remedial instruction to be less fragmented, a major problem facing at-risk children (Allington, 1992).

A second reason for teaching themes is that they offer such good opportunities for combining the different facets of language arts (*reading*, both independently and collaboratively; *writing*, in a variety of forms—taking notes, paraphrasing, writing drafts, creating final products; *speaking and listening*, to discuss work in progress, to talk about final products; and *drama*, to roleplay an aspect of a topic), and for combining, where appropriate, the different content areas (e.g., studying topics that integrate science and social studies or incorporate math, music, or art).

Third, themes offer great opportunities for balancing different kinds of reading materials. Reading in elementary school has long been dominated by the reading of narrative—mostly fictional—literature in extract or full-length form. Themes, especially if they range across the different kinds described previously, encourage students and teachers to read a wide variety of books and other literacy material that goes far beyond narrative fiction.

The same argument holds for writing. Most writing in elementary school is personal narrative. Themes encourage students to write on a wide variety of topics for different purposes (to learn, to persuade, to argue, to explain, to inform), and for different audiences that stimulate students to explore knowledge beyond their own experiences.

Fourth, themes encourage children to look at topics in greater depth and from a variety of perspectives, qualities that are critical to the development of higher level thinking abilities. When a child reads several books on a similar topic, especially books that approach the content from different directions and examine topics from a variety of perspectives, he or she is able to construct multiple links between the individual books. The sum of a child's understanding of three or four books on a given theme is always greater than the sum of their understanding of the books read individually. If teachers challenge children to examine content from a variety of perspectives, children's understanding of what they read will be deeper and more sensitive to the complexities and subtleties of ideas.

Using themes to extend children's reading and writing into areas such as nonfiction also allows teachers to bring the traditional research project (e.g., doing a book report, researching a country or a period of history) into the theme framework. Book reports will be much more satisfying to both teachers and children if they are not isolated exercises attached to individual books. Research projects, too, can be incorporated into themes that focus on nonfiction topics and be placed in a more meaningful context.

On the surface, a theme-based approach offers teachers more efficient ways of organizing the language arts curriculum and integrating content areas with language arts. Underneath, however, themes represent a fundamentally different way of approaching the elementary curriculum in which enlarging children's knowledge of their world is the primary aim, with the development of literacy and other skills subsumed within the content. In this approach, children learn about their world by engaging in genuine projects that explore topics that interest and challenge them. They learn skills and strategies as they need them in their explorations of knowledge, not as a separate or a prerequisite curriculum with its own scope and sequence. This approach is not new and untried: its philosophy and practice stem directly from the work of John Dewey nearly a century ago. It believes that children best learn in an apprenticeship model, engaging in real-world activities as opposed to preparing for them.

PUTTING THEMES TOGETHER

Choosing Topics for Themes

Given the amount of time and effort it takes to create a theme, it is worth spending some time thinking about various topics to explore as themes. Over the years, I have noticed that themes are more successful if they have the following characteristics: (1) if drawn from the content areas, themes are relevant to the content of the curriculum and represent important and genuine dimensions of that content; if drawn from other areas—concepts, calendar, current events, etc.—the themes represent topics that are substantive and worth exploring; (2) themes are appropriate to the children's experiences and yet offer them challenges to seek knowledge beyond what they already know; and (3) themes excite children's curiosity and imagination.

I have already suggested several different kinds of themes: content area, calendar-related, conceptual, biographical, current events, and form. Let's now explore each of these in more detail.

Content Area Themes

Content area themes are those drawn from science, social studies, English, math, health, music, and art. One of the things I have noticed in helping teachers draw themes from the content areas is that not all content areas are alike. For example, why does it seem more difficult to draw themes from math than from social studies? For a long time I thought it was because I knew more about history than math, and so I found it easier to create history themes. Recently, it's dawned on me that math, reading, writing, drama, art, and music are primarily—but not exclusively—processes, and it's hard to create content out of a process unless you are reflecting on or explaining the process. For example, it's easy to define the topic of "neighborhoods," because it's out there to be explored and it has dimensions (e.g., people who live there, types of businesses, and so on). But is "doing fractions" as easily defined as a topic? What about "getting the main idea" or "editing"? It's further complicated by all the subject areas having both content and process. For example, science has "frogs" (content) and "making hypotheses" (process); music has "jazz" (content, as in "jazz as a music form"), and "jazz" (process, as in "listening to or playing jazz"); art has "Impressionist Period" (content), and "sculpting" (the actual process of forming something with clay or some other material). Generally, themes are easier to create from subject-area-as-content, while subject-area-as-process seems to work better as a component of doing a theme. In other words, exploring frogs as a theme, with "making hypotheses" incorporated into it, is easier than exploring hypotheses as a theme, and incorporating "frogs" into it. Thus, it might make sense not to draw themes directly from math, reading, writing, physical education, and the process aspects of music and art, but instead use these processes liberally while carrying out the theme. Gamberg et al. (1988) said they found it too difficult to fully incorporate math into their themes in this way, making it necessary to have regularly scheduled math periods and creating special mini-themes that focus heavily on math—for example, math is a major aspect of their restaurant business project. Others who have written on themes (Haggitt, 1975; Walmsley et al., 1992a) also acknowledge this difficulty: Haggitt has a theme on containers for very young children that indirectly teaches about measurement; Walmsley et al. (1992b) tuck what they call a concurrent theme on measurement into a theme on giants. One of my graduate students, a physical education teacher, recently did a physical education theme on the cardio-vascular system, but this too focused on the content side of physical education.

Having said this, I'm aware that a graduate course I teach is called "Reading and Writing," in which my students and I examine the processes of teaching and learning reading and writing. At some point, it must be possible to focus on processes as content. But I wonder if that's because the processes of reading and writing are topics (content) at the college level—there are all sorts of books and articles written on them, from a variety of perspectives. Really what has happened is that we've turned reading and writing processes into a content area so as to study them directly.

Another problem surfaces when teachers think of English as an appropriate subject area from which to draw themes. While reading, writing, and composition are covered by the discussion above, what about literature? Literature poses a different dilemma: it isn't so much a process as it is a major vehicle for the content of almost any theme drawn from any subject area. Should literature's role in creating themes simply be to provide the books for other subject areas' themes, or might it be used as a theme itself? I think the major use of literature is as material for themes, although literature is also an excellent stimulus for themes, both directly and indirectly. For example, Jean Craighead George's *Julie of the Wolves* is a fictional account of a girl's journey across northern Alaska, but it could easily be used as a stimulus for a theme on the geography of that region, on the sociology of Eskimo family life, or even a conceptual theme on "Coming of Age." Marc Brown's *Arthur's Eyes* could easily lead to themes on vision, on eye doctors, even on diseases of the eye. Sheila

Burnford's *The Incredible Journey* could be used as an introduction to a theme on dogs or cats, or, more appropriately, to the more abstract topic of courage. Many teachers have told me that their themes most frequently come from literature (especially conceptual themes), but that once a theme has been created, literature returns to its role of supplying the books. For older students, however, literature itself can become the theme with a specific book as the sole focus of a theme or part of a particular genre (for example, a collection of poems, a group of short stories, or a set of mysteries).

If the distinction I have made between subject-area-as-content and subject-area-as-process makes sense, then it is not difficult to think of appropriate topics drawn from social studies, health, and from science; these subjects lend themselves easily to themes. Social studies yields topics such as neighborhoods, local government, battles of the Civil or Revolutionary War, Native American houses, Canada. Health produces topics such as fire safety, care of elderly, and human sexuality. In science there are topics such as magnets, solar system, minerals and fossils, and plants and growing.

Calendar-Related Themes

Elementary teachers have traditionally used the calendar as the basis for themes, and it remains an important and useful source for them. There are several dimensions to explore: themes drawn from the *seasons* (fall, winter, spring, and summer) or from the weather associated with seasons—although these could also be classified as science themes (thunderstorms, snow); themes drawn from *national holidays* (Presidents' Day, Veterans' Day, Martin Luther King, Jr. Day) or *designated days, weeks, or months* (National Library Month, National Dairy Week); from "folk" *festivals or celebrations* (Mother's Day, Father's Day, Valentine's Day, Groundhog Day, Halloween); from *religious holidays* (Christmas, Easter, Hanukkah, Chinese New Year); or from *birthdays/deaths of significant people* (death of Justice Thurgood Marshall) or *anniversaries of specific events* (500th anniversary of Columbus's voyage to the New World; 200th anniversary of the U.S. Constitution).

I have several concerns about calendar-related themes. One is that too many children end up studying the same calendar-related themes over and over again across the grades. Children often study George Washington and Abraham Lincoln each year in grades K–5, while other presidents of equal importance (Thomas Jefferson, for example) are barely studied at all. Another is that many teachers aren't exploiting the potential for calendar-related themes. It doesn't take much to capitalize on children's interest in Valentine's Day and extend the topic into sending letters, which in turn leads to learning about the post office or perhaps other forms of communication; or to start with Groundhog Day, and turn it into a science theme on shadows (see Walmsley et al., 1992b). Almost every day is designated as a day (or part of a week, or month, or year) devoted to honoring or celebrating something. Rather than always stick with the same few "days," why not branch out and invite children to learn about less publicized events? Why not deliberately introduce children to different folk festivals or celebrations across the grades so that over the course of several years they learn about a variety of these customs? There are two excellent sources to use for this purpose. One is *Chase's Annual Events* (Contemporary Books, 1993), which lists special days, weeks, and months on an annual basis (available at most public libraries); the other is *Do You Know What Tomorrow Is?* (Hopkins & Aranstein, 1990), which lists events like birthdates of famous Americans according to the calendar.

If variety is not possible, then at least can we delve deeper into the same topics if they are repeated each year or explore different dimensions of them? For example, kindergartners can participate in Halloween, but they can also listen to some fine literature on the topic (e.g., Eve Bunting's *In the Haunted House)* and draw their favorite costumes or Halloween characters; first graders can write about their Halloween trick-or-treating; fourth graders can explore Halloween traditions in other countries; seventh graders can examine the issue of the thin line between playful trick-or-treating and delinquent behavior. Perhaps we could focus on Washington and Lincoln in grades K–1; study Jefferson in grade 3; examine Carter, Reagan, and Bush in grade 7.

Conceptual Themes

Conceptual themes are organized around abstract concepts that generally cross subject area boundaries and offer teachers and children a unique opportunity to explore issues and topics that touch on some of the most important aspects of the human condition. For example, the conceptual theme "Walk a Mile in My Shoes" (a sixth grade theme developed in North Warren Schools, New York), explores the differences between people of different abilities, religious beliefs, cultural backgrounds and experiences, and so on. The conceptual theme "Growing and Changing Relationships" (a third grade theme from North Warren Schools) examines the different ways in which family members relate to one another (young with young, young with old) and how those relationships change over time, how humans relate to animals, and how animals relate to other animals. The conceptual theme "Courage" can examine the thin line between courage and stupidity, the courage that manifests itself in war, the courage of individuals battling long-term illnesses, the courage of a person's political or religious convictions in the face of oppression, the everyday circumstances that lead to acts of courage, and recognizing courage in all of us, rather than just in the superheroes. "A Day in the Life" is a conceptual theme that looks at a single day from the vantage points of children and adults in several walks of life across the United States and in other countries.

While conceptual themes offer limitless possibilities for exploration, I have learned that conceptual themes seem to work better if they have some tension or direction built into them. The "Walk a Mile in My Shoes" theme works well because it looks at life from markedly different points of view; a child's understanding of the notion of individual differences is considerably strengthened by these different perspectives. A theme on journeys works well too because journeys always have a direction to them (from earth to moon and return, from innocence to maturity) and a real purpose (to explore the unknown, to recapture one's past). A conceptual theme on energy, however, is too flat and abstract. Unless some tension is built into it by introducing the contrast between the users of energy and its producers or between the benefits and dangers of energy, the topic is extremely hard to come to grips with. "Friendship" is a common theme in the early grades that is easily made meatier by building into it some tension—perhaps by contrasting it with its opposite. In the early grades, conceptual themes are best kept fairly concrete; also, building into them a reasonable amount of tension or direction makes it easier for children to grasp them and to profit from them.

Another issue that frequently comes up is making themes out of topics that potentially or actually invade children's privacy or have the potential to cause them psychological harm. I have seen children who are overweight become increasingly embarrassed as their class spends a week or so on the topic of obesity as part of a nutrition theme. I wonder, too, about themes that focus on topics such as divorce, loneliness, or other topics that bring out into the open what children may prefer to keep private. Generally, I try to focus on conceptual themes that deal with issues and topics that lie outside, rather than inside, the children themselves. This doesn't mean we should avoid books, for example, that deal with divorce, but rather we shouldn't make divorce itself the focus of a theme. I don't think conceptual themes should moralize or deliberately attempt to solve children's psychological or physiological problems. I'm always glad if a child reads a book that has been particularly comforting in dealing with the loss of a pet, but I would never create a theme on losing pets, or on death, especially in the early grades. In secondary school, however, death as a topic isn't as gruesome as it sounds (see Hillkirk, 1982; McClaren, 1987).

Biographical Themes

Biographical themes examine the lives and contributions of individual people. Students in the upper elementary grades are used to doing biographical reports ("Choose a significant person, and write an essay that details their life and contribution."), but biographical themes can be used at all grade levels, allowing students to learn about people whose talents in politics, medicine, invention, civil rights, writing and illustrating, music, painting, architecture, sports, and other areas make them especially interesting to know about. The current interest in children's authors and illustrators have made author/illustrator themes very popular in the elementary grades. Children are naturally curious about the lives and writing/illustrating techniques of the people who compose and illustrate the books they read. (See Endersbee, 1987 and Lionetti, 1992 for good examples of how to put author themes together.) Again, I have a concern that the same few people—authors, illustrators, politicians, historical figures, sports personalities—get most of the attention in biographical themes. It would be good for children, during their elementary years, to explore the lives and contributions of a wide variety of people from all walks of life. Biographical themes need not be limited only to famous people; children may want to learn about people in their own family or community whose contributions are as significant locally as famous people's are nationally. Biographical themes stand well on their own, but they also work well tucked inside a current events theme, or a calendar-related theme.

Current Events Themes

I have listed current events separately from social studies because so often teachers don't get to current events in their social studies curriculum. Listing them separately increases the chances they will actually be used. Current events make particularly good themes partly because they are inherently stimulating, and partly because there is so much information readily available. One way to create a theme from a current event is to start with a specific incident and explore it geographically, economically, politically, and historically. When I first wrote this section, the San Francisco earthquake, Hurricane Andrew, and the dissolution of East Germany were very much in the news. At that time, teachers and students might have started with the California earthquake and traced it backwards. Some might have ended up investigating plate tectonics; others might have researched the 1906 earthquake or the topic of making buildings earthquake-proof. An investigation into the events in East Germany would have quickly led to a study of the Second World War and its aftermath; a study of the situation in Europe would quickly have led into the history, geography, and economics of the region. As this book goes to press, the Los Angeles earthquake, the Hubble telescope repair, and the civil war in Bosnia are making the headlines. By the time you read this book, these events will have been replaced by others. The events may change, but the possibilities for exploring what is currently happening around the world are always there, and they make excellent topics for themes.

Current events do not need to be restricted to world politics, however. There are always interesting things going on in the community, in the school, in the classroom, or at home from which a theme could naturally and spontaneously arise. For example, a few years ago, a local inner-city school was threatened with demolition, and the students and faculty created a theme centered around saving the school, a part of which was devoted to gathering together all the collective memories of the school from its nearly one hundred-year history. Bill Ordway, a sixth grade teacher in North Warren, was recently doing an environmental project that involved studying energy conservation, pollution, and so on. At the same time, the local community was debating whether to close the local landfill to meet new state environmental regulations. Bill and his students researched things like how long it takes for garbage to decompose, how much refuse the local community generates, and what kinds of things were in the garbage. After gathering the information, the students made a documentary called "A Landfill Speaks Out" that became part of the community's discussions on the future of landfills.

There is a tendency, I think, for some elementary teachers to focus on the "human interest" stories in the world, especially stories that deal with the unusual or the bizarre. Children's appetites for these kinds of stories are more than satisfied in the media, especially on television, and so it might be useful to concentrate on those current events that help children enlarge their knowledge of more important things that are happening around the world. In the early grades, current events won't be particularly interesting to children unless they are concrete and can be understood within the context of what they already know about history, geography, politics, and religion. (Weaver et al., 1993 exemplify this point well in their account of a first grade theme on weather and a fourth grade theme on robots; they argue that themes need to be focused on topics that children can understand and relate to.) But I find myself constantly underestimating children's interest in and capacity for understanding what is happening in distant places, and the more they deal with world events, the more they develop an appetite for them. Done with sensitivity, current events themes work very well even in the earliest grades, and they will be important sources of children's growing understanding of the world around them.

Form Themes

Unlike all the previous themes, a form theme focuses on form, style, or structure rather than content—at least its initial organization is by form. One of the most widely used form themes is organized around one of the major genres (e.g., traditional literature—myths, legends, fairy or folk tales, fables or epics; concepts—counting, alphabet, colors; realism—realistic fiction, historical fiction, adventure, mystery, humor; fantasy—science fiction and fantasy; nonfiction— reference, biography, and informational; poetry; and short stories). In New York, the state language arts curriculum guide is organized by genre, and so it is a popular method of organization in many of the schools I work in. Most teachers that do genre themes are trying to enlarge students' knowledge of the genre, but they also are interested in enlarging their students' understanding of the authors and illustrators of the books in the chosen genre(s) and of the topics about which the books are written. Even though often the only thing that holds the books together in a genre theme is their genre (as opposed to a common topic or content), I am always surprised how well received some of these themes are by the students. One of the most successful genre themes I recall is one on humor (called "What's So Funny?") created by Gail Sirrine for her third grade class; I also remember an excellent mystery theme run by a fourth grade teacher in Manchester, Vermont. But genre themes in the early grades are really closer to conceptual themes. For example, breaking down humor into the various humor "types" (irony, sarcasm, etc.) doesn't work very well at third grade. What does work well is basing the theme on the notion that people have different senses of humor, and that what's funny to one person isn't funny at all to someone else. The humor theme explores humor, but it doesn't analyze it as a genre. I think the same is true of mystery themes in elementary school; they are more conceptual than genre based.

Another kind of form theme is one that focuses on an aspect of language such as characterization, personification, or dialect. In these themes, typically only done in upper elementary grades or in junior or senior high school, a teacher will gather books and other materials that exemplify the particular construct and focus the reading, discussion, and writing on that construct. These themes can provide upper elementary students and teachers unique opportunities to explore quite sophisticated literary concepts.

There's one kind of form theme that troubles me. Many kindergarten teachers organize their language arts curriculum around form themes (although that's not what they call them), focusing on a letter each week. I have two concerns about this practice. One is that if all the themes in a year are form based—and they frequently are in these kindergarten classrooms—then the curriculum will be seriously out of balance. Another is that letter-a-week themes tend to focus children's attention on the narrow skills of letter recognition and sound-symbol association, which are a very small part of becoming literate, and such themes make it very hard for the teacher to focus the children's attention on substantive topics. For example, how are books easily related to one another when they are selected on the basis of the first letter of the authors' last name? Organizing themes around colors presents similar problems, severely constricting the range of possible activities. There's nothing wrong with occasionally focusing on a form theme in kindergarten, provided that the majority of themes are drawn from other kinds of topics (see Walmsley et al., 1992b).

Crossing Theme Boundaries

I don't want to leave the impression that teachers should be sticking rigidly to the various theme categories I have suggested. Many topics are hard to fit neatly into one theme category or another. Is weather a science theme or a calendar-related theme? It really doesn't matter. On the other hand, sometimes it makes sense to deliberately blur the boundaries between categories. Conceptual themes automatically do this. Content area themes frequently lend themselves to it. For example, studying the literary, musical, and artistic aspects (writers, composers, artists; styles of writing, music, and art) of a historical period will enrich children's historical understandings and enliven the connections between politics and culture. Looking at the differences between people in the "Walk a Mile in My Shoes" theme brings many different subject areas together. I don't think we should overdo the connectivity of subject areas—it can easily overwhelm young learners—but themes do offer genuine opportunities for making sensible connections between the humanities and the sciences, and teachers shouldn't be afraid to exploit them.

Who Should Decide on Themes?

Teachers and the curriculum traditionally have dictated the topics for themes (e.g., a Canada theme because Canada is what we are studying in social studies). Recently, the idea of children selecting their own topics has become very popular, partly as a reaction to teacher-dominated topic selection.

It is true that letting children select their own topics does maximize their ownership of what they explore; it is also inherently motivating for a child to explore a topic that he or she has interest in. But there's another reason to let children select their own topics: if they are interested in a topic and have some knowledge of it, they don't become overwhelmed by a task that not only asks them to explore something they know little about (nor have much interest in) but also expects them to obtain information from sources such as books that they aren't familiar with. Self-selecting topics reduces the cognitive demands on the young reader and writer and makes it quite a bit easier to obtain information from books and other sources.

On the other hand, if students select all their topics, they will not necessarily choose topics from the curriculum, nor will they necessarily choose topics that challenge them to explore beyond what they already know. I think letting children choose all the topics they explore is as bad as having teachers choose them all. Children need to explore topics of their own choosing, and they need to explore topics they didn't necessarily choose; this combination is healthy for growing minds, and it mirrors the kinds of experiences adult learners typically encounter in the real world. My experience is that many of the topics that children love are ones that someone else introduced them to at an earlier time. But I acknowledge that many teachers are fearful that if they decide on the themes, their children will lose ownership. (See Weaver et al., 1993 for a discussion of this issue.) I would argue for a balance between child-chosen themes and teacher-directed ones. Children can become interested in a topic that a teacher has chosen if the topic is inherently motivating, if the teacher is knowledgeable and enthusiastic about it, and if the teacher takes the time to provide the right kinds of initiating activities. A good compromise is for the general theme to be decided by the teacher, but the specific subtopics—the ones that children actually explore—be chosen by children. This doesn't solve the ownership issue, however, and there should be ample opportunities within and across the grades for children to explore topics entirely of their own choosing.

A third choice is for teachers and students to negotiate topics for theme study. In this approach, teachers and students could decide among predetermined topics, or they could jointly create new ones from scratch, as suggested by

Altwerger and Flores (1991; 1994). Altwerger and her colleagues invite us to think about "theme cycles" in which questions and problems are posed and addressed jointly between teachers and students, leading to new questions and problems, hence the notion of "cycles." Altwerger and Flores specifically argue against predetermining topics for themes.

Teachers also need to have choice in what they explore through themes. One of my constant concerns about helping schools develop a theme-based curriculum is that it's frequently more my curriculum than it is the teachers', despite efforts to put into place a mechanism for teachers to make the curriculum their own. One technique devised by Trudy Walp and her colleagues at North Warren School is to have available more themes per grade level than can be used, and let teachers and students choose the ones they want, always encouraging them to create new ones. Teachers also have a choice in the read-alouds and guided reading books they use in a theme. This has the added bonus of reducing the possibility of teachers getting tired of doing the same readings year after year.

How Long Should Themes Last?

Themes can last less than a single day or take as long as a year—I've seen a number of examples of themes at these two extremes—but most themes in elementary classrooms typically last between two to three days and twelve weeks. Some teachers get carried away with themes: I have seen a year-long theme on animals (it should have lasted a month at most; everyone was thoroughly sick of animals before the end of the first month), and a semester-long theme on an autobiography (unfortunate for the sixth grader whose memories of early childhood were brief or painful! The children didn't even read other people's autobiographies as a model for writing their own). Almost any theme can be extended indefinitely because there's always more to explore, more to read, and more to write. But there's also the law of diminishing returns, and after a while, even the keenest student begins to lose interest. Also, the time devoted to one topic prevents others from being explored, and so a few lengthy themes are likely to result in very lopsided coverage of the curriculum. Further, it isn't fair to students who neither like nor are profiting from a particular topic to spend too long on it.

I think of "mini-themes" that last less than a day or two in kindergarten (perhaps slightly longer in the upper grades) as being appropriate for studying a small topic very briefly. "Regular" themes (lasting up to a week in kindergarten, up to a month in the upper grades) are the most typical in length, and probably would be the most frequently used in elementary school. "Major" themes (lasting up to two weeks in kindergarten, up to twelve weeks in the upper grades) are for delving deeply into important topics. Semester-length or year-long themes should only be undertaken with a great deal of preparation and foresight, mostly because they run the risk of having insufficient material and student interest to last that long. I have seen a few successful year-long themes, but they tend to be rather global (e.g., "Friendship," "Respect," "Ecology"), and most of them have a number of smaller themes tucked inside them. I cannot imagine a "Dinosaurs" theme being stretched out to three months, let alone a year, but with some imagination I could see an overarching theme of "Year of the Child" or "Prejudice" working well across a year provided that there was plenty of variety in the specific topics being explored in a given time period. I would find it hard to justify devoting an entire year to a single topic, but I do like the idea of having shorter and longer themes, so that I can adjust the time I spend on a topic to the students' interests, the materials available, and the relevance of the topic to important goals of the elementary curriculum.

Should the Entire Curriculum Be Theme-Based?

This question has only arisen recently, because theme-based instruction is so rare. Very few teachers have experience with it across a single class year, let alone across an entire elementary curriculum. A theme-based curriculum might, like the basal readers it supplements or replaces, become repetitive and boring if it is simply instituted without regard to how it relates to other themes within and between the grades. Since there is no long-term evidence of the effectiveness of theme-based instruction across the grades—at least none that I know about— any attempt to build an entire theme-based elementary curriculum should be mindful that what works in one classroom may not work across the whole school. I would never insist that any teacher be required to use a theme-based approach against his or her professional judgment. I am reminded of Bill Ordway, the sixth grade teacher in North Warren Schools I wrote about earlier. Bill's approach to his sixth grade language arts class is to start with one or two books and see where they lead the students. He rarely repeats himself. One year, his students did a lengthy project in which they mapped the entire area; another, after reading Betsy Byars's *Summer of the Swans*, the students first rewrote it as a play, then rewrote it again and produced it as a videotape. The last time I was in his classroom, he was doing a theme on immigrants, exploring the conditions on the journey across from Europe and in the Pennsylvania coal mines, from the journals and letters of the immigrants to the families they left behind. To have forced Bill into a theme-based approach would have robbed his students of superb—but primarily not theme-based—experiences. In another school, I am convinced that a teacher I helped make the transition to themes was actually more effective using a basal reader, but the principal wouldn't let her return to it. Teachers should be allowed to exercise their professional judgment in these instances.

   Since there are schools that have turned to themes as the major instructional framework, it might be useful to think about ways to ensure that neither teachers nor students become as tired of this format as they apparently were of the instructional approach they used before turning to themes. One way of ensuring variety is to mix the length and type of themes. Here's what I recommend: mix major themes (important topics that last perhaps up to two weeks in kindergarten, twelve weeks in sixth grade) with regular ones (smaller topics that occupy up to a week in kindergarten, up to a month in sixth grade). From time to time, drop in a "mini-theme" for a day or so. Also, occasionally have two themes going at once—a "concurrent" theme alongside a major theme that either explores a related topic or something quite different for relief.

Sometimes, when everyone is up for it, it's fun to do a school-wide theme. I recall a particularly successful theme called "Yesterday—Today," which was interpreted in a variety of ways by each grade level and was shared with the whole school community. For example, some classes concentrated on the contrast between houses of yesterday versus today; some researched the school's past and compared it to its present; some reached back into their own family's histories and compared them to contemporary families.

Another way to ensure variety is to draw themes from the different types described above—alternating between content, calendar-related, conceptual, biographical, current events, and form themes. Or let students create or choose their own themes from time to time, building on their own interests. (Do a "theme cycle" using the approach suggested by Edelsky et al., 1991; Altwerger & Flores, 1991; 1994).

Another way is to come out of themes occasionally, and just do free reading, using an approach such as Nancie Atwell's (1987), or Jane Hansen's (1987); or create literature groups around particular books, as Peterson and Eeds (1990) suggest; or team up with a lower grade and do partner reading for a while. Sometimes, it's good to break out of literacy activities altogether and do something completely different. (Do a project such as building an aquarium or an extended science project; reach out into the community and do something for senior citizens or for the local environment.) In the real world of schools, there are so many interruptions for specials (assemblies, trips, visits by artists, drug and health programs, as well as mandated academic testing) that even the most rigid theme-based curriculum will be broken up.

Provided that teachers willingly organize their curriculum around themes, create challenging and substantive themes on a variety of topics, and know when a topic has become exhausted and it's time to move on or step out of the sequence for a while, theme-centered instruction is a valid and viable option for organizing instruction within a single grade (see Walmsley et al., 1992b). Provided that successive grades build on what children have already experienced and what they know, and that children are challenged with topics that match their ability to handle increasingly sophisticated and abstract ideas and also match their need to examine things from multiple perspectives, it's possible—though difficult—to create a theme-based curriculum that extends across the whole elementary school (see Walmsley & Walp, 1990). My experience is that if the literature is enjoyable and challenging and if children with literacy difficulties are given adequate and sustained help, both teachers and children enjoy the approach and profit enormously from it.

Exploring Dimensions of a Theme

Once a general idea for a theme has been established, a useful next step is to think about the dimensions of the topic. Are there important subtopics to consider? If the topic is very broad, might it be worth breaking it up into smaller themes? Some teachers find that "webbing" a topic—laying out all its dimensions visually in a map—is very helpful. I encourage teachers to start brainstorming the topic by writing down everything that comes to mind related to the topic. This works much better if it is done with colleagues or friends because other people always see a topic slightly differently. (I don't recommend doing this with the children themselves, unless you are creating a theme with them from scratch, in which case it's a great technique.) I have brainstormed some topics hundreds of times with groups of teachers, and I'm always surprised and delighted that every so often someone in the group comes up with an angle on the topic that has never come up before. Figure 1 illustrates an example of an initial brainstorm on the topic of courage.

It's clear from this brainstorming exercise that there are several distinct subtopics on courage, each of which would not be difficult to make into a complete theme. The main ones seem to be: courage in wartime, courage of one's convictions (scientific, religious, political, artistic), courage in the face of long-term illness, courage in a natural or man-made disaster or accident, the issue of what makes something an act of courage rather than an act of stupidity, and finally, physiological aspects of courage (the issue of mind over matter). There may be others, and there almost certainly are different ways of grouping the ones I listed above. The exercise is designed not to arrive at a "correct" definition of courage and all its subtopics, but rather to bring the different dimensions of a topic out into the open so they can be examined. One of the problems with the exercise is that it almost inevitably makes the topic bigger than it was before the exercise was started, and so the topic may have to be brought down to size again afterwards. Then why brainstorm it in the first place? Because brainstorming a topic forces the teacher to think through a number of possibilities for approaching a theme as opposed to simply using the first notion that comes into mind. Also, my experience is that themes are more interesting and more substantive if they are thought through ahead of time. But brainstorming does yield a larger set of subtopics than typically can be used, and so some paring down has to be done. In making decisions about which subtopics to explore with the students, which to spin off into another theme, and which to drop altogether, we have to take into account the age and grade of the children, what themes they have already explored, what literature is available on the subtopic, and whether suitable activities can be generated. We can also

FIGURE 1. Brainstorming the Topic "Courage."

delay this paring down until after (or during) the next step in the process—what I call "bumping up" one's knowledge of a topic.

Bumping Up One's Knowledge of a Topic

While I was writing this section, I kept rearranging this section and the previous one—exploring dimensions of a theme—because I couldn't decide which came first. I even tried writing them as one section, but they are distinct activities, even though they are highly related. It really doesn't matter whether a teacher establishes a tentative set of subtopics first and then enlarges his or her knowledge of them or whether a teacher starts by enlarging his or her knowledge of the topic and then creates the subtopics. Whichever way it is approached, the theme itself will be immeasurably enriched by the teacher's additional knowledge. I call this "bumping up" one's knowledge of a topic—it's learning something about a topic you know nothing about or bringing your knowledge up to date on a topic you already know something about.

I hear frequently that because young children have such little knowledge of the world—compared to teachers, that is—teachers in the early grades really don't have to know very much about the topics their students explore. There are several reasons, I think, why this view is so prevalent. One is that, unlike secondary teachers who teach one subject and are specifically trained in that subject, elementary teachers are expected to be equally well versed in all subject areas, but they rarely have strong backgrounds in all subject areas. Their training in history, science, and literature—frequently the content areas in which themes are done—is rarely as thorough as their background in language arts, and until recently, there's been little pressure to ensure substantive and sustained teaching of history and science in elementary school (see Walmsley, 1991). Another is that elementary teachers have for so long been used to teaching subject areas with textbooks, that many of them have come to see themselves as monitors of someone else's curriculum rather than as originators of their own (see Shannon, 1989). Finally, there's a question of time. Elementary teachers are busy to the point of exhaustion, and if they are going to devote additional time to something, it had better be worth their while.

I think bumping up on one's knowledge is. And here's why.

We should be practicing what we preach. We want our students to acquire new knowledge, and so we also should be doing the same. It's become a common practice for teachers to read while the students are reading and to write while they are writing. Then why not have teachers learning while students are learning? Children need to see us as learners, just as much as they need to see us as readers and writers.

It reminds us about where most knowledge resides—in books and other literacy materials. It's easy to forget, if you don't read for information yourself or if you only use textbooks for instruction, that most of the important knowledge of the world resides in books, and eventually that's where we have to go to enlarge our knowledge of the world. Most textbooks skim over the surface of this knowledge, and they frequently ignore or trivialize genuinely different perspectives on a topic. Lectures, films and discussions are useful sources of knowledge, but these too have limitations that ultimately can only be overcome by reading books (and other important written material such as journals, magazines, reports, and documents). When teachers read to enlarge their own knowledge, they send a powerful message to students about the value of reading, and the importance of books.

We need to acquire our own knowledge and not rely on others. By acquiring our own knowledge of topics, we will make these topics our own, and we'll become less dependent on textbooks for exploring the topics. For one thing, if you know something about a topic, it enables you to evaluate the adequacy and appropriateness of what's already out there. For example, if all you have read about Henry Hudson, the seventeenth century explorer, is what's in the social studies textbook, how can you possibly evaluate his accomplishments?

(Actually, you'll not even know much about his accomplishments.) But once you've read one or two of the better books on Henry Hudson—for example, E. Rachlis's *The Voyages of Henry Hudson* or R. Symes's *Henry Hudson*, you'll not only know a lot about each of his four voyages that sought to find a passage from England to the Orient, but you'll be able to evaluate the adequacy of the small piece about Henry Hudson in the textbook. Unfortunately, this cannot be done for you since it's in the process of actually reading this material that the material comes alive for you.

Children will benefit enormously from our expanded knowledge. Once a teacher knows something new about a topic, he or she will find ways to let students in on it. By knowing a topic better, a teacher will be able to help children work their way through the same topic, including giving them some advice up front about whether the topic itself is too broad or narrow. A teacher will know something about the sources for a topic, and this will help to assist children in finding their sources. (Also, this might save a child a lot of wasted time by knowing ahead of time that a topic has too few sources on it.) The more knowledgeable a teacher becomes about a topic, the more enthusiastic he or she will be about it with the children. The more enthusiastic children are about a topic, the harder they will work to explore it and make it their own.

What about the downside? There's no denying that bumping up one's own knowledge takes time. However, in all the years that I have encouraged teachers to do this, I've never had a complaint that spending this time wasn't worth it. In fact, the opposite is the case. Teachers who have taken the time to enlarge their own knowledge all say the same thing—they became engrossed with the topic, spending far longer on their own research than they thought they would, and not noticing how long it took. What seems to happen is that once a teacher starts going after a topic, she becomes absorbed by it, and one source leads to another. Indeed, the most common thing teachers report to me is that they become somewhat carried away with their newfound knowledge, and they begin to annoy their family and colleagues with their enthusiasm for their topics. I have never encountered children, however, who aren't excited about the topics their teachers have recently learned about.

There is one problem, however, associated with teaching newfound knowledge of a topic: it's the tendency to simply dump out that knowledge on the children, not realizing that the children need to make this knowledge their own through their own inquiries. It's the same with the books a teacher has found for the children to read, especially if they are doing research projects. If the teacher simply supplies all the materials, children don't have to go and find them, which makes everyone's life a little easier but robs the children of one of the most important research tasks, which is finding the sources. I think the value of teachers enlarging their knowledge of a topic far outweighs the dangers, however, because it's a lot easier to withhold some of this knowledge so that children can gain it on their own than it is to create worthwhile projects for children without this knowledge. But teachers have to be constantly vigilant not to spill the beans, as it were.

I also need to acknowledge the argument, advanced by Altwerger and Flores (1991), that teachers should not plan themes in advance but rather develop them around topics that are negotiated between teachers and students. Thus, the process of a teacher bumping up his or her knowledge would take place alongside the students' bumping up theirs, rather than ahead of time. This approach fits well with the philosophical stance taken by Altwerger and Flores.

Strategies for Bumping Up One's Knowledge of a Topic

Over the past several years, I have bumped up my own knowledge of topics and helped hundreds of teachers bump up theirs, and in the process I've learned about techniques that seem to work well and some that don't. Let me share some.

Suppose we've decided on a topic and have tentatively set out what we think are its important dimensions, or we are plunging directly into enlarging our knowledge of a topic without yet having explored its dimensions. Where do we begin?

I'm not sure one starting point is any better than another, but the following all seem to work well:

- talk to colleagues and ask for good sources.
- discuss the topic with a school or public librarian and get suggestions.
- call up a friend who knows something about this topic and ask for ideas for reading.
- look up the topic in the subject index in the library, locate one book, find it in the shelves, and then browse around it (that's my favorite technique).

I wouldn't do any serious reading yet, but rather get a sense of what kinds of books and other materials are out there and what people who know something about the topic think are appropriate things to read. I usually find that talking to more than one "expert" and visiting more than one library is necessary, otherwise what happens is that only one aspect of a topic has been tapped—the one that my colleague is interested in or the one that my school library happens to have material on. One thing I've found is that libraries tend to carry much more older material than newer, and sometimes I have to really work at finding the newer material. I know I'm missing something important if all the sources I have on a popular topic were written before 1950, but sometimes I find that some of the best material on a topic was written in an earlier period. The new CD-ROM databases that most libraries have installed to replace the old card catalogs are particularly helpful in tracking down relevant material, especially as many of them cover the holdings of all the public libraries in the area. I am also an avid user of interlibrary loan, much to the chagrin of my local librarian who has to do all the paperwork. Having the books at hand, though, makes all the difference.

At this early stage, what I'm primarily looking for are books and other materials that will enlarge my knowledge of the topic, not books that I can use with the students or have them read on their own. This isn't to say that I won't keep an eye out for these books, especially once I have started to narrow down a topic, but there's a temptation only to gather books for the children and abandon bumping up my own knowledge. There are exceptions. Children's nonfiction books on topics ranging from farms to transportation to Native American tribes are frequently so well researched that they enlarge both the teacher's knowledge and the students' at the same time, but I wouldn't want to rely only on these books to supply me with all the knowledge I need for a theme. Moreover, some conceptual themes are on topics that necessitate bumping up one's knowledge with the books that eventually children will be reading. For example, it would be hard to bump up one's knowledge of a topic like survival or bears in literature without spending the bulk of one's time reading children's books.

One of my students recently did a theme on fairy tales. To bump up her knowledge, she started by talking with a children's literature professor at a local college to learn more about what fairy tales were (she really wasn't sure about the difference between a fairy tale and a folk tale), where they came from, and what had been written about them. The professor recommended a number of books and articles, including Charlotte Huck et al. *Children's Literature in the Elementary School* (1987) and Bruno Bettelheim's *The Uses of Enchantment* (1976). She wasn't sure if she could use any of Bettelheim's book with her second graders, but she came away from these books and some articles with a much better understanding of where fairy tales came from, what they were, and what role people thought they played in children's development. Having done this, she then plunged into reading as many fairy tales as she could.

Once I've got a sense of a topic, I start into some extended reading. There's a temptation to give a topic the once-over, but ultimately this will disappoint because I'll end up with very little for the effort I've put in. So, I settle down with the material and read it carefully. As I do this, I can't resist thinking about how I might use the information either to modify a subtopic in the theme or as the springboard for an activity, but what I'm mainly doing is learning more about the topic. Sometimes this exercise begins to reveal the shallowness of a topic I originally thought was substantive, or it makes me realize that to do the topic justice, I'll have to spend more time on it. In such cases it's not difficult to lay the topic aside and move on to something else or to start thinking about making extensive modifications to the theme.

Different kinds of themes require different ways of enlarging a teacher's knowledge. Current events will send us mostly into newspapers, magazines, and contemporary books written about modern history, politics, society, business, and religion. For many teachers, this kind of reading will be very different from what they are used to, but it opens up views on the modern world and why things happen the way they do in a manner that textbooks are completely unable to do. Older students can access much of this material directly, and they too will be fascinated by it. Biographical themes will require us to read as many of the books written about or—in the case of an author theme—written by the person we have chosen for study. Form themes, on the other hand, will compel us to read a large amount of commentary about the genre we have chosen, so we have a much better sense of what the genre is about, what kinds of books fit into the genre, and what seems to emerge as patterns in them. For example, if we were to do a science fiction theme in sixth grade, we'd have to bring our own science fiction reading up to date as well as read commentaries and articles in journals about this ever-changing genre (so we know where science fiction ends and science fantasy begins, for example). Content area themes will require us to bring our subject area knowledge up to date. To do this, we might rely heavily on the kinds of materials suggested to us by professors, high school teachers, and other subject area experts.

Reading books that really are only for adults might seem at first to be an inefficient way of getting ready for a theme. But I would argue that nothing is wasted. The knowledge gained from this reading can be applied directly toward establishing the major subtopics of a theme and to deciding what it is that the teacher hopes students will learn from the theme. Even the books themselves can be used either as read-alouds (extracted or edited for readability) or they can be made available for students to pick up and read themselves. Using the books in this way is another reminder to the students that their teacher is learning alongside them.

Let me give an example of a theme I developed as a result of a challenge by the fourth grade teachers at a school where we were working on a theme-based curriculum. They said, "Show us how to prepare for a theme. We'll pick the theme, and you get it ready." They chose "Minerals of New York State." I knew absolutely nothing about minerals in New York State. To be honest, it wasn't a theme I would ever have thought of, and even if I had, I couldn't imagine it being interesting for fourth graders. How wrong I was!

I started by looking up minerals in the subject catalog at the university library. I found a book—I forget now which one it was—and then went up to the shelves. It was in a part of the library I had never been in before, and I wandered up and down the aisles looking at books on geology, mineralogy, and other subjects I had never heard of. All the books there seemed to belong to a different era, and I was completely alone. Eventually, I came across a little book that had the title, *Minerals in New York State.* I pulled it out and opened it up. It looked like an annual report that listed a number of minerals, the geographic region of New York State where they came from, the number of tons mined (or gathered in some other fashion), and many other statistics I didn't understand. But I discovered three critical things: this little book was part of a series of reports on minerals produced every five years or so; it was written by someone in the State Geology Department in Albany; and it listed all the minerals of New York State. In less than fifteen minutes, and in one little book, I had stumbled across exactly what I needed to start bumping up my knowledge. (Later, the teachers joked that this was beginner's luck, and that I really ought to prepare a number of other themes so I really knew what hard work was.) I discovered, for example, that iron ore used to be the major mineral mined in New York State, but that was long since gone, and now rock salt and gypsum are the major minerals that New York State produces. (I won't bore you with all the other details, even though I'm dying to share everything that I learned!) I had no idea that rock salt came from New York State, and I had even less of a clue about gypsum. (It's the main ingredient of gypsum board, now more commonly known as sheetrock.) I also found on the shelf, not far from the book on minerals, a fascinating book on the rock salt industry in the north of England at the turn of the century where salt was removed by pumping water into the salt layers and then pumping out the briny solution. This technique was very cost effective—you didn't need to mine the salt—but it also made the ground unstable, and entire villages in Cheshire would sink into the brine. I sat on the floor and read, mesmerized, through a large portion of the book, until the library closed. This was one book I knew the children would enjoy.

These discoveries led me to talk with the head of the Geology department at the University, who lent me samples of the major minerals, which was very helpful. I then went to the State Geology Department where I met with the very person whose job it was to update the little book on New York's minerals—he just happened to be putting the final touches on the latest edition of the report. Within a week, I not only knew all the minerals, but I had samples of many of them. In fact, I already knew what kinds of activities I might suggest for the fourth graders; they could do pretty much what I had done: find out about the different minerals, where in New York State the minerals came from, how they were extracted from underground, and what they were used for in everyday life. As I soon discovered, there really aren't many good books on minerals for the children to read, but in this instance it really didn't matter because the children could find out about their minerals in other ways: by writing away for information (we had the names and addresses of the major mineral companies, and no fourth grader in the country had ever written to any of them), by visiting local companies that used minerals, and, as a final project, by visiting the State Museum to see the state's extensive mineral collection and to talk with the state geologists. What they needed in terms of understanding the geological properties of the minerals, the children could get from their textbooks and other reference books, from the middle school science teacher, and from local geologists.

I don't see how this theme could have been successful without someone bumping up their knowledge of the topic before bringing the theme to the classroom. More importantly, by exploring the topic ahead of time, we were able to create genuine activities for the children. The theme has since become a regular feature of the fourth grade curriculum.

In another school, Rensselaer Park Elementary (in Lansingburg, New York) I was asked by Kathy Town, the third grade teacher, and Christine McGurrin, the Gifted and Talented teacher, to demonstrate how to put together a theme on Henry Hudson. As with minerals, I really knew very little about him other than his reputation for having given the River Hudson its name. I went about researching Henry Hudson primarily through books written about him, but this time I wrote a set of notes to help me remember what I had read and to organize a fairly complicated topic (keeping the voyages distinct from one another was a real headache). Here are the notes I made on Hudson, and the sources I used to create them:

Notes on Henry Hudson, Explorer

As I see it, Henry Hudson (about whom almost nothing is known until 1607) was a single-minded explorer with one burning ambition—to find a northern route from England to the Orient. You can think of his four voyages as four different attempts to accomplish that goal:

Voyage 1 (1607): To get to the other side by sailing straight over the top (it was thought that because the sun shone during a major part of the year over the Pole, the Polar Cap would be warm). Undertaken under the sponsorship of the Muscovy Company, Hudson sailed the *Hopewell* straight up to Spitzbergen, along its West coast, and bumped straight into ice. Along the way, he also bumped into what is called Whale Bay (Cove?), finding thousands of whales. He also found coal on land, too (and saw the first walruses, before they were called walruses). Having hit the ice, he turned around and came home. The significance of this voyage to Hudson was that you couldn't go straight over the top. The significance of the voyage to others was that there were enormous numbers of whales in Spitzbergen; this discovery led to the beginnings of serious whaling. (Coal from Spitzbergen never did catch on, apparently.)

Voyage 2 (1608): To get across the top of the north pole by going slightly to the right of it, via Navaya Zemlya. Again in the *Hopewell*, Hudson tried to find a way through the middle of the two islands above Norway, but he found that it wasn't possible.

Voyage 3 (1609)—the "big one," as far as the United States is concerned: To get across the top of the north pole by going slightly to the left of it. This trip is a little complicated because Hudson made a deal with the Dutch, who sponsored it, to go north, but actually he wanted to go across the top of what is now the United States. Eventually, the Dutch got wind of his plan, and made him sign a contract, but Hudson had no intention of following it. He set off north to Norway in the *Half Moon*, then he turned and headed to the United States, past Newfoundland, and down the Maine coast. Thought to have made landfall in Penobscot Bay, where he had encounters with Indians. Traveled south along the coast down to Cape Hatteras, then northwards to New York. He was looking for the river that he believed led through to the Great Lakes and straight out into the Pacific. Eventually found the Hudson River, and traveled up it as far as Albany. By November, he was back in England, and put under house arrest because the Hudson river had been discovered for the Dutch. Eventually, through the king's son's "good offices," he was released and set up with everything he needed to explore what he originally wanted to in the first place. (Note: Hudson's exploration of the Hudson River was driven only by his desire to get through to the Pacific, not to discover the Hudson River.)

Voyage 4 (1610)— the "big one," as far as the British are concerned: Hudson set off to find the northern route (through Hudson Bay) to the Orient, in the *Discovery*. He got caught in Hudson Bay while trying to get out of it to the south, and he had to winter over in bitterly cold conditions without adequate supplies. In June of 1611, he set sail north, but at the top of Hudson Bay decided to go left (west) to see if there was another opening, but the crew had had enough. They mutinied and cast Hudson off in the ship's gig. The nine crewmen left on the *Discovery* barely made it back (attacks by Eskimos, poor condition of the ship), and they cleverly blamed the First Mate (Robert Juet) who conveniently died on the way back, so they all escaped hangings on their return.

Some of the interesting things I learned about Hudson:

- apparently he never was interested in making money, and made deals for voyages that his wife bitterly complained about.
- he was a superb sailor but a rotten captain (he had several incidents, which normally would have resulted in hangings, but he always compromised, or maybe he was the first democratic skipper).
- for some strange reason, he took Robert Juet on several of the voyages, even though Juet absolutely loathed him and plotted mutiny on more than one trip (it sounds like Hudson was a poor judge of character as well as a poor captain).
- he failed in his missions (all of them) to find the short route to the Orient, but he brought back incredibly good maps and information from all the voyages (his real accomplishment was finding out there wasn't a northern route).
- his wife was impoverished during Hudson's brief career, but eventually she landed a job with the East India Company and made herself a small fortune (I like that!).

Possible activities:

- making maps of the four voyages (each voyage should have two maps, one large one that plots the route overall and one close-up that shows Spitzbergen, Navaya Zemlya, Hudson River, and Hudson Bay respectively). Children might want to include dates on the plots and small descriptions of incidents they thought were particularly exciting.
- choosing a character, incident, etc. from Hudson's voyages and writing a piece about it.
- writing reaction pieces on each of the books, choosing favorite extracts and saying what they learned from the books.
- drawing one or more of the ships.
- visiting the *Half Moon* the next time it's in Albany (this would be a great culminating activity for the whole class, wouldn't it?) [Some entrepreneurs have built a replica of the *Half Moon* in the port of Albany, and offer tours].
- getting a local historian to talk to the class about the theories of what points Hudson reached on the Hudson.

References

Asher, G. M. (1964). *Henry Hudson. the Navigator.* New York: B. Franklin. *[Originally published in 1860, this is a collection of the chief original documents, annotated with an introduction.]*

Baker, N. (1958). *Henry Hudson.* New York: Knopf.

Harley, R. (1979). *Henry Hudson.* Mahwah, NJ: Troll Associates. *[Fictionalized account of Henry Hudson's expeditions, written for children. Excellent illustrations. Writing style is rather choppy, and the author has latched onto what is felt to be the more "exciting" parts. Historically accurate, nevertheless.]*

Janvier, T. A. (1909). *Henry Hudson. A Brief Statement of His Aims and Achievements.* New York: Harper. *[This book covers the trial of the mutineers after the fourth and final expedition.]*

Murphy, H. C. (1909). *Henry Hudson in Holland: An Inquiry into the Origin and Objects of the Voyage Which Led to the Discovery of the Hudson River.* New York: B. Franklin.

O'Connell, R. (1978). *Hudson's Fourth Voyage.* New York: Atlantis Edns. *[This may be the most recent work on this voyage.]*

Polking, K. (1964). *Let's Go on the Half-Moon with Henry Hudson.* New York: Putnam.
[*Fictionalized account of the 1609 expedition from the son's (John) perspective. Very easy to read, but historically accurate.*]

Powys, L. (1928). *Henry Hudson.* New York: Harper & Bros.
[*Covers the trial in some detail, and has bibliography.*]

Rachlis, E. (1962). *The Voyages of Henry Hudson.* New York: Random House.
[*Fictionalized account of Henry Hudson's four voyages, written at a fourth- to fifth-grade level; well illustrated and clearly written.*]

Symes, R. (1955). *Henry Hudson.* New York: Morrow.
[*Fictionalized account of Hudson's voyages, written for children but drawn from records. Fairly large print.*]

Vail, P. (1965). *The Magnificent Adventures of Henry Hudson.* New York: Dodd, Mead.
[*Fictionalized account of Henry Hudson's four voyages. Written at a fairly adult level, it uses primary source materials and is extremely well written.*]

Again, I don't see how this theme could have been successful unless the teacher had taken the time to learn about the topic. I worked directly with the children (third graders) on this project, and found out firsthand how valuable it was to have thoroughly understood the four voyages.

The final step in this phase of theme development is to revisit the original "web" (or create one, if the reading was done first) and make some decisions about which aspects of the topic are to be used in the theme and which aren't. This is a crucial step because these subtopics will dictate how long the theme will run, what books and other material will be gathered, and what activities will be pursued by the students. For example, if we were doing a courage theme, now would be the time to decide if we were going to include all the subtopics (e.g., courage of one's convictions, courage in the face of long-term illness, and so on), or focus on one or just a few of them. We may be unsure of the availability of books and other materials on any or all of these subtopics, and so a final decision may have to be postponed until after we have assembled the classroom materials, but at least we now have a pretty good idea of how the theme is shaping up and what its major dimensions are.

One final thing we need to think about is what we want the students to accomplish through the theme. I shudder at the thought of behavioral objectives, but I don't see anything wrong in articulating the theme's major goals. For example, Candy Fischer, the seventh/eighth grade English teacher in North

Warren, recently created a science fiction theme called "Back into the Future." She listed the following objectives:

1. To introduce students to science fiction and science fantasy as literary genres.

2. To study the elements of science fiction and science fantasy in order to compare and contrast their literary characteristics, as well as to build comprehension and composing skills.

3. To expand reading interests and to stimulate independent reading.

4. To provide a context in which students can examine their views of the future; how technological advances have implications for society as a whole, as well as implications for their personal lives.

Articulating goals in this way not only lets others know that the theme is purposeful and meaning-driven, but it also helps to focus the theme's activities. It also comes in handy when it's time to assess what students have accomplished through their theme studies. But there's always a danger that laying out goals and objectives will become an end in itself, and when this happens, the value of articulating what we hope students will accomplish through the theme will be lost.

Assembling Materials for a Theme

The next step in developing a theme is gathering materials for use in the classroom. Once the major subtopics of the theme have been decided, the next step is to ensure that there are enough books and other source material available for each of them. What some teachers do is devote separate pages of a journal to the major subtopics and list sources in each of them as they find them. Others simply gather all the materials they can and then sort them all afterwards. It really doesn't matter, provided there are enough materials for each major dimension of the theme.

What Kinds of Books and Other Materials Should Be Used in Themes?

If children are to enlarge their knowledge of the world, they are going to need books and other materials. Let's examine these in more detail:

Books. Ultimately, most of the important knowledge about the world is contained in books. There are several kinds of books that students and teachers may wish to use in their themes.

1. *Reference materials* (e.g., encyclopedias, books that list sources, book reviews, and so on) are useful to get an idea about where to find information about a given topic and to obtain some preliminary information about the topic. For example, a student (or teacher) might use *Books in Print* to see what books are currently available on the topic of dinosaurs; or they might use the *World Book Encyclopedia* to obtain some general information on a topic they are just

beginning to explore, finding an entry about the different kinds of whales or a brief synopsis of the Civil War.

2. *Textbooks* can also be quite useful in providing some preliminary information about a topic, especially in science and social studies. To be honest, though, I see encyclopedias and textbooks playing a very minor role in themes.

3. It is *trade books* (i.e., full-length books, both fiction and nonfiction, routinely sold to bookstores and libraries) that should make up the bulk of reading material to be used in themes, especially in the upper elementary grades.

Trade books come in many shapes and sizes. Some books are strictly for adults; they contain information at a level that students could not possibly understand on their own. Such books will be useful to students only indirectly, mediated by the teacher by explaining their major points, perhaps by reading some selections aloud, perhaps just showing illustrations with explanations. Except where it is obviously inappropriate, I think that teachers should make these books available to students to read or consult if they choose. For example, in a fifth grade class studying a theme on the Westward Movement, the teacher read aloud from Lewis and Clark's original account of their expeditions, and several students read this book independently, even though it was thought to be far too difficult for fifth graders to read. Some books are written for adults but are nonetheless suitable for use by students directly due to their simple prose or rich illustrations, or because they represent some of the only written material available on a topic that a student is anxious to learn about.

Other trade books are written directly for children. There are many kinds of books in this category, ranging from traditional literature (myths, legends, folk tales, fairy tales, and epics), realistic and historical fiction, fantasy, poetry, and nonfiction. Many teachers find it quite hard to fit traditional literature into content area themes, and they prefer to incorporate it into conceptual or genre themes instead (e.g., a conceptual theme called "Larger than Life" that explores primarily myths and legends; or a genre theme on folk tales, fairy tales or mythology). Content area themes can use both fiction and nonfiction. For example, there are books that fictionalize factual events so as to bring history, science, or current events to life. For example, Laura Ingalls Wilder's *Little House on the Prairie* series is a dramatized account of her own family's westward movement, R. Symes's account of Henry Hudson's voyages is based on fact but is told as a story, David Macaulay's *Pyramid* is a fictionalized account of the building of a pyramid, based on current archaeological knowledge. Another kind of book especially suitable for content area themes is purely factual but has been written with students' interests and perspectives in mind. For example, David Macaulay's *The Way Things Work* takes major scientific principles such as levers, movement, and light, and explains them in everyday terms that young students can understand; Aliki's *Dinosaurs* explains theories of dinosaurs in a manner that brings them to the students' level without compromising scientific knowledge. There are nonfiction books written even for the youngest students, for example, David Drew's *Skeletons* and Barbara Taylor's *Look Closer: Coral Reef.*

Nonfiction books will also make up the bulk of books for use in current events themes, especially if they focus on national and international events.

Realistic fiction and fantasy books seem better suited to conceptual themes, given that most of these books are about topics such as friendship, going on adventures, growing up, and so on. Very few realistic fiction books are directly related to a content area, but many of them are related to the calendar (Christmas, Valentine's Day, etc.), and so they are ideal candidates for calendar-related themes.

Trade books selected for use in biographical themes will depend on the person under study. An author or illustrator theme will of necessity include all the books written or illustrated by that person, while a theme that focuses on sports people will probably be made up mostly of nonfiction.

There are thousands of trade books published each year, and increasing numbers of books are now available to help students and their teachers enlarge their knowledge of topics ranging from dinosaurs to lighthouses to chicken farming to rain forests. The problem for a teacher these days is having to exclude fine literature because there isn't enough time to include it all.

Magazines and journals. A second major source of information are the hundreds of magazines and journals published each month on various topics. Again, there are several different kinds.

1. Journals written strictly for teachers and professionals in the various disciplines. These journals communicate current knowledge about the disciplines. For example, *Nature* is a primary journal for communicating knowledge in the earth sciences; its audience is assumed to have quite advanced prior knowledge of the earth sciences.

2. Journals aimed at communicating knowledge in a given area to a broader public. For example, *Scientific American* contains articles on very sophisticated topics, but they are written for readers that have only a general understanding of science; *National Geographic* magazine is aimed at an even broader readership, but its articles are well researched and they are written for quite capable readers. Its illustrations are so good, however, that it can be enjoyed by even quite young readers.

3. Magazines intended for young readers. These include publications such as *Cobblestone* (a journal with a historical bias), *National Geographic World, Zoo Books, Ranger Rick, My Own Backyard* (magazines about animals and nature), *Penny Pincher* (a children's version of *Consumer Reports*), *3–2–1 Contact* (based on the public TV program of the same name), and *Scholastic Scope* (a current affairs magazine sold directly to schools). Stoll (1989) has compiled and annotated a list of more than one hundred twenty-five children's magazines, many of which can be used in themes.

Primary Source Documents. A third source of information involves the use of primary source documents such as diaries, records (e.g., court transcripts, house deeds, legal documents), letters, plans (e.g., architects' blueprints, artists' drawings), maps, family trees, and so on. In studying Christopher Columbus's journey to the new world, for example, students in the upper elementary grades might enjoy and profit enormously from studying translations of the original logs kept by Columbus (e.g., Peter Hanson's *I Columbus, My Journal*). In studying the architecture of an early village or learning about their own family's roots, students might explore house deeds and family trees. In trying to understand rulings by the Supreme Court on issues such as abortion, segregation, or the burning of the American flag, having the actual ruling available for study is particularly important.

Obviously, there are real limitations involved in the use of primary source documents; many are extremely hard to find, and once found, they are extremely hard to read, even by adults. Careful preparation by the teacher, however, frequently pays off with the discovery of documents that reveal something about a topic from a child's perspective. In any event, even if the source documents are too hard for students to read independently, they can always be read to students, and just having them (or copies) physically present is enormously helpful to students.

People. Especially for young students, people represent one of the best sources of information, and one of the easiest for them to obtain information from. Children are used to asking others for information. In contrast, they aren't used to getting information from books. People can be used as sources in a variety of ways. They can be used as primary sources themselves, as in the case of children finding out about the history of a village from the town historian, discovering one's family history from a grandparent, or learning about how a fire engine works from a firefighter. They can also be used as a guide to primary sources, as in the case of children asking a town historian for advice on which books to consult for specific architectural information, asking a school or public librarian for help in selecting appropriate sources, asking a state geologist's advice on where to get up-to-date information on salt production in eastern New York. Parents, relatives, community members (caregivers, older citizens, local and county government personnel, church leaders, members of organizations such as Lions, Red Cross, chamber of commerce, volunteer ambulance and fire, police), business people (from utility companies, merchandise stores, manufacturing, banking), schools, colleges and universities, and state agencies (education, cultural, etc.) are all possible "people" sources for students to use in their projects. Students should also be reminded that fellow students are valuable resources, too.

While exploring people as possible sources for a theme, it pays to find out how experienced they are with children at your grade level and what might be the best way to seek out their knowledge. Some experts are superb writers but dreadful speakers; others are superb with young children and know exactly how to relate to them. Some experts are very good interacting with individual

children but very uncomfortable with a whole class. Knowing this in advance—
by talking with the expert personally, observing the person in someone else's
classroom, or talking to other teachers who have had this person in their
classroom—is very helpful in avoiding awkward situations during the theme
itself.

Direct Observation. Other than the required chick-hatching experiment, the
growing of beans (or grass, squash, etc.), and field trip(s), elementary students
are rarely asked to use direct observation in their theme studies. As with people
as sources, direct observation of phenomena is already one of the major ways in
which students acquire information about the world around them, but it is
underused in school. The field trip is a fairly common activity in elementary
school, but students rarely get opportunities on field trips to make careful,
extended direct observations; they are typically shuffled from one exhibit to
another. Almost every kind of theme can benefit from children having an
opportunity to make direct observations of things that are relevant to their
topics: spending time observing birds migrate, walking around a battlefield,
handling archaeological artifacts, observing a manufacturing process, attending
a concert, and so on. There are three important aspects of direct observation, and
they are hard to reconcile with the typical way in which a field trip is organized:

1. Children need extended periods of time to immerse themselves in the
observations.

2. Children need, when it is appropriate, to have ample opportunities for
discussions with people on the scene so their questions can be fully addressed.

3. Children need to have the means for recording what they have
experienced.

In thinking about using direct observation as a source of knowledge, teachers
need to decide if they want to take the children out of the classroom or bring
someone or something in. If going out, it really pays to have been on the field
trip yourself and to talk with people at the site about what you want to
accomplish. Otherwise, what you frequently get is the give-them-the spiel-and-
get-them-out-of-here treatment. You'll know you have succeeded when children
come back from a field trip and want to write about the things they went to see
rather than about the bus trip, lunch, or the fight that erupted between Billy and
Fred.

Electronic Media (Film, Videotape, Radio, TV, CD-ROM). Electronic media
are more commonly used as stimuli for themes than they are during projects
themselves, but they do have a useful role to play. Some themes (e.g., an inquiry
into a period of art history, a biography of a painter or sculptor, an analysis of
comedy in an earlier period of TV or radio) require students to use electronic
media for obvious reasons, but films or TV documentaries have been made on
almost every subject, and these will always provide students with both
knowledge and a perspective on a given topic. While these media cannot

completely substitute for written sources—nor should they—they can supplement written materials, and they offer students not only information but also ideas for ways to present what they have learned. The biggest obstacle to using these media sources—and it's ironic, given that we are apparently so far into the "information" age—is that they are so hard to access. Most school libraries' collections of films, filmstrips, and videotapes are often meager and out of date, and it is expensive and time-consuming to get access to the latest and the best in film and video media. Compare this with the ease of obtaining books through interlibrary loan!

In the past few years, however, there's been an enormous rise in the use of compact discs (CD-ROM) for the storage and retrieval of information of text, sound, still and motion photography. For a while, all that could be found on these CDs were electronic versions of encyclopedias and games. But recently, there's been some serious development of interactive programs that allow children to explore a variety of topics in ways that they choose. For example, children can now explore multimedia encyclopedias (e.g., *The New Grolier Multimedia Encyclopedia*, CEL Educational Resources' *Video Encyclopedia of the 20th Century)*, and a range of other topics, including music (e.g., Voyager's *Beethoven Symphony #9)*, medicine, politics, geography, and sports, to name a few.

But the downside of this new technology, as Borrell (1992) points out, is that the promise is still far ahead of the reality: what he and his colleagues from the magazine *MacWorld* found from their visits to schools across America was "antiquated computers; unused computers; computers used for games and not for teaching; schools and teachers unprepared to use computers that they own;" and so on (p. 25). But I remain optimistic that the CD-ROM, with its enormous capacity for storing text, sound, pictures, music, and film, will emerge as a major new source of information, and if teachers can take advantage of it for their themes, they should.

Locating the Materials to Use in Themes

I have always found this stage of the development of a theme to be the most enjoyable because it involves reading so much children's literature. But the task isn't all that simple, especially if a teacher wants to be sure that the best sources available have been tracked down. To make the search easier, it really pays to enlist the support of a school or public librarian, especially those with experience in selecting materials for a theme; but there's plenty of help available even if school or public librarians aren't close at hand. Also, there are several sources for obtaining the books themselves that need to be considered.

There is no substitute for a knowledgeable school or public librarian who is enthusiastic about theme-based instruction. In the schools where I have helped teachers create themes, we've usually been able to rely on librarians, and they are worth their weight in gold. Most librarians are willing to search for books on themes, thereby saving many hours of the teacher's time, but I prefer that when possible, teachers should involve the librarian in the development of the themes right from the beginning. Then they become part of the curriculum planning, not merely recommenders or suppliers of books. Most children's librarians have accumulated over the years an extensive knowledge of children's literature. Since they have to deal with clients with a wide variety of interests, reading abilities, and habits, they are generally resourceful and accommodating. They keep up with the reviews of children's books, and although they primarily serve children and parents directly, increasingly they are sensitive to the needs of classroom teachers. Bringing a school or public librarian into the theme planning stage is one of the most important things a teacher can do (see Hansen, 1993).

Even if there is no librarian at hand (some schools don't have them, and some librarians are too busy or unwilling to help), all is not lost. Fortunately, there are some excellent guides to choosing literature, and some of these are particularly useful for selecting books on a given theme (see Gillespie & Naden, 1990; Yaakov, 1991). Pillar (1987) is an excellent resource; she reviews all the major sources for finding books, including those that list books by subjects. For example, she refers to the massive *Children's Books in Print*, one of whose volumes lists titles by subject; to the American Association for the Advancement of Science's *AAAS Science Book List for Children*, which lists thousands of science books for children; and to a number of other subject-specific bibliographies. She also refers to indexes, subject encyclopedias, publishers' newsletters, directories, and handbooks. Major libraries carry these reference books, and they should be one of the first sources to consult for a theme. Also, most children's literature textbooks (e.g., Huck et al., 1987), and books on themes (e.g., Moss, 1984; 1990) have excellent bibliographies of both sources for books and books themselves. And every year, more reference books are published (for example, see Freeman and Person's 1992 sources for nonfiction books).

Another technique is to do with children's books what I recommended for adult material: visit school and public libraries (visit several to ensure thorough coverage), look up one book on a subject, and then browse through the shelves. This works well if the library organizes its collection by subject, but it doesn't if all the books are arranged alphabetically, as most fiction is. Books for genre themes, however, are sometimes easy to find because some libraries (especially school libraries) organize their collection alphabetically by genre. If the books are arranged purely alphabetically by author, I start with the CD-ROM catalog, jot down (or print out) the titles/authors of likely candidates, and then roam the library. This is time-consuming, but occasionally other titles pop out of the shelves, especially if the librarians have made displays of books. On more than one occasion, I have found new titles for a theme I wasn't preparing.

Libraries aren't the only place to look for materials. Bookstores (especially those with a big children's section) are especially useful because they always have the latest and newest books. My favorite bookstore in the world is the Northshire Book Store in Manchester, Vermont; it not only has one of the finest collections of books for adults and children, but also its staff are themselves experts in children's literature. (Recently, Borders bookstore opened a branch in Albany, New York, and my experience there rivals Northshire. If this is a trend, those of us looking for quality source material for themes will be well served.) Unlike car dealerships that sell both new and previously-owned automobiles, the major bookstores generally sell only new books, and so it's also necessary to scour second-hand bookstores and garage sales for books.

School book clubs (Scholastic, Trumpet, Troll) are excellent sources for books. They provide a wide range of books suitable for theme-based instruction, and they are easy and inexpensive to purchase either through participating in the clubs, or ordering through their catalogs.

Teacher supply stores and mail-order catalogs (e.g., New York's Metropolitan Museum) are also good sources for ideas, especially for nonprint materials (e.g., posters, kits, models).

Finally, collections of books at home (the teacher's, children's, and their relatives') are excellent sources for books.

Characteristics of Materials to Use in Themes

As I put together a set of books for a theme, I am looking for books that meet a number of different criteria, although obviously not every book needs to meet all of them. I assume a book fits the theme, but I also have in mind to search for books that are suitable for three different kinds of reading in the classroom: read-aloud, independent, and guided. The mix of these three will depend on the grade level—in kindergarten, most of the books will be read-alouds; by sixth grade, most will be for independent reading.

Teachers also will need a range of books (especially for independent and guided reading) that meet the different interests, reading abilities, and background knowledge of the students in their class. They will also want books to represent other dimensions—for example, cultural diversity, format, and genre.

Cultural Diversity. Teachers need to include within and across themes books and other materials that challenge children to appreciate and understand different cultural perspectives and that represent the writings and illustrations of minorities and women. These include books that focus on members of a minority language and/or cultural community such as African Americans (including Caribbean cultures), Amish Americans, Asian Americans (including Chinese, Japanese, Vietnamese, and other Eastern cultures), Hispanic Americans, Jewish Americans, Arab Americans, and Native Americans. Of particular importance are books in which the ethnicity of the characters is of central importance to the story line or very apparent through the illustrations; books based on the folklore and true-life experiences of a country of origin of these American ethnic communities, such as Africa, Japan, etc.; and books written or illustrated by individuals who may or may not be members of the ethnic groups represented (definition taken from Strickland and Walmsley, 1993). Galda and Cotter (1992) have some excellent suggestions not only for specific book titles representing cultural diversity, but also for grouping these within themes.

Book Formats. Children need to be exposed, across the grades, to a range of books with different formats (e.g., wordless picture books, picture story books, illustrated chapter books, chapter books, and anthologies).

Book Genres. Even if genre themes are to be created, there's a need to ensure that children are exposed to books representing the major genres in content area, conceptual, and other themes. Authorities in children's literature (e.g., Huck et al., 1987; Lukens, 1982) generally divide genre into six major categories (Traditional Literature, Concepts, Realism, Fantasy, Nonfiction, and Poetry), although there's some debate over the divisions within these categories. These discussions have significance to academics, but in the classroom they aren't quite so important. What matters is that children are exposed to a wide range of genres in their theme reading. But in case a teacher wants to ensure a balanced coverage of genres within or across themes, Figure 2 lists the genre categories, divides each category into sub-genres, and explains each sub-genre. This list was based on Huck's and Lukens's schemes and was compiled originally by the author and Trudy Walp for a study of second graders' literary experiences (Walmsley et al., 1991); after analyzing over three thousand books from the school book clubs (Strickland & Walmsley, 1993), it has been further modified.

Obviously, not every theme needs to have all these criteria filled in even numbers—it would impossibly restrict the development of any theme—but there should be a balance, and where appropriate a progression, across the year and especially across the grades so that children are exposed to a broad spectrum of books meeting these various criteria.

Since books for read-aloud, independent reading, and guided reading occupy a major part of a theme, it makes sense to consider them separately.

Books for Reading Aloud. Some books—poetry for example—cry out to be read aloud (Diane Siebert's *Train Song*), and others that have strong rhythmic or poetic qualities to them (Joyce Maxner's *Nicholas Cricket*, J.R.R. Tolkein's *The Hobbit*) are especially suitable for reading to children. But I think we often miss important pedagogical opportunities that reading aloud affords. In his book *Wordstruck*, Robert MacNeil traces the origins of his love for the language, and in one passage he talks about the notion of "layering," the process by which we accumulate knowledge of words, stories, and language over time. Just before this extract, he's talking about what he remembers of stories by Kipling and Defoe. He goes on:

All these stories were laying down little lessons in psychology, as well as language, and this material was not being laid down in an empty place. New pieces triggered responses from material that was already there, for example, the pleasure it gave me as Crusoe provisioned his cave.

Laid down is a term with many associations—the keel of a ship to be built; fruits preserved for the winter; wine laid down to age. It is the term they use in sound and videotape editing when one track or sequence has been recorded and others will be added and mixed together.

It must be with words as it is with music. Music heard early in life lays down a rich bed of memories against which you evaluate and absorb music encountered later. Each layer adds to the richness of your musical experience; it ingrains expectations that will govern your taste for future music and perhaps change your feelings about music you already know. Certain harmonic patterns embed themselves in your consciousness and create yearnings for repetition, so that you can relive that pleasurable disturbance of the soul. Gradually, your head becomes an unimaginably large juke box, with instantaneous recall and cross-referencing, far more sophisticated than anything manmade.

It is so with words and word patterns. They accumulate in layers, and as the layers thicken they govern all use and appreciation of language thenceforth. Like music, the patterns of melody, rhythm, and quality of voice become templates against which we judge the sweetness and justness of new patterns and rhythms; and the patterns laid down in our memories create expectations and hungers for fulfillment again. It is the same for the bookish person and for the illiterate. Each has a mind programmed with language—from prayers, hymns, verses, jokes, patriotic texts, proverbs, folk sayings, clichés, stories, movies, radio, and television.

I picture each of those layers of experience and language gradually accumulating and thickening to form a kind of living matrix, nourishing like a placenta, serving as a mini-thesaurus or dictionary of quotations, yet more retrievable and interactive and richer because it is so one's own, steeped in emotional colour and personal associations.

The earliest of those layers must date from the first words a baby hears, and certainly from the time a child can understand connected speech and can be read to. (pp. 23–24)

If parents read to children before school, and if teachers continue to read to children throughout the elementary years, layers of literary understanding will accumulate inside children's heads, and if MacNeil is right, these experiences will have profound effects on children's literacy and on their literary knowledge. Reading aloud to children plays a major role in this layering process. Reading aloud is also one of the few techniques that allows teachers to place in front of children topics and syntax that are slightly beyond their current grasp—something that is essential for children's language development,

FIGURE 2.
Genre
Categories.

Genre	Sub-Genre	Explanation
Traditional	Myths/Legends	Myths frequently explain natural phenomena through religious or ritualistic plots. Legends are stories presented as true accounts of past secular events or heroes.
	Folk Tales	Fictional stories with predictable plot structure (e.g., "Once upon a time"). They often depict conflicts between good and evil where good eventually "lives happily ever after."
	Fairy Tales	Fairy tales share many of the same characteristics as folk tales but are often longer and contain romantic elements.
	Fables	Fables are very short stories, usually with animal characters depicting human behaviors, that teach a lesson or moral.
	Epics	Epics are long narratives with the adventures of a heroic figure at the center of the action.
Concepts		Stories or collections of pictures or photographs that focus on a concept area such as letters of the alphabet, numbers, colors, or shapes.
Fiction	Realistic Fiction	In realistic fiction, the plot, the setting, and characters depict "real life" situations and issues but are not actual, true accounts. (The book's characters may be humans or animals.)
	Mystery	Mystery contains elements of suspense and involves the reader in solving the problem that drives the plot.
	Scary	In a scary book, the purpose is to tell a horrifying or frightening story, frequently involving ghosts, aliens, or "creatures."
	Humor	Literature which, through the situations depicted, the language used, or sheer nonsense, is written to make children laugh.
	Adventure	Adventure stories are fast-paced and include elements of excitement. The plot may center around overcoming difficulties, journeys, or quests.
	Historical Fiction	Literature based on historical settings and events but fictional elements, such as the characters, are used.

FIGURE 2
continued

Genre	Sub-Genre	Explanation
Fiction	Science Fiction	Science fiction draws upon hypothesized scientific and technological advances in telling stories about the future of humankind.
Fantasy		Fantasy creates an imaginary world which departs from what is real and expected, yet is made believable through the characters' experiences.
Informational	Reference	A variety of printed materials that present factual information about particular events or topics, typically in a list.
	[Auto]biography	Stories or accounts of the lives of people, particularly famous ones, told by self (autobiography) or by others (biography).
	Informational	Informational text is factual and may be supported by detailed descriptions, definitions, illustrations and examples to clarify the information presented.
Poetry		Individual poem, or collection of poems (as opposed to story, myth, fairy tale told in verse).

according to Vygotsky (1986)—without any fear that children will become frustrated. Because teachers can instantly judge whether children are indeed comprehending what is being read, they can make adjustments as they read aloud (use gestures, change the pitch and phrasing, stop and explain something, reword, show pictures), and so mediate between the author and the listener. In selecting books for read-aloud, then, teachers may want to seek out books that have the potential for exposing children to new information or topics, material that is conceptually more difficult than the children handle on their own, and material that is written with syntax and vocabulary that's slightly harder than they can understand independently. Occasionally, a teacher will want to select a book for reading aloud that might otherwise be suitable for guided or independent reading, only the high price of the book makes it impossible to have more than one copy. For example, only the wealthiest teacher could afford to obtain multiple copies of Peter Lourie's book *Hudson River: An Adventure from the Mountains to the Sea*, a book that would nicely complement the purely historical books in a Henry Hudson theme.

   Books for Independent Reading. I assume that teachers will generally make read-aloud books available to the children for independent reading, but children will also need to have available a good selection of books on each theme that they can read on their own. In choosing books for independent reading, teachers need to ensure that they cover the various subtopics, represent different formats, genres, and cultures, and especially that there are sufficient numbers of books that challenge the most able reader (in content, not just syntax), and meet the needs of children who have less knowledge of the topic and weaker literacy skills. Finding books that enlarge children's knowledge of a topic and are still able to be read independently by a weaker reader is difficult but not impossible. Weaker readers (especially those with very limited exposure to books) need a great deal of help at first, but each book they read helps them with the next, and eventually they build up sufficient literary experiences that enable them to cope more easily with the independent reading. A combination of providing much assistance and selecting relatively easy books—without resorting to books that have been stripped of their content—seems to work well in most cases (see Fielding & Roller, 1992; McGill-Franzen, 1993; Walmsley & Walp, 1990). Another thing to remember is that longer books take longer to read, and therefore they will be out of circulation longer than shorter books will; this means that more copies of longer books will be needed, especially if there's limited time available for independent reading.

Books for Guided or Shared Reading. Books for guided reading (reading that is shared between the teacher and the students, often as a vehicle for literacy or literary skills instruction) need to be chosen very carefully, especially if they are to be the focus of what Peterson and Eeds (1990) call "intensive reading," which "gives deliberate thought to the literary experience" (p. 12). Peterson and Eeds define the criteria for selecting books for intensive reading in this way (their use of "layers" is somewhat different from MacNeil's, quoted earlier):

> Teachers of literature want children to be more than plot readers. They want them to get beyond bookjacket reporting to interpreting a story at different levels of meaning. Plot readers will know who lived, who died, and who broke a leg, but they will not reap the true rewards of attending carefully to what is evolving at various levels in the story. For literature studies we restrict our choices to books that have *layers* of story action and meaning. Multi-layered books contribute more dramatically to the feelings readers experience and the thoughts they create, and make the resolution of the central story conflict more compelling. It is possible to read MacLachlan's *Sarah, Plain and Tall* without attending to how the story is moved along by the simplicity of the prairie setting, without being aware of the part music plays in symbolizing the loss felt by Caleb and Anna, or without being aware of the importance of color in building our anticipation as well as bringing unity to the text, but much of the richness of the book will be lost if these levels are not explored. (p. 26)

Guided reading books should be meaty, but they shouldn't be too long. For example, in a fourth grade theme in North Warren Schools on people and animals on the move, Trudy Walp and her colleagues chose Laura Ingalls Wilder's *Little House on the Prairie* for guided reading. It's three hundred thirty-five pages long, and the teachers eventually realized that their students were becoming bogged down in it, so they moved it to independent reading.

The only exception to these criteria will be so-called "Big Books" chosen for guided reading by kindergarten and perhaps first grade. Big Books are not necessarily multilayered (although a few are), but they have proved themselves to be invaluable for initiating children into the beginning stages of reading, and their use in the early grades is truly an example of guided or shared reading.

Obtaining the Books

If life were fair, all the teacher should need to do is fill out a purchase order and wait until the books arrive. In the real world, obtaining books is one of the hardest parts of putting a theme together, and often teachers abandon themes simply because of the hassle of finding appropriate material. I have worked in schools with (almost) unlimited resources and in those with almost none (one didn't even have a school library while I was there), and so I'm sensitive to this issue. But in both types of schools, there were plenty of books available to the children and the teachers. Here are some ways to obtain books, starting with the least expensive:

- Borrow them from the school or public library, or educational agency (In New York State, teachers can borrow theme sets of books from local BOCES—Boards of Cooperative Services). It's a rare library that won't allow teachers to borrow copies of books in sufficient quantity to stock a classroom for the duration of a theme. But there are problems. Who pays for books that are lost, and how do you ensure books don't get lost? One way is to keep these books in the classroom, and only loan out books that you can afford to lose; another is to use only paperbacks, so replacing them doesn't cost an arm and leg. A variation on this approach is to take the children to the library and do a major part of the theme right where the books are.
- Get them from the school book clubs (Scholastic, Trumpet, Troll). It doesn't take long to build up bonus points in these clubs to earn free books for the classroom, and the range and quality of books offered by the clubs is excellent (see Strickland & Walmsley, 1993). Even the books you pay for from the book clubs are so cheap that a classroom library is quickly built up. Problems? You can't get free books unless children order on a regular basis, and some teachers are concerned that even the cheap prices are too expensive for some children.
- Purchase them with textbook money through the school. Increasingly, school districts are allowing teachers to buy trade books with money that used to be reserved only for textbooks. This is by far the most

effective method of getting books, but there are many districts in which this is still not possible. In New York State, a school has to demonstrate that the trade books are being used as "primary instructional materials," otherwise they cannot be purchased with textbook funds. This technique might not work well in other parts of the country.

- Obtain books through a grant, donations from local businesses, or through fund-raising by local parent-teacher organizations. It's sad when we have to raise our own funds to purchase classroom necessities, but raising funds for books is not difficult, and it is so visible and rewarding that few organizations can resist participating.
- Ask parents and community people to donate books. This requires a lot of organizing, but it can yield large quantities of books. Unfortunately, what it generally doesn't yield is new books. A variation on this is to ask parents and others to donate new books to celebrate birthdays or special school occasions such as graduation.
- Purchase books for one theme at a time, while borrowing the rest. What this does is build up a collection without requiring a huge lump sum all at once. It doesn't take long before all the themes are well stocked and can easily be supplemented by borrowing books.

Children Finding Their Own Books

I might have given the impression that teachers should be the sole source for the books. They shouldn't be. Just as teachers sought out books to enlarge their knowledge of a topic, children need to be seeking out their materials, too. Here's the dilemma: it's extremely difficult and time-consuming for children to seek out all the materials for a theme, and yet if they simply read what's placed in front of them, they won't learn how to select materials or even think of it as an essential part of enlarging their knowledge. Here are some ways to resolve this dilemma:

- Create some themes in which children are responsible for seeking out all the source material.
- Always encourage children to read beyond the materials supplied and to bring in materials for read-aloud, independent, or guided reading.
- Insist that some of the sources that children use for their projects go beyond what has been provided for them.

Alternating between projects in which the bulk of the materials are provided and those in which children have to go out and find the materials, or progressing from one to the other, will ensure that children aren't either insulated from the real world task of finding sources or overwhelmed by having to do everything on their own. Also, there's nothing wrong with occasionally holding back some of the sources a teacher has located so as to encourage children to find them on their own.

Fitting the Books to the Theme

One thing that frequently happens to themes is that what starts as a coherent and focused unit begins to fall apart because the original web and the theme's objectives are laid aside in the rush to obtain books. Figure 3 illustrates a technique used by Donna Norton (1982) for reminding the teacher how the books are to fit with the various aspects of the theme.

She attaches the titles of books to the various branches of the web. In this way, a teacher can instantaneously see which books belong where and if any are missing. The only addition I would suggest is marking which books are for read-aloud, which are for guided reading, and which are for independent reading.

Getting a Theme Organized

Blocking the Theme

Once the books and other sources have been found, the next step is to start thinking about how to organize the day-to-day activities that make up a theme. This is easier said than done because there are so many things to juggle into place. Is the theme meaty enough to be set up as a major theme (up to two weeks in kindergarten, perhaps up to six weeks in sixth grade), or is it more suitable for a regular theme (a day or two)? One way to decide this is by seeing how well this theme fits with major aspects of the curriculum or by looking again at the books and the subtopics and seeing how substantive they are. Also, what about the themes that come before or after this one? What interest have the children shown in the topics already explored? Would it be best to balance a longer theme with a shorter one?

Once a rough estimate of the theme's duration has been decided, it's time to start blocking in the periods to be devoted to the major subtopics. Figure 4 shows how the conceptual theme courage might be blocked.

Of course, this isn't the only way of blocking this theme: we might instead deal with the major subtopics all at once in the first week, and then let the children explore a chosen topic on their own, to return in the last week to share what they've learned. Or, we might want to have the class break up into groups, each group exploring a different subtopic for a week. (This works well when there are only a few books available.) Then, we might start going through the read-alouds, independent reading, and guided reading books and other material suitable for each of these topics; and finally, we might think about the major activities we want the children to pursue—or choose—in each of these areas. We will also need to think about the amount of time we can devote to the project. Should it consume all the time outside of the daily routines in a language arts

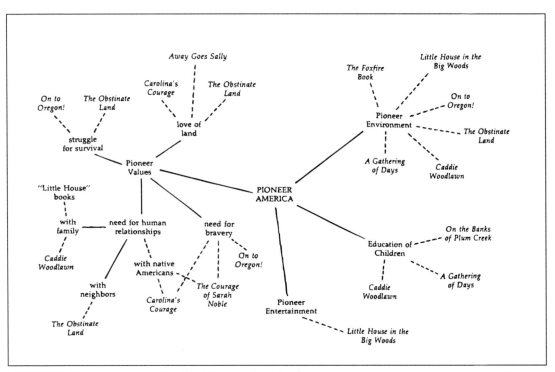

FIGURE 3. Donna Norton's Web for "Pioneer America."

class, or is it to be spread across the whole day (in a self-contained classroom), or across subject areas, or even across individual periods in a departmentalized grade? Some teachers prefer to immerse themselves in a theme for a time and then come out of it altogether, while others like to borrow smaller amounts of time from their regular curriculum and do themes concurrently.

Two Examples: A Conceptual Theme and an Author Theme. It's time for some concrete examples. Here's how two themes ("People and Animals on the Move," and an author theme on Patricia Reilly Giff) were blocked out by Trudy Walp and her colleagues at North Warren. "People and Animals on the Move" started out as the "Journeys" theme described in Walmsley and Walp (1990), but it has evolved since then into a six-week conceptual theme for fourth grade. The theme is designed for children to explore important concepts related to people and animals that make various kinds of journeys. Figure 5 illustrates the web used for this theme.

In blocking this theme, Trudy and her colleagues wanted to be sure to expose children to the major subtopics before going on to explore one or two of them in depth. Basically, the plan was to spend the first week sampling all the subtopics, using guided readings of shorter pieces—mostly articles from magazines—to

FIGURE 4.
Blocking the
Conceptual
Theme
"Courage."

Week 1	Week 2	Week 3	Week 4
General notions of courage	Courage of one's convictions	Courage in face of long term disability or illness	Courage in war

introduce the children to the various topics of the web. In the next two weeks, the teacher would pick (on her own or with the students) one or two topics to explore in depth, using both read-alouds and guided reading. The students would also be reading independently across all the topics and doing short pieces of writing across the topics. After this was completed, the students would then pick topics related to the theme to explore in depth as a project for two weeks. Major pieces of writing would accompany this project, as would sustained reading of books and other materials. Finally, a week would be devoted to sharing and presenting the individual projects.

The first thing the teachers did was to gather a number of short selections from magazines for the first week's guided reading. For example, the following article was selected to introduce students to the subtopic on journeys to challenge:

> Butcher, S. S. (1983). A woman's icy struggle. *National Geographic, 163*(3), 411–422.

The following was chosen to introduce students to the subtopic on exploration of unknown territories:

> Duryea, W. (1990). In pursuit of the Pole. *Cobblestone, 11*(11), 9–11.

The following were chosen to introduce students to the subtopic on migration:

> Gore, R. (1976). The fiery Brazilian bees. *National Geographic, 149*(4), 491–501.
> King, D. (1984). *Puffin*. New York: Lothrop.
> May, J. (1970). *Why Birds Migrate*. New York: Holiday House.

In the second and third weeks, the teacher would pick a subtopic and do extended read-alouds and guided reading on it, while the students did independent reading on books they chose from all the topics.

Suppose the teacher and students chose the subtopic "Journeys to Escape Oppression." The teacher could choose from a wide selection of books and other materials for extended read-alouds and guided reading that were aimed at

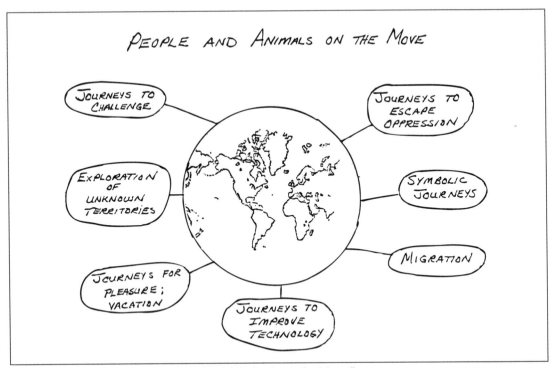

FIGURE 5. Web for the Theme "People and Animals on the Move."

building students' background information. For example, in order to build students' background knowledge of the journeys taken by oppressed black slaves in the antebellum South, the teacher might read aloud an article about Harriet Tubman in *Cobblestone*, (the February 1981 issue is devoted entirely to Harriet Tubman), a short book on following the North Star to freedom (*The Drinking Gourd* by F. N. Monjo), a poem about the dangers of escaping to freedom (*The Whippoorwill Calls*, by Beverly McLoughland), and an article from a current newspaper describing the plight of oppressed people today. For guided reading on the same topic, the teacher might choose the play *Escape to Freedom: The Story of Young Frederick Douglass* (Ossie Davis). These readings aren't limited to a single oppressed group, and they typically will include material on religious, political, and economically oppressed people from different parts of the world and in different points in history.

The fourth and fifth week would be devoted entirely to students doing projects on a subtopic of their choice. Students first decide which subtopic to explore. For example, Jason, a fourth grader, chose the subtopic "Migration" for his project. This topic is very broad, and Jason could spend the rest of his life exploring all the animals and insects that migrate. So, with his teacher, Jason begins his study of migration by narrowing down the topic to an aspect of migration he's truly interested in. He does this by plunging into reading about all kinds of migrating animals and insects until one or two start to emerge as his particular interest. In Jason's case, this turned out to be the migration of whales, and one in particular—the gray whale. Once having chosen this topic, he then explored it through additional readings (*Whales: Giants of the Deep* by Dorothy Hinshaw Patent; *Gigi* by Eleanor Coerr) that helped him become an "expert" on the gray whale. He then proceeded to write an illustrated account of the migration of the gray whale as it travels back and forth from the Bering Sea to the Baja Peninsula.

The sixth and final week would be given over to sharing and presenting the projects. Projects would be shared and presented in a variety of ways, including publishing books and reports, annotating maps (particularly appropriate for the "journeys" projects), making models, creating journals (of a journey, written by one of the characters who took it), drawing time lines of journeys, and so on.

Another example is of an author theme. Since they only had room in the curriculum for one author theme, the fourth grade teachers in North Warren decided on some criteria for selecting the particular author. One was that the author had to have written enough books to make the theme possible (for example, Madeleine L'Engle is well known, and her books are outstanding, but there aren't enough of them to sustain an author theme devoted to her work); another was that the author had to be popular with the children (plenty to choose from here!); a third was that the books themselves could be read by children of differing reading abilities. This criterion is especially difficult to meet. For example, most of Jean Craighead George's books are too challenging for some of North Warren's fourth graders to read independently. Also, it was important that the books appeal to both boys and girls. After some lengthy lunchtime discussions, the teachers decided on Patricia Reilly Giff as a suitable subject for an author theme. She is popular and prolific, her books are widely available, they appeal to both boys and girls, and there's a good range of reading and interest levels among them.

First, the teachers assembled all Patricia Reilly Giff's books and read them. What emerged from these readings was that the books fell into a number of categories. Giff has written several series (The Kids of the Polk Street School, The New Kids of the Polk Street School, Casey-Tracy, Abby Jones, Junior Detective, and The Polka Dot Private Eye); some of these are mysteries, others are contemporary realistic fiction set in schools. One way to organize the theme, then, was by the series themselves. The teachers couldn't find enough information about Patricia Reilly Giff's life to make it possible to organize the theme around her life. (This would be much easier to do for authors such as Roald Dahl or Beatrice Potter, about whom much more has been written.) So this author theme focused on Giff's writings more than on her life. Figure 6 shows how the teachers mapped out the theme.

They then decided which books to use for which kinds of reading. They selected *Fourth Grade Celebrity, Left-Handed Shortstop,* and *Rat Teeth* from the

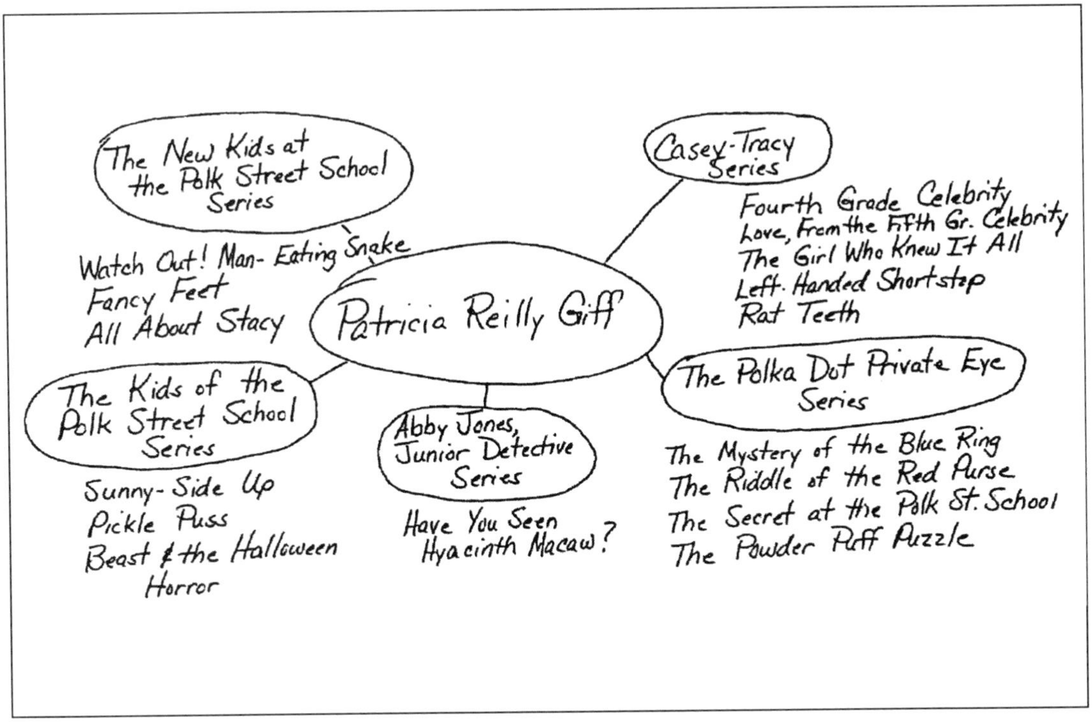

FIGURE 6. Web for Patricia Reilly Giff Theme.

Casey-Tracy series for guided reading. (They would use only one of these books for guided reading; the others would be offered as independent material.) These books are Giff's most challenging and meaty, according to the teachers, and so they made ideal candidates for guided reading. The Polk Street series—both old and new—and the Polka Dot Private Eye series were designated as independent reading material. The Abby Jones series, and additional titles from the Casey-Tracy series were also included as independent titles so that the children who wanted to read all of Giff's books could do so. One title, *The Gift of the Pirate Queen*, is not part of any series, and it's offered as an independent reading title in the sixth grade theme "Walk a Mile in My Shoes" so it wasn't included in this author theme.

For read-aloud, the teachers would select one or two books from the independent reading list.

The theme was planned to run six weeks at the beginning of the school year. One of its goals was to bring the students in from a long summer vacation, and have them be immersed in independent reading. In the first week, the teachers would introduce the web, and would "sell" independent titles. Then the students would settle into an extended period of independent reading. The guided reading would begin in the second week, with three days of guided reading along with two days of independent; this pattern would prevail for the rest of the theme. Since the theme has Giff's books rather than Giff herself as its central idea, the writing and extension activities were based on the books themselves. A typical writing activity would be for students to write about their becoming a celebrity after reading *Fourth Grade Celebrity*. An activity based on *All About Stacy* has the students collect items they feel represent themselves and put them in an All About Me box. The students tell the class about these items and about themselves, just like the main character Stacy does in the book. After planning some of these activities the teachers came across a booklet written by Patricia Reilly Giff (Giff, 1990), that suggested several activities along the same lines. It's reassuring to find out that the activities you have created for an author theme are compatible with the author's own recommendations.

Not everything can be planned and mapped out ahead of time, and there should always be room for spontaneity and the unexpected. In the Giff theme, for example, several of the children borrowed an idea from the main character Casey Valentine in *Fourth Grade Celebrity* and started their own class newspaper using many of the same techniques described by Giff in her book. This turned out to be one of the very best extension activities in the theme, and it was completely unplanned by the teachers. But the theme's major goal, to have children thoroughly explore the work of a single author, could not have been achieved without careful preparation.

Planning for Integration of Other Areas

One of the questions I get asked a lot is how important is it in designing activities to integrate as many areas as possible. Some teachers think that a theme is better if it integrates more, and so they try to think of ways in which to incorporate as many math, art, music, science, and other activities into each theme as they can. I'm not so sure we need to do this. The goal is not to see how many things can be integrated, but rather to create activities that are meaningful and encourage the children to explore different dimensions of the topic. If exploring an aspect of a topic is enhanced by doing some math or by drawing something, then by all means incorporate math and art. If not, don't feel compelled to. For example, if we do a theme on the local community that explores its industries and its geography, we will probably want to incorporate math (doing charts that show what kinds of industries there are and how many people work in them), art, and geometry (drawing scaled maps, freehand drawings of buildings or people). We'd be less likely to incorporate music in this theme. On the other hand, if we were doing a theme on the Erie Canal, we might explore canal songs and canal poetry as a major component of the theme because folk songs are an integral part of the building of the canal and of its continued use. If we burden activities with all kinds of subprojects, especially those that don't naturally fit the theme, the students will quickly become overwhelmed and they'll lose sight of the main point of the activities, which is to enlarge their knowledge of the theme.

Planning for Skills Integration

Another question that arises is whether skills instruction can be built into the activities. If the curriculum doesn't require that skills be covered, then my advice would be to teach skills as they come up in the activities rather than try to cover them explicitly and deliberately. If the curriculum does require the teaching of skills, then they will need to be built into the activities from the outset. For reading skills, I would generally try to build them into the guided reading rather than into read-alouds or independent reading. (Use these for exposing children to books and for practice of reading and listening.) For example, suppose we had created a survival theme and had picked Jean Craighead George's book *Julie of the Wolves* for guided reading. And suppose our skills curriculum demanded that we cover metaphors and similes at the same time. I would incorporate these skills as follows:

- Go through *Julie of the Wolves* and pick out metaphors and similes. One of the nice things about good literature is the ease with which good metaphors and similes can be found. There are plenty of examples within the first several pages of the book: "The Arctic sun…was a yellow disc"; "ponds and lakes freckle its immensity"; "like the beautifully formed polar bears and foxes of the north, she was slightly short-limbed."
- Prepare a general lesson on metaphors and similes, drawing definitions of metaphors and similes from the language text, but examples from *Julie of the Wolves* and other books being read during the theme (it wouldn't be that difficult to modify the practice worksheets to incorporate examples from trade books).
- Point out metaphors and similes in all of the books read on this theme, and have children keep track of ones they find and record them in a notebook, labeling them as metaphors or similes—perhaps displaying the children's favorite metaphors and similes on a large bulletin board. (These examples could also serve as items for skills assessment.)

If I had to fit writing skills into a theme, then I would probably begin by ensuring that children explored particular writing functions (expressive, transactional, persuasive) that are appropriate to the theme we are doing. For example, in our courage theme, we might deliberately have students write expressively (reflecting on the notion of courage, exploring family stories of courage), transactionally (writing to find out about what others have written on the topic), even persuasively (writing to persuade a foundation that a particular act of courage is worthy of an award). If I had an editing curriculum I had to follow, I might focus on particular editing conventions within the compositions children wrote. These are not things I'd do if I had freedom to pursue skills within the context of children's own reading and writing, but many teachers neither have the freedom, nor sometimes the confidence, to incorporate skill teaching in this way.

It does take a little preparation—as well as some confidence—to incorporate skills teaching into the books, but the result is that the skills are well integrated into the theme and have a much higher chance of being understood and remembered by the children because all the examples are taken from the books they are reading and from the pieces they are writing.

Planning for Options

Another thing we need to do while creating activities is to think about options. By this I mean that the activities we create should accommodate not only the range of children's interests, but also their differing language abilities. All children should be able to participate in the activities, and they all should be able to profit from them. This sounds like a tall order if there's a wide range of interests and abilities represented in the class, but it isn't really that difficult to do. Here's how:

- Make sure there is a sufficient range of books for each theme, especially for independent reading, that challenge the best readers at one end and accommodate the weakest readers on the other—although I would never restrict any reader to particular books, especially on the basis of readability.
- Create broad activities, with plenty of options within them, so that different children can be doing different things, even though everything they do is related to the broad topic. For example, if the topic is courage, you could ask students to explore and write about an act of courage in wartime, not restrict them to a particular war or a particular act of courage, and allow them to explore the topic in their own way. Or you could make it even broader by asking students to explore any aspect of courage they wanted, drawing on the subtopics read about and discussed in class—courage of convictions, courage vs. stupidity, and so on.

Teaching Routines

Getting Started with a New Theme

I think it's very helpful at the beginning of a new theme to give students a good idea of what they'll be exploring during the next week, month, or however long the theme will last. It's what I call "framing" the topic—giving students a general notion of the dimensions of the topic, the various directions from which we'll be approaching it, and an overall idea about what we hope they'll learn from it.

How this is done will depend partly on the age and grade of the children and partly on the topic itself. I might start a kindergarten theme by letting the children know that for the next week or so we'll be reading and talking about farms, and then I would plunge into a brief discussion about what they know about the topic, what they've read, and what they want to explore. Then I would start straight into the first read-aloud. With a more complex topic such as courage, with upper elementary students I might start the theme by briefly announcing its topic, then lay out for them the major elements of the theme, explaining how we will be approaching the topic, what kinds of activities and projects we will be doing, and what I hope the students will learn from the theme. If I have a major project in mind, this is when I'd describe it in broad terms and tell the students when it was due. This introduction might take less than thirty minutes, and then we'd plunge directly into the first activity.

There is no correct way to begin a theme, but somewhere embedded in the initial activities we should try to *stimulate* students' interest in the topic, and then *focus* their attention on different aspects of it. By stimulating, I mean that we try to open up the topic and its possibilities, partly by relating it to what students already know, and partly by drawing the students into it with interesting stimuli. By focusing, I mean that we try to get students to examine aspects of a topic more closely.

One good stimulating activity is reading aloud from a book, a poem, newspaper, or magazine, or showing a film that raises a provocative question about the topic or is inherently exciting. Beach (1983) describes a project in a remedial reading program for third and fourth graders: the teacher started by reading aloud Baylor's book *The Desert Is Theirs*. Hess (1989) describes a project in her fourth grade class in which students were researching an animal of their own choice: she read them an animal story from the children's science magazine *Chickadee*. Our theme on courage might begin with a read-aloud from Gary Paulsen's book *Hatchet*.

Another good stimulating activity is relating the topic to the students' own prior knowledge. A technique that's become very popular is getting children to tell (or write on a large sheet of construction paper or chart) "What We Know" and "What We Want to Know" (Harste et al., 1987, p. 367). In our courage theme, we might start by asking, "Can anyone tell us about an act of courage that you've witnessed or a book you've read about courage or one that has a particularly memorable act of courage in it?" Or, "What does the word *courage* mean to you?" Karen Lynch, a sixth grade teacher in North Warren, tapped her students' prior knowledge just before they started a theme on Russia: she asked them to write down everything they knew about the Soviet Union. These statements were discussed and posted on a bulletin board. Graves (1989) draws on more immediate stimuli for children to start their explorations: writing about what happened to them, about how they work and learn ("Tell me about how you used the scissors to cut this out."), about classmates' preferences ("Which do you prefer: breakfast, lunch, or dinner?"). Haggitt (1975) describes a kindergarten teacher in England who brought into class a picture of a milkman delivering milk:

> The children were able to tell the teacher how often milk was delivered to their homes, the name of the basket used for carrying milk, and why the milkman needed a van to carry his deliveries. The teacher told them that the van was called a "float"... Peter, whose father was a milkman, offered to find out more about milk floats. (p. 2)

The purpose of this introduction was to draw children into a theme on containers. Wilen and McKenrick (1989) suggest that teachers open up a topic by

> Creating some cognitive dissonance related to an issue, topic, concept, fact, event, generalization, or some other aspect of the content under study. In other words, students expect one thing, based on their current knowledge and beliefs, and something different is read, seen, heard or experienced. The discrepancy is the root of a problem and the teacher seeks to exploit the differences between what students expect and what actually happens. The more puzzlement involved, and the greater the extent of personal attachment or relevance the students have toward the problem, the better the potential for inquiry. (p. 52)

Creating a web is another good technique for getting started on a topic: webbing is especially good at opening up a topic. Here's where already having made a web as part of the preparation for the theme pays off. Instead of simply laying out the web for the students, I'd suggest starting the web from scratch, using the students' suggestions, but nudging them into aspects of the topic that they haven't thought of. This way, the students take a major responsibility in formulating the topic, but they also benefit from the teacher's bumped-up knowledge of the topic. This exercise often results in a web that's somewhat different from the teacher's original version, and sometimes it opens up aspects of a topic that the teacher had never thought of and that might be worth exploring either in addition to or instead of aspects already decided on. Katz and Chard (1989), Tchudi and Tchudi (1984), and Walmsley and Walp (1990) have practical suggestions for webbing, and several examples of webs will be found in the themes described later in the book. Katz and Chard have a particularly good technique for webbing in the early grades. They suggest doing the initial brainstorming on small slips of paper, then organizing these into the various categories, and finally constructing a permanent web, as shown in Figure 7.

Focusing is the opposite of stimulating; it helps students narrow down a topic, and makes it more manageable and better defined. A good focusing activity is revising a web that has already been generated, especially if this is done a day or two after the original web was created. Once children become adept at creating webs, they almost always will create ones that have overlapping categories, categories that really don't belong to the theme, or ones that seem, on reflection, not to be feasible or sensible to explore. So it makes

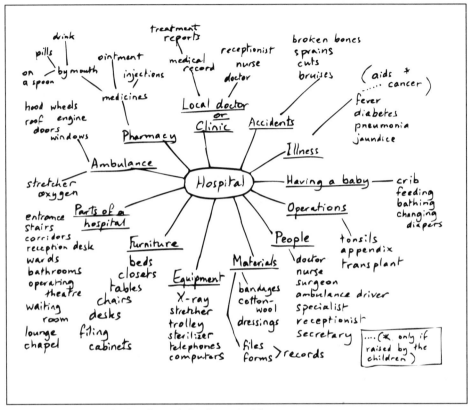

FIGURE 7. Katz and Chard's Web for "Hospital."

sense to get the web down to size and end up with, as far as possible, categories that don't overlap. Revising a web is an excellent exercise in its own right because it involves children in a great deal of thinking as they sort through the various options for combining, adding, and deleting categories.

Another popular method for getting students to narrow their focus on a topic is to ask them a series of questions (e.g., "What's the difference between bravery and courage?" "Can you tell me all of the different kinds of farms?" "Are dolphins whales?"), or have them generate a list of questions. Suid (1988) has some good advice:

> Be sure your students understand that having a *subject* is not the same as having a *question*. "Termites" is a subject, and as such, leads no place in particular. But "Are people winning the war against termites?" is a question that gives direction and focus to the quest for information. Sometimes you can provide the question. But you're better off providing a general subject, getting your students to think up lots of questions, then

helping them pick the most interesting ones. As they practice, they'll begin to see which questions lead to the most successful research. (p. 74)

While developing a list of questions is valuable, it also can have undesirable effects. One of them is the tendency of children to use their questions or treat the teacher's questions as a rigid, unbendable outline for their projects, as though the only purpose for the questions being asked is to answer them—and only them—in their projects. Another is for teachers and children to only ask certain kinds of questions, for example, "What is...?"; "How does it feel to be...?", while ignoring questions that raise other questions and encourage deeper thinking (e.g., "Why do you suppose...?", "What will you need to explore if you address that question?", "Is that the same as...?"). Some teachers are very good at acknowledging children's questions without answering them (answering them simply leads children to think that their job is to get the right answers to the right questions); answering children's questions with more questions is a good strategy, too:

Child: "Is bravery the same thing as courage?"

Teacher: "I wonder. And what's the difference between courage and heroism?"

A third approach to focusing, which is suitable for children in second grade and above, is having students write down things they want to explore or questions they want to answer now that they have had some preliminary discussions on the topic. Writing is by its very nature a focusing activity, and it also provides a permanent and individual record of what was discussed, unlike brainstorming, which typically leaves no residue after the discussion is over and the chalkboard erased.

There are several things I'm trying to get accomplished in these initial exercises:

- I want to generate some excitement and enthusiasm for the theme, especially if it's one that takes a little getting into (but is well worth the effort once the ice is broken).
- I want students to know what I hope they'll learn by exploring this theme.
- I want students to understand the broad dimensions of the topic and also the major subtopics (and I want their assistance in defining what these are).
- I want them to have a good idea about the major activities, projects, and assignments (so they know what's involved and can start thinking about their projects/assignments, especially if this involves selecting topics of their choice).

With younger children, generating excitement and enthusiasm and letting them know what I hope they'll learn will probably suffice; they'll understand the subtopics and the projects as they explore them.

Now we are ready to settle into the daily routines.

Settling into the Routines

Whether we are teaching a half-day kindergarten, a ninety-minute language arts block in third grade, or a thirty-seven-minute English or social studies period in seventh grade, there are some basic routines associated with theme studies. Essentially, what we'll be doing throughout a theme is enlarging children's knowledge of topics by reading about them (out aloud, independently, and shared), writing about them, talking and listening about them, doing things with them (e.g., dramatizing, drawing, making models, filming), and presenting them. Along the way, we may include activities that involve math, music, art, and combine subject areas. We will certainly teach children the skills and strategies they need in order to gain access to the topics and communicate that knowledge to themselves and others, although some teachers will work on these skills and strategies more directly, while others will tuck them into the various reading and writing activities.

Reading Aloud. Most teachers need no encouragement to read aloud on a regular basis, and I would expect daily read-aloud sessions of an average of at least fifteen minutes throughout a theme. (In situations where the schedule is broken up into thirty- to forty-minute periods, I would suggest that reading aloud account for about ten to fifteen percent of the time devoted to the theme, and done two or three times a week for fifteen minutes, rather than three to four minutes each class period.) I have already made the case for reading aloud and suggested criteria for selecting books for read-alouds (see pp. 43–46). The most important things about reading aloud during a theme are that:

- All children in the class participate in the theme read-alouds (in other words, we don't have separate read-alouds for differently able readers).
- We select material for read aloud that enlarges children's knowledge of the topics in the theme.
- We select a sufficient number of books and other material that are slightly ahead, in terms of content and syntax, of where children currently are (we can mediate between the text and the children).
- We read straight through the material, pausing not at all, or only to address students' questions (not stopping at the end of each paragraph or page to ask comprehension or vocabulary questions).

Independent Reading. Again, most teachers don't need their arms twisted to have their students read on their own, and providing an average of fifteen to thirty minutes daily for children's independent reading is now commonplace. In a theme, independent reading plays an important role in helping children gain access to new knowledge (even in kindergarten, but increasingly as children get older and are more capable of reading independently). What's different, however, between regular independent reading (e.g., uninterrupted silent sustained reading, or "drop everything and read") and the independent reading done as part of a theme is that in the former, children generally bring in and read anything they want, while in the latter, children will be reading material related to theme (whether they chose it or it was chosen for them). What's important about theme-related independent reading is:

- Children have access to a wide range of reading materials related to the theme for their independent reading.
- We do not restrict children to particular books on the basis of readability or children's reading abilities, but we do give children guidance and assistance in choosing appropriate books.
- We encourage children to seek out and read books related to the theme beyond those we have provided for them (from school and public libraries or from home collections).
- We provide uninterrupted time for children to read independently, and in the higher grades we extend independent reading into homework.
- We keep track—or, better still, the children do—of what children have read independently.
- We talk informally to children about their independent reading, and beyond kindergarten, we have them react to what they have read and learned (e.g., in response journals, discussion groups, book conferences with teacher, and so on).

Shared or Guided Reading. Themes are, by their very nature, intensive explorations of topics, and so we should expect children to be involved in close readings of books and other materials. Shared or guided reading is especially important in classrooms where the bulk of skills teaching is to be done within the context of the reading and writing activities, as opposed to being taught separately, because it is in these intensive studies of books that many of the skills and strategies will be taught. In kindergarten and first grade, guided reading primarily consists of "Big Books"; they may not meet Peterson and Eeds's (1990) criteria for books with multiple layers of meaning, but they are ideal for teaching book reading strategies in the early grades. At the second grade level and beyond, we would be looking for books that had sufficient depth that makes studying them closely worthwhile. What's important about guided reading beyond second grade is:

- We choose books with multiple layers of meaning that allow children to study them intensively and gain literary insights from them.
- We choose books from genres appropriate to the theme (for example, in a historical theme, we can do guided reading with both fiction and nonfiction material; in a current events theme, we can use newspapers, nonfiction books, even documents for guided reading).
- We read these books or other literacy materials deliberately and closely with the children, working through their layers of meaning, examining literary elements where appropriate (e.g., characters, time, settings), and

resolving reading difficulties (word identification, vocabulary, comprehension) as they arise.

- We can teach all, or the bulk of, reading skills through these guided books, or we can use them to practice or strengthen skills taught independently of the theme.
- We can use the same books with the whole class (provided that the less able readers are given additional assistance to help them keep up with the others in the class), or have smaller groups of children read different books (provided that children are not permanently assigned to a group on the basis of their reading ability).

Techniques for guided reading are extensively explored in Routman (1988; 1991); Walmsley and Walp (1990); Peterson and Eeds (1990).

Writing. In a typical process writing program, children choose their own topics to write about; writing in a theme, on the other hand, will almost always be focused on the topics being explored. This doesn't mean that children have no choice in their writing topics; within the area broadly defined by the theme, children will have considerable freedom to explore topics of their own and to explore them in unique ways. I see two kinds of writing in a theme: one consists of shorter pieces such as response journals or logs or as exploratory essays assigned by the teacher to get children to think through an aspect of a topic (for example, a short piece on an act of courage in the student's family or community; a brief summary of two or three of the books read on courage in war). The other is writing done as part of a major project for a theme (for example, writing a research paper on the physiology of courage after reading several books and journal articles). In a theme in which there are many books read, writing plays a particularly important role in helping children articulate their reactions to what they have read.

The major purpose of writing in a theme is to help students learn more about the topics they are pursuing and to communicate to others what they are learning. Over the course of several themes, students will have written a number of pieces that explore different aspects of topics, and they will have written for a variety of functions (e.g., expressive, persuasive, referential) and audiences (self, trusted others, wider audiences). The themes themselves will suggest genuine topics, functions, and audiences: for example, writing letters to a state geologist to ask if he could explain something in a pamphlet on minerals that the class didn't understand; submitting poems written on the topic of courage to *Merlyn's Pen*, the national magazine of student writing; reflecting on what was learned in the theme "Walk a Mile in My Shoes"; engaging in the struggle to stop whale hunting as part of the "Whales" theme; writing a major referential report on an endangered species.

As with reading, we need to set aside time for children to write. In the early grades, writing—like everything else—is a highly social activity, but as children become more proficient with their writing, and as writing plays an increasingly larger role in their thinking, they need more time alone to compose. It is generally acknowledged that writing is harder than reading: in reading, all you have to do is figure out what someone else has written, but in writing, you not only have to think of something to say but also get it down using the appropriate written conventions, and do it in such a way that others will understand what you have written. So we need to give students plenty of uninterrupted time for their writing. Since their writing is connected to the theme, we really don't have to assign separate blocks of time for reading and writing—children can easily read and write on their own in the same physical space and at the same time—but we do need to ensure that adequate blocks of time are available for writing, especially during a major writing project. I think we should devote an average of fifteen to thirty minutes daily to independent writing. Revision and editing conferences can be scheduled during this time, provided they don't disturb the other children. Older children should be encouraged to take their writing home and work on it independently outside of school.

In addition to helping students enlarge their composing repertoire, these written pieces make excellent candidates for post-writing activities, so they can be used to help students improve their composing and editing abilities, too. Provided that students have written extensively, all—or at least the bulk of—revision and editing skills can be taught within the context of their own compositions. Here's how:

- Select, or have the children select, pieces for revision conferences; it helps if over time different kinds of pieces have been revised.
- Hold revision conferences using techniques suggested by Graves (1983); Calkins (1986); Calkins and Harwayne (1990); Harwayne (1992).
- Analyze and take notes on the child's editing strengths and weaknesses (spelling, handwriting, usage, punctuation/capitalization, grammar), then hold editing conferences, focusing on a manageable number of editing issues.
- Have children (with the exception of kindergartners and beginning first graders who may not be ready to handle this task) correct all editing errors before a piece is published.
- If need be, do mini-lessons on specific editing problems (see Atwell, 1987; Calkins, 1986), but only with children who need them.
- Keep track of each child's progress in revision and editing, noting growth in the child's mastery of written conventions.

Activities/Projects. Reading and writing are, of course, activities. What I mean by an activity is teachers and children doing something concrete with theme-related topics that extends what has been read or puts a concept into practice. The difference between an activity and a project is that a project lasts over a period of time, and it involves sustained and focused inquiries into an aspect or aspects of a theme, while an activity is usually brief and fairly narrow in its scope. Projects, however, will always be made up of activities that extend what children have read about, written, or discussed. In the early grades, a project and a theme are really the same thing because what kindergartners and first graders do is a series of activities that contribute to the theme, even though they aren't formally engaged in a project. In later grades, a project is more likely to be part of a theme, but it is not the whole theme.

In kindergarten or first grade, we would expect children to be engaged daily in activities related to the theme. For example, in a farm theme, activities might involve children in drawing barns, making farm animals out of clay, keeping a journal to follow the progress of chick-hatching, making butter, working on puzzles with a farm motif, or doing counting with farm animals (Walmsley et al., 1992b). Activities at this level need to be concrete, brief in duration (no longer than twenty to thirty minutes), and engaging.

Activities are always better if they relate to the theme and not just to a book that is read as part of the theme. For example, it isn't appropriate to do a pasta cooking activity after reading Tomie de Paola's *Strega Nona* if the book is part of a theme on folk tales. *Strega Nona* is a cautionary tale about a boy who is naughty—it isn't really about making pasta—and so an activity in which children write or tell about a time they didn't listen to their parents, and something that happened as a consequence, would be much more appropriate than a cooking activity.

As children become older, they have the capacity and appetite for longer and more complex activities, what I call projects. By third grade, children can do projects that last over three or more weeks, which involve them in reading, writing, and other activities such as art and music. In a theme on humor, children might be asked to gather a number of humorous family stories by interviewing family members and writing down the stories. They might then collate the stories into a folder and participate in a reading of their favorite ones to the entire class. This project sounds simple, but it's quite involved. Children have to seek out family members who have stories, listen to them (perhaps record them), write them down (which will involve drafts, revisions, editing, and final copies), and then make a presentation. A theme on Russia at the sixth grade level might involve the careful reading of a number of books, followed by choosing a topic to research, further reading, and then writing up the whole project as a report. Our theme on courage might have multiple projects from which students could choose: one that explores the physiology of courage, another that researches commonalties among acts of courage during war (or acts of courage across different wars), another that describes in detail the anatomy of a single act of courage, another that examines the lives of people whose courage of their convictions makes them memorable, and so on. Each one of these projects involves substantial reading and writing, and presenting them might also involve art, music, and drama. We wouldn't abandon activities beyond first grade—they are very useful to drive home a point or to see how well a child has grasped the details of something he or she has been reading—but we might want to ensure that each major theme has associated with it at least one substantial project.

One of the most important things to bear in mind when creating projects for a theme is that in doing them, students will substantially enlarge their knowledge of the topics they explore. Projects, if done well, take a lot of time, and there should be intellectual returns on the investment of this time. Many of the projects I see in elementary classrooms don't show much evidence of substantive learning, which is sad given their potential.

Another point to be made about projects is that they don't necessarily need to be thought of only as a culminating activity. Projects can start off a theme, go on for the duration of a theme, or wind one up.

Different kinds of projects require different ways to acquire, organize, make sense of, and present information. In creating projects, we might want to vary these so that children experience this variety. If we ask students to read extensively on a topic and then write an essay that pulls these readings together, the students will mostly be engaged in reading and writing. On the other hand, if we ask students to interview family or community members to learn about family or community traditions, then they will be relying more heavily on gleaning information from people rather than from books. If we ask students to participate in an event (volunteering in a nursing home, learning how to milk cows, assembling items for a museum collection, building a piece of playground equipment, constructing a model of a Native American longhouse), then they will be transforming information taken from direct experience into written or spoken form. For each of these projects, the information lies in different locations, and its transformation requires quite different mental operations.

Choice is also important in project work. There's nothing worse than to see a child slugging through a six-week project on a topic he or she dislikes intensely and one that has to be done exactly the same way as everyone else in the class. It might be easier for the teacher to compare performances on projects that have identical topics and requirements, but it's misery for the students and ultimately quite boring for the teacher, too. Why not instead set out the general parameters of the project, and then encourage students to explore subtopics of their own in ways they find interesting and appropriate? This will involve more work for the teacher, both in giving students assistance and in reading and grading the final products, but it's inherently more satisfying, and it brings with it some unexpected bonuses. One is that it forces students to take responsibility for their own projects (rather than simply comply with the project requirements). It also yields projects that take different slants on the same topic and explore a variety of topics from which all students will eventually profit. (For a good example of the results of such an approach, see Five and Rosen, 1985.) They will see, for example, how other students approached the same topic, and they will learn about topics they didn't explore. One of my graduate students, Bill Failing, recently created a theme on diversity in which he explored the lives and contributions of a large number of minority Americans. If his students each explored the life and contribution of a different person, then came together and shared what they had learned, all the students would benefit enormously from the variety of people they had explored. Contrast this with everyone doing the same project on the same person. Another bonus is that if students explore different aspects of a topic, they won't be falling all over each other to find and read the same materials. But most of all, this approach acknowledges that different students have different interests and ways of learning, and their enthusiasm for project work will be enormously enhanced by giving them genuine choices about what to pursue and how to pursue it.

Should students work alone on projects, or should the projects be collaborative efforts? I would suggest a balance between the two. Project work is ideal for students to work together in small groups, especially with activities in which pooling resources and sharing the tasks have good payoffs. For example, if a project involves interviewing a number of people in the community, a team of students could share the work: one student asks the questions, another records the conversation; they all share in writing up the interview. At other times, students with particular talents in photography or art could work together with students with writing abilities so that the final product is both well written and well illustrated. That's the way adults typically work, so why shouldn't students? But there will be times when students need to work alone on projects. If we've decided to explore a number of smaller projects—learning about all the domestic birds in our community—then we might want each student to pick a favorite bird and research it by themselves. Here's where sharing the tasks makes less sense. I also like the idea of letting students decide, on occasion, whether they want to work alone or in a group of their own choosing (or mine, if their group really gets bogged down).

Finally, when do you know that a project has gone on long enough? As with themes themselves, no project is ever truly completed, but after a while they no longer sustain our interest, and from that point on, they yield less and less. Inexperienced teachers should start with activities and small projects (probably only one per theme) in order to become comfortable with the approach. Later, experiment with longer projects, ones that require more reading, more integration, and deeper explorations. I still wouldn't do more than two projects in a major theme lasting more than four weeks, and I might avoid projects all together in smaller themes (just do activities).

Activities and projects are essential components of themes, and if they are done right, will certainly enlarge students' knowledge of the world. They are also excellent vehicles for nurturing students' growing language abilities. They are not easy to put together, but they yield such excellent returns that the effort is well rewarded for teachers and their students.

Presenting, Sharing. As students and teachers, all of us have suffered through interminable presentations of projects in which children who have copied information straight from encyclopedias attempt to read this information to an assembly of their classmates. While substantial reading of books and other materials will almost certainly improve the quality of these oral reports, varying the format of the presentations themselves is also a good idea. The first thing to do is give up insisting that children all report on their projects in the same way; instead, we should encourage them to present their projects in ways they think are appropriate both for the project and for the audience and give them help as they do so. The most important thing about presentation formats is that they are appropriate to the project at hand. Short projects should probably be shared and either be displayed for everyone to look at or be briefly talked about by the author in a share session. Longer projects should probably have more elaborate modes of presentation. If done imaginatively, preparing a project for presentation can involve students in a number of language and other activities (e.g., artistic, graphic design, word-processing, film-making, multi-media) that flow naturally from their projects and match the presentation format with the project itself. For example, Karen Lynch's sixth grade students in North Warren recently did a poetry theme. As a culminating activity, the students recorded their poems on audiotape. They then chose music and slides to accompany the readings, and so their presentations were truly multi-media. If it is a project that attempts to explain a process in which much of the material is visual (e.g., the making of automobiles, manufacturing everyday materials out of minerals, the process of growing rice), then it would be more appropriate to think of a filmstrip (either an actual one or one made with overheads). If it's a project on the lifestyles of several Native American tribes, then a diorama or model might be more appropriate. Geographical projects lend themselves more to posters, maps, and three-dimensional displays. Compiling an autobiography might lend itself to an album format. As students get older and their research becomes more formal, they most likely will want their reports to look like reports, properly bound and word-processed. (I like using models from the real world, such as company annual reports, brochures, magazines, and professional journals.) James and Barkin (1983), Tone (1988), and Beach (1983) have some excellent ideas to pass on to students as they do their projects.

Oral presentations will be improved greatly if students can be persuaded not to simply read "essays" aloud in front of the class. A sixth grade teacher I observed several years ago encourages students to bring to the class one or two exhibits from their project, talk about them, and then answer questions. This seems to me to be particularly effective.

I recommend that students rehearse their formal presentations and teachers coach them as they would in directing a play so that students not only make a formal presentation but also learn how to. It's as important to revise presentations as it is to revise writing. Otherwise, how will a student who isn't already naturally gifted at presenting become proficient at it?

Assessment

There are several things we need to assess, or rather know about, during and after a theme. First, we need to know where students are in terms of their knowledge of the topics they are exploring. If a child already knows what we were going to explore in a theme on Russia, then we need to make appropriate adjustments to the theme—like finding more challenging material that explores aspects of Russia that the child doesn't know about but still would find interesting. If children's prior knowledge of a topic is very scant, we may have to make adjustments in the other direction. This doesn't require formal pretesting; it can be found out through initial discussions with the children and in their reactions to the material presented at the beginning of the theme. As a theme progresses, we need to keep track of what children are learning about the topic so that at the end of the theme we can assess what they did learn. One of the problems of trying to measure this knowledge too precisely is that what children acquire during a theme may not truly sink in until much later when connections are made between information gained in one theme and information learned later. Children assimilate information over time, so there isn't a tidy connection between the focus of a particular theme and what eventually is acquired from it. Nonetheless, it is useful to be able to characterize what knowledge we think a child has taken away from a theme. For example, if we have been studying farms, what can we say that children know now about farms that they didn't know before? One way is go back to our original web where perhaps we'll find that we set out to explore four aspects of farms: different types of farms (dairy, vegetable, etc.), dairy farms (a detailed exploration of breeds of dairy cows, milking cows, and dairy products), farm animals (cows, pigs, chickens, etc.), and egg-to-chick (a mini-project on hatching chicken eggs) (Walmsley et al., 1992b, p. 385). It shouldn't be too difficult to find out what individual children have learned about these four aspects of the topic. We can get this information from a variety of sources: from children's reactions to books and other materials we have shared with them, from their written products, from observing them in the small group activities dotted throughout the theme, and from the conversations we have with them.

Thus we might be able to say that a child named Deanna came into this theme with quite a lot of information on farms because she told us early in the theme that her grandparents have a farm, and she's visited it many times. She knew a lot about dairy farms but little about other kinds of farms, as we found out when we explored the different kinds, but she quickly assimilated this new information. Even though she had been on her grandparents' dairy farm, she knew little about the process of dairy farming, but after this theme she had an excellent grasp of the grass-to-milk transformation, as we learned from an explanation she gave during a "reading" of Ali Mitgutsch's book *From Grass to Butter*. We acquired this knowledge about Deanna without a single paper-and-pencil test, just by observing her during activities, noting the responses she gave to questions, and looking at her written products. Obviously, we don't know whether Deanna's knowledge of farms will strengthen or diminish as we move on to other topics, but we have a fairly clear idea of what she has gained from this topic. And if we routinely communicate with parents, we should get confirmation of our assessment of Deanna's knowledge from her parents, unless Deanna keeps her new-found knowledge to herself.

We can also ask children what they have learned from the themes. Very young children have some difficulty reflecting on their own knowledge, and they might be puzzled why a teacher is asking them, but as children get older, their capacity for reflection increases, and they are excellent sources for this information.

We also need to keep tabs on children's processing abilities—their ability to gain access to the materials and their ability to communicate orally or in writing what they have been learning. Again, this requires no formal testing, but it requires careful observation during read-alouds, independent, and guided reading; during writing; in book and writing conferences; and in share sessions and formal presentations. Some of this information comes from an analysis of children's actual reading (in, say, a miscue analysis or a running record), some comes from our notes on their composing and editing abilities (taken from their own compositions), and some comes from our notes on working directly on skills or strategies in mini-lessons. Thus we might say of a child called David that at this point his reading is characterized by excellent comprehension provided that the book is narrative fiction and illustrated, but he has continuing difficulties with nonfiction and with chapter books that aren't illustrated. In particular, he has difficulty figuring out longer passages that aren't directly related to the overall story line. His writing is technically fine, with the exception of his spelling, but he hasn't yet tackled topics that require a sustained focus, and so it's hard to say if he can handle them. His oral abilities are excellent; even though his project was thin in substance, he presented it clearly and effectively. Again, all of this information comes from observation and from analysis of conversations and samples of his reading and writing.

We also need to assess the theme itself. Is this theme appropriate for the children? What about its subtopics? What about the reading materials and the activities and assignments? Was it about the right length? Did it accomplish what it set out for enlarging children's knowledge? We will get some of this information from doing the theme—books that fall flat either because they are too hard or too easy; projects that seem too hard for the children (frustration levels will be high), or not challenging enough (boredom will show); writing activities that don't seem to work; activities that "bomb." Sometimes things go so badly that the best thing is to abandon them right away and move on. Other times, a project starts off on the wrong foot, but it recovers after some tinkering or after the children get into it. Also, things that bomb for us aren't necessarily disasters for children. Conversely, we'll see which books excited, stimulated, and challenged (the "must repeats"); projects that children became so engrossed in they didn't want them to end; writing and other activities that clearly were just right for the children.

Even if adjustments have been made to the theme as it goes along, it's still worthwhile to reflect on it after it's done. Take a look at samples of all the children's work laid out across the floor. What do they tell you about the appropriateness of the activities for all the children? Your recollection of the theme was that it went very well. For you. What about for the children? Was it effective for the brighter children or those with prior knowledge or interest in the topic but disappointing for those with less ability, knowledge, or interest? Did the boys profit from it, the girls less so, or vice versa? This exercise doesn't take long, and it should address two questions: are all children profiting from the theme? If not, what changes could be made to this theme, or the one coming up, to ensure that they are?

How is all of this actually done? First, lay out the major subtopics or goals for children's learning in a theme. This is probably best done before starting the theme, as I have suggested earlier, but if the theme has been created as it went along, then it will have to be done after the fact, as it were. One of my graduate students, Nancy Mulcahy, recently created a fifth grade theme on endangered species, and she had three things she wanted her students to come away with:

1. Knowing which species are endangered, their physical characteristics and habitats, reasons why they are disappearing, and what is being done to help them survive.

2. Knowing why changes in people's behavior towards endangered species and their habitats are so slow in coming.

3. Encourage students to become actively involved in working towards saving endangered species.

Because her theme is organized around these three major subtopics, her evaluation instruments should to be organized around them, too. Figure 8 shows a chart that would allow her to note the progress being made by each student towards these goals.

The evidence for children's progress toward these goals will come from a variety of sources: from direct observation (e.g., students answering teacher's or other students' questions, discussing topics in small groups, presenting to or sharing with the class), from written products (logs of books read, reaction pieces to books, activities and projects), and from one-on-one conferences (e.g., book, writing).

From the same activities and through the same means (direct observation, examination of written products, and one-on-one conferences), the teacher can also track each student's progress in literacy skills. This progress can be charted on a check list, as seen in Figure 9, or transferred from teacher notes to a narrative, as seen in Figure 10.

It helps also to solicit feedback on the effectiveness of a theme from parents of younger children and from the students themselves, especially as they get older. A simple sheet that explains what the theme was intended to accomplish, with

Student	Species	Changes in people's behavior	Involvement in saving species
J.S.S.	manatee	conflict between recreation and manatee's inability to get out of way.	sent away for materials to the Center for Marine Conservation (Wash, D.C.)
D.P.W.	whales	whales still hunted for their bones & blubber	became involved in green Peace

FIGURE 8. Example of a Student Progress Chart.

Language Arts
Reading Record

Student Name _Dan_   Grade _5_

Date	Title & Author	Reading Activity	Notes
10/8	If You Want to Scare Yourself — Sommer-Bodenburg	___ Shared Rdg ___ Guided Rdg ✓ Independent Rdg ✓ Book Conference ___ Project ___ Other ___	Dan said the book was hard but he read it slowly he understood it. He also said he reread parts when he didn't get them the first time. He did organized unaided retelling of plot. Liked book.
11/23	The Crows of Pear-Blossom — Huxley	___ Shared Rdg ___ Guided Rdg ✓ Independent Rdg ✓ Book Conference ___ Project ___ Other ___	Picture book. Dan really liked it. Did detailed unaided retelling. Compared death of main character to death of Sadako.
12/7	Freckle Juice — Blume	___ Shared Rdg ___ Guided Rdg ✓ Independent Rdg ✓ Book Conference ___ Project ___ Other ___	Dan did accurate & detailed retelling of plot - no prompts needed. Dan described how sometimes he reads parts over when he doesn't understand. Oral reading was accurate & fluent.
		___ Shared Rdg ___ Guided Rdg ___ Book Conference ___ Project	

FIGURE 9. Example of a Child's Reading Record.

FIGURE 10.
Example of a
Narrative
Report Card.

Language Arts

Word recognition continues
to be Dan's stronger area
in reading but his com-
prehension is improving.
Dan has been doing a lot
of independent reading in
school. He retells the plot
of books without any prompts.
His retellings are accurate
and detailed. He is also
monitoring his comprehension
and can describe what he
does to understand a part
that initially confused him.
These are the beginnings
of solid independent
reading behaviors.
    In writing, Dan's drafts
are improving in organization.
Continued work is needed to
develop his ideas more. The
mechanical aspects of writing
are difficult areas for Dan.
Dan seems to rely almost
exclusively on phonics to
spell words. He often is
unsure as to whether
or not he has spelled
words correctly.

Math
Progressing Successfully ☐

Needs More Time & Experience ☐

Social Studies
Progressing Successfully ☐

Needs More Time & Experience ☐

Science
Progressing Successfully ☐

Needs More Time & Experience ☐

space for the parent or student to write their comments and suggestions, is probably sufficient for this task. For younger students, it might be helpful to ask parents if their children have remarked on or shown evidence of having learned new information about the current or previous themes. These informal evaluations are easy to conduct and they provide extremely valuable information.

In this first section I've tried to make the case for a theme-centered approach to the elementary curriculum, and I have laid out in some detail the various elements of putting a theme together and carrying it out. If the reader is only allowed to take away from this section two things, I'd like them to be these:

- Make themes substantive in the sense that they pursue knowledge worth spending time on.
- Bump up your own knowledge of the topic before doing the theme with children because your enlarged knowledge will have profoundly positive effects on enlarging children's knowledge.

If themes are substantive and if teachers have enlarged their knowledge ahead of time, there'll be no need to insist that the activities and projects during a theme be genuine and worthwhile because they already will be if these two steps have been taken.

Although I have given many practical examples along the way, I felt that it might be useful to provide examples of themes in action. In Part 2, teachers from grades K–6 describe themes they have developed and have used with their children. In their different ways, these teachers exemplify the principles and practices I have described in Part 1, but it will become clear right from the outset that they define themes and what they consider to be appropriate activities in their own way. This is as it should be. There is no single right way to create and carry out a theme, and I hope that these seven themes demonstrate a range of ways to approach theme-based teaching across the elementary grades.

REFERENCES

Professional Resources

Allington, R. L. (1992). Reducing the risk: Integrated language arts in restructured elementary schools. In L. M. Morrow, L. C. Wilkinson, & J. Smith (Eds.), *The integrated language arts: Controversy to consensus* (pp. 193–213). New York: Allyn & Bacon.

Altwerger, B., & Flores, B. (1991). The theme cycle: An overview. In K. S. Goodman, L. B. Bird, & Y. M. Goodman (Eds.), *The whole language catalog* (p. 295). New York: American School Publishers.

Altwerger, B., & Flores, B. (1994). Theme cycles: Creating communities of learners. *Primary Voices K–6, 2*(1), 2–6.

Atwell, N. (1987). *In the middle: Writing, reading, and learning with adolescents.* Portsmouth, NH: Heinemann.

Beach, J. D. (1983). Teaching students to write informational reports. *Elementary School Journal, 84*(2), 213–220.

Bettelheim, B. (1976). *The uses of enchantment.* New York: Knopf.

Borrell, J. (1992). America's shame: How we've abandoned our children's future. *MacWorld, 9*(9), 25–31.

Bracey, G. W. (1991). Why can't they be like we were? *Phi Delta Kappan, 73*(2), 104–117.

Bredekamp, S. (Ed.). (1987). *Developmentally appropriate practice in early childhood programs serving children from birth through age 8* (Expanded ed.). Washington, DC: National Association for the Education of Young Children.

Byrum, D., & Pierce, V. L. (1993). Bringing children to literacy through theme cycles. In B. Harp (Ed.), *Bringing children to literary: Classrooms at work* (pp. 105–122). Norwood, MA: Christopher Gordon.

Calkins, L. McC. (1983). *Lessons from a child: On the teaching and learning of writing.* Portsmouth, NH: Heinemann.

Calkins, L. McC. (1986). *The art of teaching writing.* Portsmouth, NH: Heinemann.

Calkins, L. McC., & Harwayne, S. (1990). *Living between the lines.* Portsmouth, NH: Heinemann.

Contemporary Books. (1993). *Chase's annual events: Special days, weeks, and months, 1993.* Chicago: Contemporary Books.

Cullinan, B. E. (Ed.). (1992). *Invitation to read: More children's literature in the reading program.* Newark, DE: International Reading Association.

Edelsky, C., Altwerger, B., & Flores, B. (1991). *Whole language: What's the difference?* Portsmouth, NH: Heinemann.

Emig, J. (1977). Writing as a mode of learning. *College Composition and Communication, 28,* 122–128.

Endersbee, B. (1987). In the library with Roald Dahl. In J. Hancock & S. Hill (Eds.), *Literature-based reading programs at work* (pp. 107–116). Portsmouth, NH: Heinemann.

Fielding, L. & Roller, C. (1992). Making difficult books accessible and easy books acceptable. *Reading Teacher, 45*(9), 675–685.

Finn, C. (1991). *We must take charge.* New York: Macmillan.

Five, C., & Rosen, M. (1985). Children recreate history in their own voices. In J. Hansen, T. Newkirk, & D. Graves (Eds.), *Breaking ground: Teachers relate reading and writing in the elementary school* (pp. 91–96). Portsmouth, NH: Heinemann.

Freeman, E. B., & Person, D. G. (Eds.). (1992). *Using Nonfiction Trade Books in the Elementary Classroom: From Ants to Zeppelins.* Urbana, Il: National Council of Teachers of English.

Galda, L., & Cotter, J. (1992). Exploring cultural diversity (Children's books). *Reading Teacher, 45*(6), 452–460.

Gamberg, R., Kwak, W., Hutchings, M., & Altheim, J. (1988). *Learning and loving it: Theme studies in the classroom.* Portsmouth, NH: Heinemann.

Giff, P. R. (1990). *A teacher's guide to "The new kids at the Polk Street School books" and "The kids of the Polk Street School books."* New York: Bantam Doubleday Dell.

Gillespie, J. T., & Naden, C. J. (1990). *Best books for children, pre-school through grade six.* New York: R.R. Bowker.

Goodman, K. S. (1986). *What's whole in whole language?* Portsmouth, NH: Heinemann.

Graves, D. H. (1983). *Writing: Teachers and children at work.* Portsmouth, NH: Heinemann.

Graves, D. H. (1989). *Investigate nonfiction.* Portsmouth, NH: Heinemann.

Grosvenor, M. (1985). Geographic ignorance: Time for a turnaround. *National Geographic, 167*(6), iv.

Haggitt, E. M. (1975). *Projects in the primary school.* London: Longman.

Hansen, J. (1987). *When writers read.* Portsmouth, NH: Heinemann.

Hansen, J. (1993). Synergism of classroom and school libraries. *The New Advocate, 6*(3), 201–211.

Harste, J., Short, K., & Burke, C. (Eds.). (1987). *Creating classrooms for authors: The reading-writing connection*. Portsmouth, NH: Heinemann.

Harwayne, S. (1992). *Lasting impressions: Weaving literature into the writing workshop*. Portsmouth, NH: Heinemann.

Hess, M. L. (1989). All about hawks or Oliver's Disaster: From facts to narrative. *Language Arts*, 66(3), 304–308.

Hillkirk, R. K. (1982). Death as a theme in literature. *English Journal*, 71(4), 48–49.

Hirsch, E. D. Jr. (1987). *Cultural literacy*. Boston: Houghton Mifflin.

Hopkins, L. B., & Aranstein, M. (1990). *Do you know what tomorrow is?* New York: Scholastic.

Huck, C., Hepler, S., & Hickman, J. (1987). *Children's literature in the elementary school, 4th edition*. New York: Holt.

Jacobs, H. H. (Ed.). (1989). *Interdisciplinary curriculum: Design and implementation*. Alexandria, VA: Association for Supervision & Curriculum Development.

James, E., & Barkin, C. (1983). *How to write a great school report*. New York: Lothrop, Lee & Shepard Books.

Katz, L. G., & Chard, S. C. (1989). *Engaging children's minds: The project approach*. Norwood, NJ: Ablex.

Kostelnik, M. L. (Ed.). (1991). *Teaching young children to use themes*. Glenview, IL: Goodyear Books.

Kyle, W. C., Jr., & Shymansky, J. A. (1988). What research says about teachers as researchers. *Science & Children*, 26(3), 29–31.

Lionetti, J. (1992). An author study: Tomie de Paola. In B. E. Cullinan (Ed.), *Invitation to read: More children's literature in the reading program*. Newark, DE: International Reading Association.

Lipson, M. Y., Valencia, S. W., Wixson, K. K., & Peters, C. W. (1993). Integration and thematic teaching: Integration to improve teaching and learning. *Language Arts*, 70, 252–263.

Lukens, R. J. (1982). *A critical handbook of children's literature*. Glenview, IL: Scott, Foresman.

MacNeil, R. (1989). *Wordstruck: A memoir*. New York: Viking.

Manning, G., Manning, M., & Long, R. (1994). *Theme immersion: Inquiry-based curriculum in elementary and middle schools*. Portsmouth, NH: Heinemann.

McClaren, A. W. (1987). Thanatology: A thematic approach to teaching. Paper presented at the 77th Annual Meeting of the National Council of Teachers of English, Los Angeles, CA.

McGill-Franzen, A. (1993). "I could read the words!": Selecting good books for inexperienced readers. *The Reading Teacher, 46*(5), 424–426.

Moffett, J., & Wagner, B. J. (1992). *Student-centered language arts, K-12 (4th edition)*. Portsmouth, NH: Boynton-Cook.

Moss, J. F. (1984). *Focus units in literature: A handbook for elementary school teachers*. Urbana, IL: National Council of Teachers of English.

Moss, J. F. (1990). *Focus on literature: A context for literacy learning*. New York: Richard C. Owen.

Mullis, I. V. S., & Jenkins, L. B. (1988). *The science report card: Elements of risk and recovery. Trends and achievement based on the 1986 National Assessment*. Princeton, NJ: Educational Testing Service.

Murray, D. M. (1989). *Expecting the unexpected: Teaching myself—and others—to read and write*. Portsmouth, NH: Heinemann.

Norton, D. E. (1982). Using a webbing process to develop children's literature units. *Language Arts, 59*(4), 348–356.

Norton, D. E. (1993). Webbing and historical fiction. *The Reading Teacher, 46*(5), 432–436.

Pappas, C.C., Kiefer, B. Z., & Levstik, L. S. (1990). *An integrated language perspective in the elementary school: Theory into action*. White Plains, New York: Longman.

Parker, F. W. (1894/1969). *Talks on pedagogics*. New York: Arno Press.

Peterson, R., & Eeds, M. (1990). *Grand conversations*. New York: Scholastic.

Pigdon, K., & Woolley, M. (Eds.). (1993). *The big picture: Integrating children's learning*. Portsmouth, NH: Heinemann.

Pillar, A. M. (1987). Resources to identify children's books for the reading program. In B. E. Cullinan (Ed.), *Children's literature in the reading program* (pp. 156–164). Newark, DE: International Reading Association.

Ravitch, D. (1985). *The schools we deserve: Reflections on the educational crises of our time.* New York: Basic Books.

Ravitch, D., & Finn, C. E. J. (1987). *What do our 17-year-olds know? A report on the first National Assessment of History and Literature.* New York: Harper & Row.

Routman, R. (1988). *Transitions: From literature to literacy.* Portsmouth, NH: Heinemann.

Routman, R. (1991). *Invitations: Changing as teachers and learners, K–12.* Portsmouth, NH: Heinemann.

Rudman, M. K., & Rosenberg, S. P. (1991). Confronting history: Holocaust books for children. *New Advocate, 4*(3), 163–177.

Shannon, P. (1989). *Broken promises: Reading instruction in Twentieth-Century America.* Portsmouth, NH: Heinemann.

Stoll, D. R. (1989). *Magazines for children.* Newark, DE: International Reading Association.

Strickland, D. S. (1989). A model for change: Framework for an emergent literacy curriculum. In D. S. Strickland & L. M. Morrow (Eds.), *Emerging literacy: Young children learn to read and write* (pp. 135–146). Newark, DE: International Reading Association.

Strickland, D. S., & Morrow, L. M. (1990). Integrating the emergent literacy curriculum with themes (Emerging Readers and Writers). *The Reading Teacher, 43*(8), 604–605.

Strickland, D. S., & Walmsley, S. A. (1993). *School book clubs and children's literacy development: A descriptive study.* Albany, New York: Center for Teaching and Learning of Literature.

Strube, P. (1993). *Theme studies: A practical guide.* New York: Scholastic.

Suid, M. (1988). Put the 'search' back into research. *Learning, 17*(2), 73–75.

Tchudi, S., & Tchudi, S. (1984). *The young writer's handbook.* New York: Macmillan (Aladdin) Books.

Thompson, G. (1991). *Teaching through themes*. New York: Scholastic.

Tone, B. (1988). Guiding students through research papers. *Journal of Reading, 32*(1), 76–79.

Venezky, R. (1987). *The subtle danger: Reflections on the literacy abilities of America's young adults*. Princeton, NJ: Educational Testing Service.

Vygotsky, L. S. (1986). *Thought and language*. Cambridge, MA: MIT Press.

Walmsley, B. B., Camp, A., & Walmsley, S. A. (1992a). *Teaching kindergarten: A developmentally-appropriate approach*. Portsmouth, NH: Heinemann.

Walmsley, B. B., Camp, A., & Walmsley, S. A. (1992b). *Teaching kindergarten: A theme-centered curriculum*. Portsmouth, NH: Heinemann.

Walmsley, S. A. (1991). Literacy in the elementary classroom. In A. C. Purves & E. M. Jennings (Eds.), *Literate systems and individual lives: Perspectives on literacy and schooling* (pp. 139–164). Albany, New York: SUNY Press.

Walmsley, S. A. (1992). Reflections on the state of elementary literature instruction. *Language Arts, 69*, 508–514.

Walmsley, S. A., & Walp, T. P. (1989). *Teaching literature in elementary school* (Report No.1.3). Albany, New York: Center for the Learning and Teaching of Literature.

Walmsley, S. A., & Walp, T. P. (1990). Integrating literature and composing into the language arts curriculum: Philosophy and practice. *Elementary School Journal, 90*(3), 251–274.

Walmsley, S. A., Fielding, L. F., & Walp, T. P. (1991). *Home and school literary experiences of second grade children*. (Report No. 1.6). State University of New York at Albany: National Center for the Teaching and Learning of Literature.

Weaver, C., Chaston, J., & Peterson, S. (1993). *Theme exploration: A voyage of discovery*. Portsmouth, NH: Heinemann.

Wilen, W. W., & McKenrick, P. (1989). Individualized inquiry: Encouraging able students to investigate. *Social Studies, 80*(2), 51–54.

Wilson, L., Malmgren, D., Ramage, S., & Schulz, L. (1993). *An integrated approach to learning*. Portsmouth, NH: Heinemann.

Wray, D. (1985). *Teaching information skills through project work.* London: Hodder & Stoughton.

Yaakov, J. (Ed.). (1991). *Children's catalog* (16th edition). New York: H. W. Wilson.

Children's Books and Other Materials

Aliki. (1981). *Digging up dinosaurs.* New York: Harper & Row.

Baylor, B. (1975). *The desert is theirs.* New York: Macmillan.

Brown, M. (1989). *Arthur's eyes.* New York: The Trumpet Club.

Bunting, E. (1990). *In the haunted house.* New York: The Trumpet Club.

Burnford, S. (1988). *Incredible journey.* New York: Bantam Books.

Butcher, S. S. (1983). A woman's icy struggle. *National Geographic, 163*(3), 411–422.

Byars, B. (1985). *Summer of the swans.* New York: Penguin Books.

Coerr, E., & Evans, W. E. (1980). *Gigi, a baby whale borrowed for science and returned to the sea.* New York: Putnam.

Davis, O. (1978). *Escape to freedom: The story of young Frederick Douglass.* New York: Viking Press.

de Paola, T. *Strega Nona.* New York: Scholastic.

Drew, D. (1990). *Skeletons.* Crystal Lake, IL: Rigby.

Duryea, W. (1990). In pursuit of the Pole. *Cobblestone, 11*(11), 9–11.

George, J. C. (1972). *Julie of the wolves.* New York: Harper & Row.

Giff, P. R. (1979). *Fourth grade celebrity.* New York: Dell Publishing.

Giff, P. R. (1980). *Left-handed shortstop.* New York: Dell Publishing.

Giff, P. R. (1982). *The gift of the Pirate Queen.* New York: Dell Publishing.

Giff, P. R. (1984). *Rat teeth*. New York: Dell Publishing.

Giff, P. R. (1988). *All about Stacy*. New York: Dell Publishing.

Gore, R. (1976). The fiery Brazilian bees. *National Geographic, 149*(4), 491–501.

Hanson, P. (1990). *I Columbus, my journal, 1492–1493*. New York: Scholastic.

King, D. (1984). *Puffin*. New York: Lothrop.

Lourie, P. (1992). *Hudson River: An adventure from the mountains to the sea*. Honesdale, PA: Boyds Mills Press.

Macaulay, D. (1975). *Pyramid*. Boston: Houghton Mifflin.

Macaulay, D. (1988). *The way things work*. Boston: Houghton Mifflin.

Maxner, J. (1989). *Nicholas Cricket*. New York: Scholastic.

May, J. (1970). *Why birds migrate*. New York: Holiday House.

McLoughland, B. (1981). The Whippoorwill calls. *Cobblestone, 2*(2), 30.

Mitgutsch, A. (1972). *From grass to butter*. Minneapolis, MI: Carolrhoda Books.

Monjo, F. N. (1983). *The drinking gourd*. New York: Harper & Row.

Patent, D. H. (1984). *Whales: Giants of the deep*. New York: Holiday House.

Paulsen, G. (1987). *Hatchet*. New York: The Trumpet Club.

Rachlis, E. (1962). *The voyages of Henry Hudson*. New York: Random House.

Siebert, D. (1989). *Train song*. New York: The Trumpet Club.

Symes, R. (1955). *Henry Hudson*. New York: Morrow.

Taylor, B. (1992). *Look closer: Coral reef*. New York: Dorling Kindersley, Inc.

Tolkein, J. R. R. (1937). *The Hobbit*. Boston: Houghton Mifflin.

Wilder, L. I. (1941). *Little House on the Prairie*. New York: Scholastic.

Part Two

Themes in Action, Grades K–6

Chapter 1

Insects: A Kindergarten Theme

Bonnie Brown Walmsley and Anne-Marie Camp

Young children are naturally fascinated by nature, and so many of the themes we do in kindergarten are built around aspects of nature. One of these themes is insects. We do this theme either in late spring or in early autumn when insects are most abundant.

PREPARATION FOR THE THEME

When we first developed the theme on insects, we started our preparations several weeks in advance. First, we gathered all the books we could find relating to the topic. We looked for both fiction and nonfiction books appropriate to read to kindergartners. Ten years ago, we would have been hard pressed to find many nonfiction books suitable for primary age children; today, they are in abundance.

We also sought books that had good photographs or illustrations but whose text was intended for older children or adults. These books we read primarily for our own information, but we often would make them available to the children so they could learn from the illustrations and pictures.

Teachers often assume that teaching five- or six-year-olds requires the teacher to have only some very general knowledge on a topic that is being studied. We feel it is quite the opposite. Because young children cannot go off and gather information through reading, it is important that the teacher become a knowledgeable source. Also, just because a child is five or six doesn't mean that he or she won't ask thoughtful questions or won't be interested in learning quite specific information.

The second phase in our preparation was to contact local museums, universities, the U.S. Forest Service, and Cooperative Extensions (agricultural institutions associated with Cornell University) for information, posters, and collections of specimens. These sources turned out not to be particularly useful because of their reluctance to lend fragile collections to young children.

We then collected and mounted photographs of insects taken from children's nature magazines such as *Ranger Rick, Your Big Back Yard,* and *ZooBooks.*

Finally, we gathered small insect containers (baby food jars, petrie dishes, plastic peanut butter jars) and some larger ones (aquariums, gallon jars, plastic

87

buckets); an ant farm; straight pins, labels, and corrugated cardboard (which we cut into twelve-inch squares for mounting insects; rubber stamps of insects; playdough; clay; tracing paper; folders (for holding drawings, tracings, and notes on insects); magnifying boxes and magnifying glasses; and materials for "creating" insects (pipe cleaners, wax paper, cellophane, popsicle sticks, paint, glue, etc.).

WHAT CHILDREN SHOULD GAIN FROM THE INSECT THEME

We live in an age in which insects are generally perceived as pests that need to be eradicated. In this theme we want the children to learn more about the insects that live around them, to be able to name them, and to know something about their habits. We also want the children to develop a better understanding of the role of insects in nature. For example, mosquitoes and flies are usually regarded as nuisances—even dangerous—to humans, yet they are an essential part of the food chain for other creatures such as fish and birds. Some insects, such as praying mantises and ladybugs, are especially helpful to gardeners. Bees, which children often regard as mortal enemies, are essential to the life cycle of plants. Bees and ants are especially interesting to learn about because they live in colonies and depend on each other for survival. It's hard to find any redeeming qualities about Colorado beetles, cockroaches, or Japanese beetles, but these are common sights in the world our children live in, and they benefit from a better understanding of what these insects are and what they do.

There are four major areas that we explore in this theme: the physical characteristics of insects, the life cycle of insects, different kinds of insects, and insects in literature. This might sound a bit ambitious for kindergarten, but by using developmentally appropriate activities (see Walmsley et al., 1992), children can work at their level of ability and interest.

Children need to be able to distinguish insects from other creatures. Insects have three pairs of legs, a pair of antennae, and a body that is divided into three parts: head, thorax, and abdomen. Many insects have one or two pairs of wings. Contrary to what most children (and many teachers!) believe, spiders are not insects, and bugs and insects are not one and the same. During our most recent spring Insect theme, one child, Caitlin, brought in several insects to school. Upon closer inspection, it became obvious that one specimen had more than six legs. I asked the children to have a look in the insect books in the classroom during Relax and Read to see if we could find this "creature." Suddenly, Tommy came rushing up to me with a copy of *Eyewitness Explorers: Insects* (Parker, 1992) to show me a picture of the very insect that Caitlin had brought to school. It turned out to be a woodlouse, and it was in a section especially labeled as "Not Insects." The woodlouse has fourteen legs!

The life cycle of insects is another aspect we want the children to learn about. Most insects go through a complete metamorphosis: egg, larva, pupa, adult. Some insects, such as the grasshopper, do not go through all these stages; they are said to have incomplete metamorphoses.

We want the children to be able to identify the most common insects found around them (bees, ladybugs, ants, grasshoppers, butterflies). We also want them to know something about the color, size, diet, habits, and habitat of these insects.

Finally, we want to expose the children to good literature about insects. There are a number of fine books that happen to have insects as their main characters (for example, Eric Carle's *Very Hungry Caterpillar*, and his *The Grouchy Ladybug*, Chris Van Allsburg's *Two Bad Ants*), and every book about insects, whether fiction or nonfiction, helps to enlarge a child's knowledge of insects.

ORGANIZING THE THEME

In our kindergarten, we organize all our instruction around themes, which are integrated into various daily routines. We have opening activities, which include Attendance, Calendar, Daily Message, Show-and-Tell. Then we have Music and Movement when we sing songs, and do fingerplays, games, and drama. Next comes Theme Time, when we talk about our theme and read theme-related books to the children. Then we take about ten minutes for Relax and Read, when all the children and the teacher find a comfortable spot to relax and read. After this, we have Activity Time during which children pursue theme-related projects. We finish the day with Closing Activities when we read another book on the theme.

While the major activities related to the theme occur during Theme Time, Activity Time, and Closing, we also focus on the theme during the Daily Message, Show-and-Tell, Music and Movement, and Relax and Read. For example, we ask the children to bring in theme-related items for Show-and-Tell. The Daily Message is frequently related to the theme. In Music and Movement, we almost always relate the songs, fingerplays, and games to the theme. During Relax and Read, children are encouraged to read theme-related books.

In planning the insect theme, we decided to focus on insects in general for the first two days then focus on individual insects (ladybugs, ants, bees, and butterflies). Our goal was to discuss these insects in detail (for example, to learn about their life cycle, their characteristics, and their role in nature), and then have the children gather additional insects to learn about. Having modeled the process ourselves, we hoped that the children would be better able to find out about the insects they had gathered.

In terms of specific activities for the week, we organized the theme around Show-and-Tell, Daily Message, Theme Time, Activity Time, and Closing.

Show-and-Tell

We asked the children to bring in and share with the class items related to insects. They could bring in insects (alive or dead), books about insects that they had at home or had borrowed from friends or from the library, pictures of insects from magazines, butterfly nets, insect containers, toy insects, ant farms, or drawings of insects they had made.

On the first day, one child brought in a live grasshopper; another brought in a bee (and a tale of having been stung by one, which led to a lively discussion about bee allergies); we also collected a number of dead insects: an earwig, several beetles, and a large Junebug. As the week progressed, we acquired a large wasp's nest (from a parent), samples of honey, an ant "city," a butterfly net, a butterfly chrysalis, a T-shirt with glow-in-the-dark lightning bugs, and a number of books including Eric Carle's *The Very Hungry Caterpillar* and his *The Very Quiet Cricket*, Judy Hawes' *Fireflies in the Night*, and Verna Aardema's *Why Mosquitoes Buzz in People's Ears*. One child brought in a poster he had made by tracing a number of insects from an encyclopedia. After the children shared their items, many agreed to leave them in the classroom for the duration of the theme.

A child can see insects every day, but the moment we begin to study insects in school, children look at them quite differently. They are no longer pesky little bugs, but they become prized possessions to be captured and proudly shared with classmates. We might have ten caterpillars in the classroom in various jars, but the discovery of an eleventh on the playground is met with great excitement.

Over the course of the theme, these Show-and-Tell items add substantially to the theme.

Daily Message

Each day, we write a "message" on large newsprint paper at an easel. We use this message to model the writing process and to teach a variety of skills in context. As we are writing the daily message, we encourage children to read along, even help us spell the words. After the message is written, we go back over it, reading it or doing things like finding all the lower case *e*s, pointing out words that begin with the letter *d*, encouraging children to read words or sentences, or identifying and counting letters, words, or sentences. We talk about punctuation and other written conventions when the children are ready for it.

While not all the messages during this theme related to insects, we deliberately wrote several that did. For example, "Today we will go outside and look for insects. We will make insects from popsicle sticks, pipe cleaners, and wax paper." We then discussed what we had written with the children. For example, William pointed out to the class that the word *will* was almost like his name; the children were amazed how quickly they were able to recognize long and complicated words like *grasshopper* and *dragonfly*.

Music and Movement

During the Music and Movement activity, we selected songs, chants, games, and fingerplays about insects. For example, we chose the song *Arabella Miller* (about a girl who has a pet caterpillar) and *The Ants Go Marching*, which is a well-known camp song. We wrote the poem "Ladybug, Ladybug, Fly Away Home" on a chart, and then read it and dramatized it with puppets. We also had the children use scarves to dance to the music of "The Flight of the Bumble Bee."

Theme Time, Activity Time, Closing

In Theme Time, we read at least one theme-related book and had a discussion about one of the theme topics. This was followed by one or two activities in which children work in small groups on theme-related projects. We closed each day by reading another theme-related book and had children share with the class the progress they were making on their projects. During this time, we would also discuss questions children had about the theme and plan the following day's activities.

We decided to introduce the general topic of insects on days one and two, then focus on specific insects (ladybugs, ants, bees, and butterflies) on days three, four, five, and six. For Activity Time, we planned specific activities that focused on the different aspects of insects and integrated reading, writing, math, and art. For example, one group of children might be drawing and writing about the life cycle of the butterfly, while another group was mounting and labeling specimens gathered the previous day. During this period, we also scheduled time for children to go outside each day and collect insects to study.

To introduce the general topic of insects on days one and two, we read *What is an Insect?* (Day, 1975) and *Bugs* (Parker & Wright, 1987). These books are particularly good for introducing children to a variety of insects and for helping them distinguish insects from other creatures like spiders. The richly colored illustrations are very large, yet they provide enough detail for identifying an insect's three body parts, three pairs of legs, and one or two pairs of wings. We followed these up with several projects. One, which lasted all week, was for each child to start a notebook in which they traced or drew insects (one per page); we encouraged the children to label and write about each insect. We talked to the children about how scientists draw insects—they draw and color them accurately with attention to detail. Even though kindergartners' drawings can't be that sophisticated, we encouraged the children to trace, draw, and color as accurately as they could (see Figures 1–1 and 1–2).

Another activity, which also lasted for the duration of the theme, was a collection board. This is a piece of corrugated cardboard about one foot square, on which children could pin insects as they collected them. (We told children about the many places they could find dead insects: under porch lights, on window sills, even on the front grilles of cars.) Under each insect, the children

FIGURE 1–1. Zachary's Drawing of a Ladybug— "This is a lady bug."

FIGURE 1–2. Meghan's Drawing of a Ladybug.

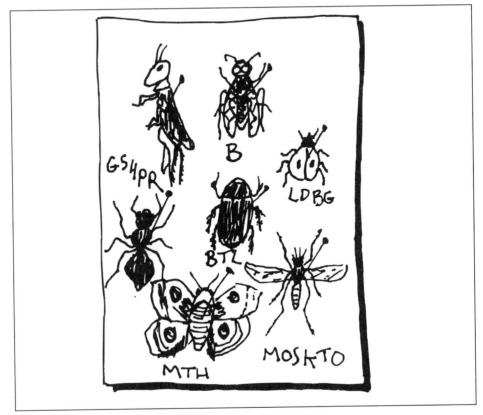

FIGURE 1–3. *Example of a Collection Board.*

placed a self-stick label and wrote the insect's name on it. As the children added to their collections, the boards became the focal point of many discussions: the children examined each other's boards and talked about what other children had collected. We noticed that many children traded insects, so their individual boards would have a wide variety of insects pinned to them (see Figure 1–3).

To help get parents and friends involved in the insect theme, we also had the children make a "WANTED" poster, to take home (see Figure 1–4).

We also created an insect center. (A *center* is part of the classroom that is devoted to a collection of books, insects—dead and alive—an ant farm, posters, insect toys, puzzles, magnifying glasses.) During the first two days of the theme, we showed the children how to use and care for the items at the center, and then gave them time to explore on their own.

At the end of day one and day two, we read Eric Carle's *The Very Quiet Cricket* (this was a book that a child brought in for Show-and Tell), and Jerry Pallotta's *The Icky Bug Alphabet Book.*

We focused days three to six on specific insects. On day three we studied ladybugs. We started out by reading Jeunesse and de Bourgoing's *The Ladybug*

FIGURE 1–4.
Kathleen's
"Wanted
Insects"
Poster.

and Other Insects. It's a superbly illustrated book with acetate overlays so that the reader can look at both sides of a ladybug and can see the various stages of metamorphosis. One project was for children to draw and paint ladybugs. Another involved reading aloud Eric Carle's *The Grouchy Ladybug* (which is about the daily goings on of a grouchy ladybug organized by time of the day), and having children follow along with individual clocks, keeping time with the grouchy ladybug. We also gave the children time to continue their insect notebooks and collection boards.

On day four we studied ants. We opened with Arthur Dorros's *Ant Cities*. We had the children add ants to their notebook, then we had them make their own ant farm using small jars and soil and with real ants collected from outside. We followed up with a math project on addition in which children used plastic ants and a piece of bread: we presented cards with simple addition facts (e.g., 2 + 2, 3 + 1), and had the children put the appropriate number of ant counters on their bread and tell the total. We closed the day by reading Chris Van Allsburg's *Two Bad Ants*.

On day five our focus was bees. We read National Geographic's *Honeybees* (Lecht, 1973), and invited Fred Ludwig, a bee-keeper, to visit the classroom. He brought some equipment with him—hat, smoker, gloves, honey comb frames— and talked about his work as a bee-keeper. He showed the children different kinds of honey (e.g., buckwheat, clover) and let them taste the different varieties. He also had with him a glass-enclosed hive containing thousands of bees, and he let the children find the queen bee. I took photographs of Mr. Ludwig and his equipment as he explained how to retrieve honey from the hives. These photos were put in plastic album pages for the children to look at in the weeks that followed. We had the children draw and write about bees in their insect notebooks (see Figure 1–5). To close we read Paula Hogan's *The Honeybee*.

On day six we studied butterflies. We started the day with Althea's *Butterflies*. After this, we had the children draw and label the life cycle of the butterfly to put in their insect notebooks (see Figure 1–6). It was interesting the see the finished products of the life cycles, but talking with the children as they drew them helped us to discover which children really understood this concept. Although the concept may not have been completely understood the first time we explored it, we revisited the concept of life cycles in many themes throughout the year. The life cycle of the chicken was examined in some depth when we hatched eggs. The life cycle of the frog was discussed when we observed frogs' eggs and tadpoles at various stages of their development. Even the life cycle of humans was touched upon in the theme on Babies.

We talked to the children about symmetry, and we had them make butterflies using pattern blocks to illustrate the concept and then paint butterflies on their own. (As is the case with all the information presented in our program, some children will not be ready to grasp the concept of symmetry, and this becomes obvious when one wing of a butterfly is totally orange, and the other is totally black. Naturally, we wouldn't tell the child he'd done it wrong. The child's

FIGURE 1–5. *David's Notes on Honey Bees—"Bees make honey."*

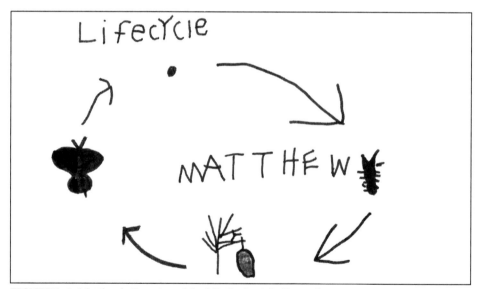

FIGURE 1–6. *Matthew's Drawing of the Life Cycle of the Butterfly.*

drawing would be displayed with all the others.) We closed the day with Eric Carle's *The Very Hungry Caterpillar*.

On day seven we wrote a thank you note to Mr. Ludwig, the bee-keeper (see Figure 1–7), and brought the theme to a close by having the children make insects from popsicle sticks, pipe cleaners, wax paper, and cellophane. Rather

FIGURE 1–7. Bethany's Letter to the Bee-keeper—"I liked it buzz!"

than reading to the children at the beginning and end of the day, we had them share their insect notebooks and collection boards.

REFLECTIONS ON THE THEME

Our kindergartners really enjoy this theme each time we do it, and we know they learn a lot from it. The children are fascinated by insects of all kinds and descriptions, and one of the nice things about a theme on insects is that they are readily available in and around almost every school in the world. Also, there's a wealth of books on insects suitable for children of this age. In fact, each time we do this theme, it seems as though there's an entirely new collection of insect books.

Before doing the insect theme, if an ant or cricket happened to wander through the classroom, some children would be bound to try and stamp on it. After the insect theme, however, the children would want to carefully capture the insect and put it safely outside or to study it for a while. So we know that children have become sensitized to these little creatures and have a new respect for them and their place in the environment. Rather than be repulsed by them, they are curious and intrigued by them. This theme doesn't pretend to teach rigorous scientific concepts, but it does introduce young children to important information about the animal kingdom that will serve as a foundation for further study and will interest them in this topic.

It wouldn't take much tinkering with this theme to adapt it to different parts of the country or to other primary grades. There are so many different kinds of insects, so much excellent literature on insects, and so many appropriate activities to do, that the same theme could easily be done in the first or second grades. We've made this theme an integral part of our kindergarten science curriculum, and we look forward to repeating it each year. It's never the same, but it always piques the interest of the children.

REFERENCES

Professional Sources

Walmsley, B. B., Camp, A., & Walmsley, S. A. (1992). *Teaching kindergarten: A theme-centered curriculum*. Portsmouth, NH: Heinemann.

Children's Literature Used in the Theme

Aardema, V. (1975). *Why mosquitoes buzz in people's ears*. New York: Scholastic. [This is a West African folk tale with a humorous twist. The artwork adds greatly to the text. The book won the Caldecott in 1975.]

Althea. (1977). *Lifecycle books: Butterflies*. New York: Longman. [This book explains the life cycle of a butterfly in clear and simple language. It's a wonderful work of nonfiction for children.]

Aylesworth, J. (1992). *Old black fly*. New York: Scholastic. [A rhyme that takes the reader through the alphabet as it describes twenty six annoying things a fly did in a day. This book lends itself to chanting or singing. The illustrations are colorful and full of expression.]

Carle, E. (1977). *The grouchy ladybug*. New York: Harper & Row. [A grouchy ladybug meets a different animal each hour, looking for a fight. This book has Carle's typically outstanding illustrations and interesting page layout. It could also be used when teaching young children to tell time.]

Carle, E. (1990). *The very quiet cricket*. New York: Philomel Books. [Throughout this story of a cricket who is unable to chirp, the reader meets a variety of insects. Eric Carle's illustrations are brilliant, and the added surprise of an actual chirping sound on the final page is a winner with children of all ages.]

Carle, E. (n. d.). *The very hungry caterpillar*. New York: Philomel Books. [There aren't many children who haven't heard this classic tale before they've gone to kindergarten. Nevertheless, it can be enjoyed over and over again. A beautiful story that teaches children about the life cycle of the butterfly.]

Day, J. W. (1975). *What is an insect?* Racine, WI: Western Publishing Company.
[*This inexpensive Golden Book offers the reader good information and realistic illustrations in a way that can be understood by young children.*]

Dorros, A. (1987). *Ant cities.* New York: Harper & Row.
[*This book explores the inside of an ant hill and provides clear and interesting information about ants. This illustrations compliment the text nicely.*]

Hawes, J. (1963). *Fireflies in the night.* New York: Thomas Crowell.
[*A beautifully illustrated book about fireflies that provides a surprising amount of information on these extraordinary insects.*]

Hogan, P. F. (1979). *The Honeybee.* Milwaukee: Raintree Children's Books.
[*This book is an excellent companion to Lecht's Honeybees. It presents information on honeybees in a way that young children find appealing.*]

Jeunesse, G., & de Bourgoing, P. (1989). *The ladybug and other insects.* New York: Scholastic.
[*This is a book that describes ladybugs and other insects in a most unusual way, using acetate sheets to reveal the insides of the various insects. The illustrations are detailed and fascinating to young children.*]

Lecht, J. (1973). *Honeybees.* Washington, DC: National Geographic Society.
[*This is an excellent book about honeybees, with photographs to illustrate the interesting text. A must when teaching about honeybees at this level.*]

Pallotta, J. (1986). *The icky bug alphabet book.* Boston: Quinlan Press.
[*This alphabet book of insects provides information about twenty-six insects with illustrations that are accurate and realistic as well as beautiful.*]

Parker, N. W., & Wright, J. R. (1987). *Bugs.* New York: Mulberry Books.
[*This book combines a silly rhyme with information about a variety of bugs. Be careful—some of them are not insects!*]

Parker, S. (1992). *Eyewitness Explorers: Insects.* New York: Dorling Kindersley, Inc.
[*This is the version of Eyewitness books for younger readers. This book is packed with information, illustrations, and photographs of various insects. It's an important resource for learning about insects.*]

Van Allsburg, C. (1988). *Two bad ants.* Boston: Houghton Mifflin.
[*This story of two ants' ordeal while trying to get some crystals takes the reader on an excellent adventure. The powerful illustrations are drawn from the ants' point of view. A wonderful picture book!*]

Additional Titles Suitable for an Insect Theme

Brenner, B., & Chardiet, B. (1993). *Where's that insect?* New York: Scholastic.

Cutting, B., & Cutting, J. (1992). *Ants*. Bothell, WA: The Wright Group.

Drew, D. (1992). *Caterpillar diary*. Crystal Lake, IL: Rigby.

Drew, D. (1993). *The life of the butterfly*. Crystal Lake, IL: Rigby.

Cutts, D. (1982). *Look: A butterfly*. Mahwah, NJ: Troll Associates.

Danks, H. (1987). *The bug book*. New York: Workman Publishing.

Garland, P. (1992). *The housefly*. Crystal Lake, IL: Rigby.

Garland, P. (1992). *The ladybug*. Crystal Lake, IL: Rigby.

Garland, P. (1992). *The marvelous mosquito*. Crystal Lake,IL: Rigby.

Hornblow, L., & Hornblow, A. (1990). *Insects do the strangest things*. New York: Random House.

Jorgensen, G. (1991). *Guess who's coming to dinner*. Crystal Lake, IL: Rigby.

Kilpatrick, C. (1982). *Creepy crawlies: Insects and other tiny animals*. London: Usborne Publishing Ltd.

Mound, L. (1990). *Eyewitness Books: Insects*. New York: Alfred A. Knopf.

Royston, A. (1992). *What's inside? Insects*. New York: Dorling Kindersley.

Sheridan, J. (1992). *Ants, ants, ants*. Bothell, WA: The Wright Group.

Sheridan, J. (1992). *How ants live*. Bothell, WA: The Wright Group.

Westcott, N. B. (1980). *I know an old lady who swallowed a fly*. Boston: Little, Brown.

Wexo, J. B. (1986). *Zoobooks 2: Insects, Volume One*. San Diego: Wildlife Education, Ltd.

Wexo, J. B. (1986). *Zoobooks 2: Insects, Volume Two*. San Diego: Wildlife Education, Ltd.

Zim, H. S., & Cottam, C. (1987). *Insects: A guide to familiar American insects*. New York: Golden Press.

Chapter 2

Fish Hatchery: A First Grade Theme

Debby Fabian, Mary Ellen Gaddy, and Margaret Wertime

For the past nine years, we have been taking our first graders on a field trip to the Warren County Fish Hatchery. For the first few years, all we did was take the children on the field trip. Our purpose was to have the children see the life cycle stages of trout, and we took the trip in the winter months because that was the only time when all the stages could be observed. We did nothing ahead of time to prepare children for the trip, other than getting permission and wearing appropriate clothing. After the trip, we wrote a class group story, which generally was of the type "First we rode on the bus to Warrensburg. Then when we got off the bus, we got into groups..." We also sent thank you notes to the Fish Hatchery staff, which the children wrote, copying the message off the board and illustrating their notes with a picture.

Seven years ago, as part of some general changes our district was making to its K–6 language arts program, we started to apply what we had been learning about process writing to field trips as a whole, and the Fish Hatchery trip lent itself well to a referential writing exercise. Instead of having children contribute to a teacher-directed group story, we let them write their own stories. As a consequence, children wrote a variety of accounts of the field trip, ranging from a sequential list of events to more detailed descriptions of specific aspects of the hatchery. What changed from earlier years was that now children were actually composing their own stories (before, they contributed ideas, but the teacher wrote them down—in fact, the children's contributions were simply answers to teachers' questions). As children began to write their own accounts of the field trip, the ownership of this writing was transferred from teacher to child. Sometimes, we would make books out of children's individual writings. What did not change, however, was how we prepared ourselves and the children for the field trip. We simply went on the trip, and all the teaching and learning came afterwards.

In the past three years, we have extended our reforms to embrace the entire first grade curriculum, with content area themes that integrate reading, writing, speaking, and listening and combine language arts with subject areas. As we began this process, it occurred to us that the fish hatchery field trip was an isolated event, not connected in any meaningful way to the curriculum. Even though the children were writing more—and more interestingly—about the field trip, the trip itself had become simply a stimulus for writing and was not in itself an integral part of the curriculum. We wondered about the possibilities of integrating it. The main connections were with the science curriculum: children could learn about fish as one of the members of the animal kingdom. But they also could learn about predators (protecting young trout against predators is one of the reasons for having a fish hatchery in the first place), about pollution (again, fish have to be raised in this protected environment to offset the ravages of manmade pollution of their natural habitat), and about life cycles. There were also connections with the social studies curriculum: children could learn about an important industry in their own community (its economy relies heavily on tourism, and sport fishing is a major tourist attraction in the Adirondacks). Of course, this topic also lent itself to the language arts curriculum, providing rich opportunities for learning and using language. With these connections in mind, we realized that what used to be just a field trip would make an excellent theme, but it needed developing.

The first step was to enlarge our own knowledge of the theme. Although we all had some general knowledge of fish, of the fish hatchery (after all, we had visited it at least eight times), and of the broader issues of pollution, life cycles, etc., we had never made it a point to know these topics thoroughly. Now our concern was: if we didn't have this knowledge, how could we share it with the children? And how could we make it pertinent to the children?

We already had some notes we took on the fish hatchery from a previous trip, and from these we had established a preliminary set of topics to explore. These included the life cycle of the trout, the fish hatchery operation (its function, how it works, and how trout are raised), and types of trout. To learn more, we contacted Bill Miller, who is head of fish management at the New York State Environment Conservation (NYENCON). Bill provided us with abundant source material, including McClane's *Fishing Encyclopedia* (McClane, 1974), a gold mine of information about types of trout, habitats, domestic versus wild strains, spawning, and survival. It also dealt specifically with trout in the Adirondack region. He also supplied us with brochures, stocking lists, pamphlets on identifying New York State's trout (Decker et al., 1978; Langan et al., 1990), and the names of other knowledgeable people in the area.

We then searched our personal collections, our own classrooms, the school library, and the public libraries for additional sources. We were looking for books and other materials suitable for enlarging our own knowledge and for using in the classroom with the children. Although there are large numbers of books on fish, there are relatively few specifically devoted to trout, and of these, even fewer suitable for first graders. In the time we had available, we found no appropriate adult books and precious few articles in magazines or journals. Later, while writing this chapter, we did locate several useful references for teachers, which we will use in future years. One of these was an excellent article on the trout of New York (McCullough & Stegemann, 1991). Others include Heacox's superb book on the brown trout (Heacox, 1974), and the most comprehensive work on trout ever written, appropriately called *Trout*

(Schwiebert, 1984). For use with the children, we located a number of good books on fish (see references), but only three directly related to our theme (Cole & Wexler's *A Fish Hatches*, Arnosky's *Freshwater Fish and Fishing*, and Say's fiction book *A River Dream*), and one indirectly related (Thomas's *Fishing Is for Me*). There are many magazines with excellent articles on trout (e.g., *Field & Stream, Outdoor Life*), but none of these provide basic information on types of trout, habitat, and so on; they are about fishing, not fish. We found many articles about fish in the popular children's magazines (e.g., *Your Back Yard, World, Ranger Rick, Boy's Life*), but none specifically about trout. The most useful source we located was, interestingly enough, provided by the fish hatchery itself: a twelve-page pamphlet on the history and operation of the hatchery, including detailed information on life cycle and the anatomy of trout. Reading these sources did a number of things for us: we "firmed up" some of our previous knowledge; we acquired new information about types of trout, anatomy of trout, and the survivability of eggs; and we found some new books for children.

Activities Before the Trip

During the month of January, we studied animals as part of our science curriculum. We had already learned about mammals, reptiles, amphibians, and birds, using the Childcraft book on animals as a primary resource. We left fish until last. In all three classes, the theme began about two weeks before the field trip. Using the book *Childcraft: The How and Why Library* ("It's a Fish" pp. 68–81) as a read-aloud, we discussed the topic of fish with the children, talking about questions such as, How can you tell what is and what isn't a fish? and What are the functions of gills, scales, and fins? We also discussed facts such as fish eyes are always open (they have no eyelids), different types of fish, egg laying habits, the roles of female and male fish, how eggs are protected by the male, what fish eat, and so on. This activity took place in forty-five-minute blocks each day. The teachers made large diagrams of trout, with the major parts labeled (see Figure 2–1).

Each session consisted of the teacher reading parts of the book aloud followed by discussion. A few of the children who fish on a regular basis shared their knowledge and experiences with the class. Facts about fish were listed on chart paper.

In Mel's (Mary Ellen) classroom, these discussions were followed by writing activities, in which children wrote about each day's topic. On the first day, they wrote about the parts of a fish (e.g., scales, fins, gills) that almost all fish have in common. On the second day, they wrote about the functions of these parts (e.g., gills are needed for breathing). The next day, children drew pictures of fish, and labeled the various parts.

In Debby's classroom, the discussions were followed by asking the children to find information about fish from a variety of sources—from *Ranger Rick, Your*

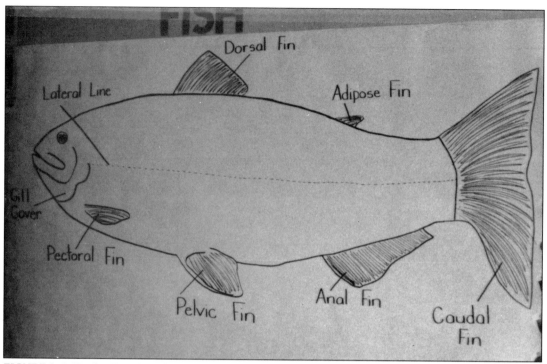

FIGURE 2–1. Teacher Drawing of a Trout, with Major Parts Labeled.

Big Backyard, and from books about fish that Debby had borrowed from the public library. Debby put out all the materials, each one having to do with fish, around the room, and then she let children select their own material. After they had spent some time looking over the material, they gathered on the rug to share what they had learned. Some children were able to read to the class from their magazine or book. Others asked Debby to read the information for them. After each child shared information, Debby would ask, "What did we learn about fish from what you heard?" This led to further discussions about fish.

Peggy followed roughly the same procedure as Debby, except that she spent a considerable amount of time on the life cycle and on how some animals look vastly different in adult versus immature forms.

In all three classes throughout the week, the children created their own "fish," by cutting out two identical fish shapes from newsprint paper, painting them during art periods, stuffing their insides with newspaper, then stapling the edges (see Figure 2–2).

The purpose of these activities was to ensure that children had some basic knowledge about fish that they could bring with them to the study of the fish hatchery.

During the week immediately before the trip, the teachers shifted the focus from fish in general to trout and the fish hatchery in particular. First, they

FIGURE 2–2. Children's "Fish."

discussed the life cycle of trout using large charts to illustrate the various stages: egg, eyed egg, sac fry, fry, spring fingerling, year-old trout (see Figure 2–3).

Next, using the Warren County Fish Hatchery booklet as a resource, the teachers discussed the fish hatchery, explaining what its purpose was, and how the trout were raised. In particular, they talked about how the trout were fed with "demand" feeders (a feature of the field trip that first graders always find fascinating), and how the hatchery brings cold, fresh water from the nearby mountain streams to use in the tanks and ponds (see Figure 2–4).

Finally, they talked about questions the children might want to ask during the field trip (for example, What is the "airborne automatic feeder" mentioned in the fish hatchery booklet?) In Peggy's class, in addition to the general discussions, the children studied photographs of previous years' field trips to the fish hatchery, so they would have some prior knowledge of the setting and layout to bring to the trip.

THE FIELD TRIP

In previous years, all three classes went to the fish hatchery on the same day. This year we decided that if we took each class on its own, the children would

FIGURE 2–3.
Teacher Chart
of the Life
Cycle of
Trout.

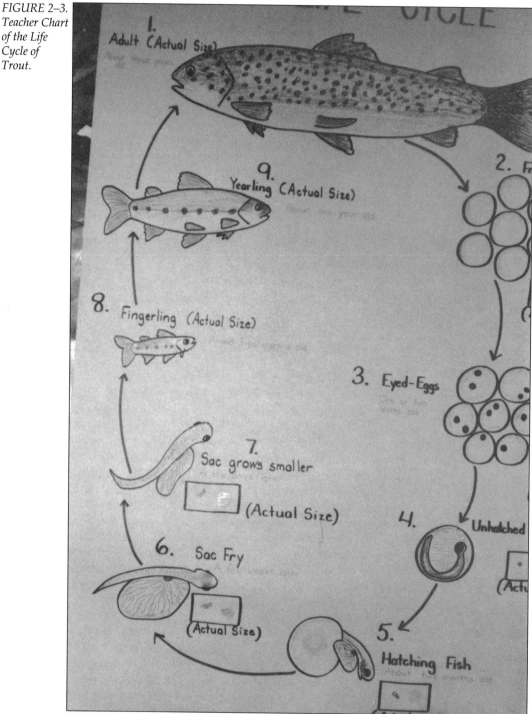

1. Adult (Actual Size)

9. Yearling (Actual Size)

8. Fingerling (Actual Size)

7. Sac grows smaller
(Actual Size)

6. Sac Fry
(Actual Size)

2. Fr

3. Eyed-Eggs

4. Unhatched

5. Hatching Fish

FIGURE 2–4. *Drawing of a Demand Feeder at the Fish Hatchery.*

be able to study the various aspects of the fish hatchery more closely, and the teachers would be able to devote more of their time to the content of the trip than to its management. The three trips were quite similar. Matt, who runs the fish hatchery, gave us a guided tour; we were the only visitors on each of the three days. See Figure 2–5 for a map of the hatchery.

The tour started at the outside ponds (Area 2 on the map), where the trout are placed when they are three-to-five inches in length, and seven-to-nine months old. There are 3,500 to 5,500 trout in each pond during the winter months, but during the summer, each pond holds between 5,000 and 7,000 trout. It is in these ponds that the trout are fed via demand and automatic feeders, but only the demand feeders are used in the winter months. Another feature of these ponds are the wooden covers to protect the fish against the sun and predators. Because we had spent some time before the trip talking about demand feeders, this station was of particular interest to the children. As they approached the ponds and realized that they would soon see an actual demand feeder, the children broke into a run. As Matt described the feeders, the children started commenting on what was happening even before Matt could explain it; he was

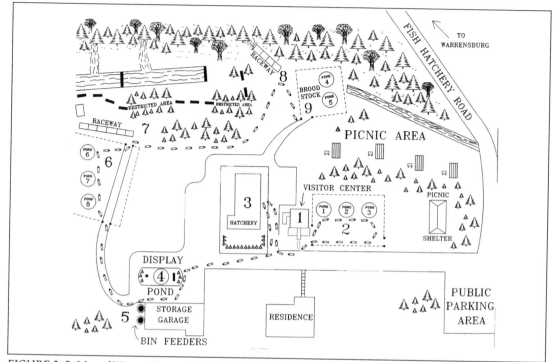

FIGURE 2–5. Map of Warren County Fish Hatchery.

pleased at how much they already knew and how interested they were in the details of how the feeder worked. The children were anxious to learn about how frequently they refilled the feeders, how many pellets each feeder held, and how long it took for the fish to learn how to bump the metal rod in order to release the pellets. But the demand feeders were not the only attraction. The children were also fascinated by the wooden shade covers. They noticed that as people approached the ponds, the fish would congregate under these covers. A child asked Matt if the fish could hear us coming, and he explained that indeed they could, and that's one of the reasons why the trout disappeared so quickly. The fish are also sensitive to shadows cast over their pool. This led to a discussion about predators and the constant battle that the hatchery fights against human and animal intrusions.

The tour then proceeded to the hatchery itself, an enclosed building where the eggs are incubated, hatched, and grow to a size large enough to survive in the outside ponds (Area 3 on the map). Inside the hatchery are shallow troughs with fast flowing, cold water (gravity-fed from nearby mountains) in which the eggs grow into eyed eggs, sac fry, and after three months or so, into fry. On the days we visited, we didn't see eggs being squeezed from the adult trout, nor the process of fertilization, but we did see eyed eggs, sac fry, and fry. It's noisy in the hatchery building because of the water running through the troughs, and it's hard to explain anything over this noise. Here, our preteaching really paid off because the children knew exactly what they were looking for, and their interest in seeing the sac fry up close led Matt to scoop some up so the children could examine them. Even teachers who had visited the hatchery many times saw details they had never really paid attention to in the past. One of the features of the troughs that interested the children were bars that sprayed cold water into the troughs to increase the oxygen (they use a similar technique in the outside ponds, but only in the summer months). Matt explained the process of oxygenation to the children, and they were fascinated by it.

Next, the tour left the hatchery building and took visitors to the display pond (Area 4 on the map). Here, children saw a variety of trout (rainbow, brook, and wild strains native to the Adirondacks, such as Little Tupper and Windfall), in various sizes and weights. This pond is very full, and mostly stocked with rainbow trout, and so it's hard to distinguish the various strains.

From the display pond, the tour then proceeded past the feed bins (Area 5, where children can see the different kinds of foods fed to trout at different stages of their growth), to more ponds, some for growing trout and others for brood stock (to supply the eggs). In these back ponds (Areas 6 and 9), which are more secluded than those by the Visitor's Center, the children noticed a fake owl perched by the fence and asked what it was for. Some of the children knew that its function was to scare off predators, and this prompted a discussion about predators in general—the hatchery has to fend off attacks by kingfishers, herons, mink, as well as human poachers. Matt explained that the ponds are one of the only nonfrozen bodies of water in the area throughout the winter, and so ducks occasionally land in them, and find a ready supply of food underneath their webbed feet.

Before returning to the Visitor's Center, we were given a private tour of the water collection system. Although the collection system is not part of the normal tour, it is an important part of our project because it is critical to an understanding of how the hatchery works, and it's fascinating for children. (What child dislikes water, especially off-limits water, flowing at five hundred gallons a minute at a temperature of forty-eight degrees?) We saw the water trickling down the mountain from a number of underground springs into the collection ditch, then through small diameter pipes into the hatchery. There are no pumps (the water flows only by gravity), and the constricted pipes create enormous water pressure and flow. Matt explained that the temperature of the water varies only by a degree or so all year long, and there's always plenty of water, even in drought years. The children were particularly interested in the screens that prevented debris from entering the pipes. They lay down on a platform over the screens so they could see the leaves and branches being trapped. Matt said they had to clear the screens every day.

Finally, we returned to the Visitor's Center (Area 2), where there was a slide show about aspects of the fish hatchery not visible in the current months (for example, although we didn't see the eggs being fertilized during our trip, we did obtain a good idea of how it was done from the slides they showed us). There were also many exhibits in the Visitor's Center.

FOLLOW-UP ACTIVITIES

After the field trip, there were several activities in which all the children participated. These included drawing life cycle charts (large diagrams of the life cycle of trout, with labels), diagrams of a trout's external and internal parts, fish poetry, reading books about fish, a hands-on lab experience dissecting a fish, and, of course, referential writing.

Life Cycle Charts

Before the field trip, all of the teachers had discussed life cycles of trout, and life cycle was a major focus of the trip itself. Now, we wanted the children to chart the life cycle of trout for themselves. To refresh the children's memories, each of the teachers briefly shared with the children the large life cycle charts they had made before the trip (see Figure 2–3), then they let children create their own versions of the chart. For each stage of the life cycle, we asked children to draw a diagram and then write a label to name it (see Figure 2–6).

Diagrams of External Parts

For this activity, each teacher created a large drawing of a trout using the diagram in Decker et al. (1978) as a model, labeling the major external parts (e.g., dorsal and other fins, lateral line, gill cover). We then asked the children to create their own diagram and labels.

A Lab Experience

This activity involved taking all the first graders over to the middle school to work with Chris Boggia, the science teacher. Chris teamed some of his seventh graders with the first graders to dissect fish. We would have liked them to dissect trout, but our budget permitted only perch. We split the children into groups of three, each group working with a seventh grader at a lab table. First, they examined the outside of the fish (scales, fins, gills, teeth), and then they tried to predict the sex of the fish from its outward shape. Next, the seventh graders cut open the fish (along the lateral line) and exposed the internal organs (stomach, air bladder, heart, etc.). The stomachs were particularly interesting because of what they contained: worms, flies, even small fish. The females had eggs, which could be removed intact. We all expected that some of the first graders would be disturbed by the sight of a fish's innards, but they weren't. In fact, they fought over possession of various parts to take home—the eyeballs

FIGURE 2–6.
Tabitha's
Drawing of the
Life Cycle of
the Trout.

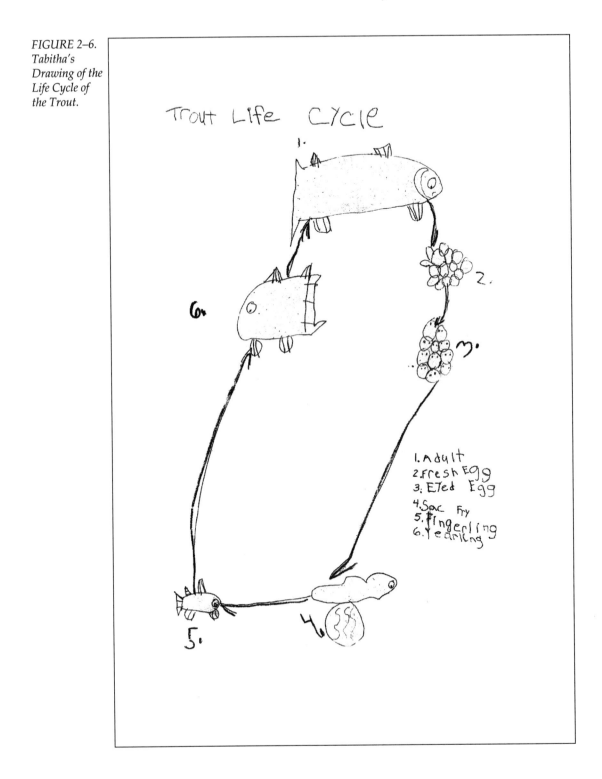

being the most prized. We also learned from one of the children that his mother regularly cooks and serves eggs from the female fish. The children learned a great deal from this exercise; they were especially fascinated by how the gills and air bladder worked and how most of the organs seemed to be concentrated in one area. Some of the children drew parallels between fish and humans—one child asked if humans had an air bladder.

Diagrams of Internal Parts

As a follow-up to the lab experience, we had children create a diagram of the trout's internal parts to accompany their diagram of the external parts. To do this, we asked the children to cut flaps in an outline of a trout and then to draw and label its internal parts (e.g., heart, swim bladder, liver, stomach) on a piece of paper stapled underneath the outline. In this way, children could create their own paper trout, and "dissect" it by opening up the flaps.

Although the children all wrote about the fish hatchery, the way in which they wrote differed across the three classrooms. In Mel's class, the writing focused on several major topics: the demand feeders, the water system, and the life cycle of the trout. Immediately after returning from the field trip, the children began writing about the demand feeders. The children were so excited about what they had seen, and with a weekend coming up, it seemed sensible to get started on this topic right away. Before the children wrote, Mel discussed the contrast between what the children thought the demand feeder would look like and what it actually looked like and the contrast between how they thought it would work and how it actually worked. After writing, the children illustrated their pieces (see Figure 2–7).

The following school day, Mel discussed the water system, reviewing what the children had seen the previous Friday by using the Fish Hatchery booklet as a visual reminder of the different parts of the water system (drainage ditch, pipes, etc.). The children wrote and illustrated their pieces on the water system (see Figure 2–8).

The next day, Mel discussed and the children wrote about the life cycle of the trout, based on the different stages they had observed at the fish hatchery.

In Peggy's class, on the day after the trip, the children wrote a general account of the field trip and illustrated it. Then, for each of the next six days, Peggy had the children write about one phase of the trip. One of Peggy's chaperones (a mother of one of the children) had made a videotape of the trip, and before the children started to write about a particular phase of the trip, Peggy showed that part of the videotape. The children also had seen a videotape at the fish hatchery that showed aspects of the hatchery operation that were not observable on the day of the trip (for example, fertilizing the eggs). Thus, children were able to write about all aspects of the hatchery using a variety of sources from which to create their own descriptions (e.g., direct observation, books and pamphlets, the hatchery's videotape, and the chaperone's videotape).

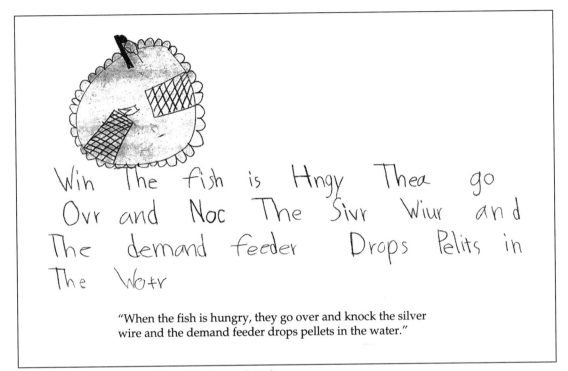

Wih The fish is Hngy Thea go
Ovr and Noc The Sivr Wiur and
The demand feeder Drops Pelits in
The Wotr

"When the fish is hungry, they go over and knock the silver
wire and the demand feeder drops pellets in the water."

FIGURE 2–7. Alon's Description of the Demand Feeder.

The first day, the children wrote about the inside of the fish hatchery building. For the next five days, the children wrote about the production ponds, the water supply, counting the fish, stocking the ponds and lakes, and writing up the dissection project (see Figure 2–9). While most of these activities primarily involved children writing about what they had observed, "counting the fish" lent itself well to a classroom demonstration by the children themselves. At the fish hatchery, fish are counted by weighing them (using the same technique that banks use to count pennies). So that the children could fully understand this process, Peggy brought a balance scale in to the class and had the children replicate the fish counting exercise using candy jellyfish. First, they put a quarter-pound weight on one side of the scale, and then they poured jellyfish onto the other side until the scales were even. Next, they counted the jellyfish to determine how many made up a quarter pound. In this way, the children were able to substitute weights for numbers and predict the number of jellyfish from a calculation of their weight, which is exactly how the fish hatchery count their real fish.

In the following week, Peggy's class made a class "Big Book" based on the information in the children's individual projects. The class broke down into groups of three. Each group selected one of the topics (inside the fish hatchery building, the production ponds, water supply, counting fish) and then started

*FIGURE 2–8.
Julie's
Description of
the Water
System.*

All the Water that Comes to
the Fish Hachrey And in ther
pons Coms From the Matins. And
then it Coms Down there the
Springs then gose there Pips. ther
An Nets to Git Owt All th
Drt. they Need Cowld Water
Becos the Fish An Cowld Blad id.
When the Fish An Owld Anof
they An takeing to A Fuwe
Pons in the Fish Hachare.

"All the water that comes to the Fish Hatchery and in their
ponds comes from the mountains. And then it comes down there
from the springs, then goes through pipes. There are nets to get
out all the dirt. They need cold water because the fish are cold
blooded. When the fish are old enough they are taken to a few
ponds in the fish hatchery."

FIGURE 2– 9.
Jaime and
Janet's
Explanation of
How the Fish
are Counted.

How to cot the fish.
Frs they put the
fish on the chale
and Wae. They the
man kots the fish
in a nat.

"How to count the fish. First they put the fish on the scale
and weigh (them). Then the man counts the fish in a net."

work on a collaborative chapter for the book. Each group decided on the various tasks that needed to be done—who was to draw the illustrations, who was to be the "scribe"—but the group as a whole was responsible for the content of their chapter. The groups used the children's individual writing as sources for their chapters, but they made extensive changes based on the discussions they had while writing their chapters.

After individual chapters were written, the children made a cover for the book, a table of contents, a list of new words the children had learned while doing the book, and a list of all the "authors" of the book. (The class Big Book was kept in the classroom, and later in the year it was read to parents and friends on "Authors' Day.")

In Debby's class, right after returning from the fish hatchery, the children wrote about the trip in their journals. They also participated in the other projects previously described, except that Debby extended the life cycle project to include creating a book made up of four sections, covering the four stages of the trout life cycle (egg, fry, fingerling, yearling).

While most of the students undertook this book project, Debby designed alternate projects for students with special needs. For several students, whose language difficulties would make the book project a complicated task, Debby suggested they first draw a large life cycle chart (using her chart as a model). On this chart, the students labeled each stage and wrote something about each of the stages (see Figure 2–10).

For one child, whose knowledge of science was already extensive, Debby decided that an independent research study would better challenge him than the book project the rest of the class was doing. Debby encouraged him to pursue the topic of gravity: he had been interested in how the fish hatchery used gravity-fed water to feed the troughs and ponds, and learning more about the concept of gravity seemed worthwhile. Debby had him read Vera Fischer's book *One Way Is Down—A Book About Gravity* (Fischer, 1967), and then she discussed with him what he had read. He wrote a story about gravity, and this led him to read about underground springs from a children's encyclopedia and write about them. After a discussion about how gravity and underground springs were related to the fish hatchery, he wrote another story called *How the Fish Hatchery Gets Its Water.* These three pieces, along with illustrations, a title page, and an author's page, became Rene's book (see Figure 2–11).

REFLECTIONS ON THE PROJECT

What We Learned

Over the years that we have been visiting the fish hatchery, we have accumulated a fair amount of knowledge about trout and about the operation of the fish hatchery itself. The reading we have recently done hasn't dramatically

FIGURE 2–10. *John Displays his Chart of the Life Cycle of the Trout.*

altered or increased our own knowledge, but it has confirmed what we already knew (which is reassuring), and in some instances has taught us things we weren't completely sure about. For example, we are now much better informed about the different kinds of trout (especially the native strains), about the anatomy of trout (in fact, of fish generally), and about the survivability of eggs. We also found some new books on trout that we could share with the children, plus a number of excellent drawings and paintings of trout from magazine articles. This topic is not well covered in literature that's accessible to first-graders, and much of what we learned from our reading really wasn't directly applicable to our classroom activities, but we have gained enough from our own reading to convince us that enlarging our knowledge of a topic is extremely worthwhile.

What the Children Learned

There is no question that the children learned a great deal from this project, far more than they would have done by just taking the field trip and then writing about it. They came away from this project with a much firmer grasp of the life cycle of trout, of the anatomy of fish, and of the fish hatchery operation than children did in previous years. One reason for this is that we explored each of

How The Fish Hatchery
Gets Its Water
by Rene Plattner

Fish Hachary
The water from the fish hachary
comes from a spring. Gravity pull's
the water down into the collection dich.
It goes into the pips and into the pools.
Sometims the fish go up the pips
And they have to fish them out. And
leves. The water alwas flose so it never
frezzies. it needs to be cold so
the fish can live.

these topics in some depth, over time, and from a variety of perspectives (reading, writing, drawing, observing, even dissecting). Because we had many opportunities to revisit topics, we were able to expose children to quite technical vocabulary (dorsal fin, sac fry, brood stock), and to take the time to explain processes that are not easily understood (e.g., how fish breathe, gravity-fed water system, how fish feed themselves). While this project by itself obviously cannot take sole credit for children's growth in reading, writing, listening, and speaking, the effects of the language activities during this project are not to be underestimated. At a minimum, each child read (or was read) several books and articles in magazines; they participated in extended discussions relating to fish; they drew three complicated diagrams (the external parts of a trout, the internal organs, and the life cycle); they did an art project involving the construction of a three-dimensional "fish"; they wrote about the field trip in their journals; and they wrote several pieces (some of which went through revision and editing phases) related to trout, the fish hatchery, and life cycles. Finally, they all participated in a hands-on dissection of a fish.

The Value of Preteaching

In previous trips to the fish hatchery, the children were excited to be away from the classroom, and they were fascinated by the sights. Looking back, however, we wonder how much the children understood or even if they were tuned in to what was being explained to them. The problem, as we see it, is that the children knew so little about fish and the hatchery beforehand that anything more than the blatantly obvious went right over their heads. This lack of knowledge may also have contributed to less than ideal behavior, although going in a large group didn't help, either. By enlarging the children's knowledge about fish and the fish hatchery before going on the trip, we ensured that the children already knew quite a bit about what they were going to see and had questions they were anxious to have answered. Thus, most of their attention was focused on things they wanted to see firsthand and learn more about. They were absorbed by aspects of the fish hatchery they came to see and had little time or energy left over for misbehaving. Their interest in specific topics also was sufficient to overcome the excitement of being away from school and the distractions of the fish hatchery itself, such as the noise in the building. We attribute these changes in attitude and behavior largely to the preteaching.

The result of preteaching was that children came to the field trip with a genuine purpose: they wanted to see everything they had learned about, and they wanted answers to unresolved questions. Under these circumstances, it isn't surprising that they were more focused than in other years; they were better listeners, better behaved, and more inquisitive. More importantly, the children's knowledge of fish and the fish hatchery was deepened and broadened though the preteaching in a way that we have never really attempted before. Children came out of this project with a far better understanding of the vocabulary, concepts, and factual knowledge than they have done in the past. In other words, not only did the preteaching help prepare children for the field trip itself, but it also played a large role in strengthening and extending children's scientific understanding, which was one of our original purposes for the project. Without this preteaching, not only would the children have benefited less from the trip, but they also would have emerged from the theme with a much more superficial understanding of the topic.

Meeting Individual Needs and Interests

A project such as this is well suited to children of widely differing abilities and interests, partly because of the wide variety of activities during the project, and partly because we encourage children to participate in activities to the extent they are able and willing. Our approach to language arts accepts individual differences in literacy development and tries to take children from where they are. While we expect that children's accomplishments in these activities will vary widely, none of the activities themselves are too difficult that less able children are unable to participate at all, nor too easy that more able children remain unchallenged. Our goal is to have children grow in their scientific knowledge and in their language abilities through these activities, not to master a set of specific scientific or language skills. The field trip offers children such a range of experiences (walking around the grounds, observing the different aspects of the hatchery, asking and answering questions about what they saw, being out in the crisp winter air), and the activities following the trip are so varied (dissecting fish, writing, drawing, being read to, reading, doing art projects, etc.) that every child can easily participate in and profit from the experiences. As we do in the normal course of teaching, we made accommodations for children with language difficulties: our Chapter 1 specialist focused on the fish theme by using theme-related books and poetry as the basis for instruction; she also assisted remedial students in the classrooms as they were reading and writing about the theme. With some children, whose knowledge of fish was extensive and whose language abilities were advanced, we provided opportunities for them to extend or deepen their knowledge. For example, we had one youngster do independent studies of gravity and underground springs; others, we encouraged to write more extensively (using more scientific information) and read additional material.

Suggestions for Adapting Our Approach to Other Topics

There aren't that many schools within easy range of a trout hatchery, and so a first grade teacher might think that the project we have described isn't appropriate to her class because there is no fish hatchery nearby. What we have learned from this project, however, isn't exclusively applicable to hatcheries.

Field trips to a factory, a hospital, a museum, a nature preserve, or a historical site have much in common with our experience because they all involve making direct observations of scientific, historical, economic, cultural, or natural phenomena. Thus, a first grade teacher could easily adapt our activities to her own field trip.

We have some suggestions to pass on that should make the field trip experience more successful. The teacher should visit the site well in advance of planning the class trip. This advance visit will make it easier to organize the trip. For example, it's useful to know in advance that in the fish hatchery building, there's so much noise that no one can hear anything that isn't shouted; that those in charge of the site insist that there be small groups, each with a chaperone; or that if arrangements are made ahead of time, groups may be allowed "behind the scenes." More importantly, the advance visit helps the teacher see how the trip can support, extend, or deepen children's knowledge of a topic—something that cannot be done "on the fly" while escorting a group of thirty children around a site. For example, by taking a trip to the fish hatchery without the children, we were able to have extended conversations with the hatchery staff, and we learned about aspects of the hatchery (e.g., the gravity water system) that eventually became an important focus of the trip.

We have already extolled the virtues of preteaching, and it is just as effective with topics such as hospitals, the pet shop, or maple sugaring. Preteaching can involve finding out what children already know about a topic and generating questions to explore. Or it may involve introducing children to the technical vocabulary of a topic (for example, explaining in advance of a hospital field trip terms such as *stethoscope, pediatrics,* and *intravenous*). It will certainly involve reading books (both fiction and nonfiction) on the topic to the children and spending time discussing both the books and children's personal experiences with the topic. It also helps to describe to the children what they are going to see on the field trip—if they have a good idea of what's involved before they go, they'll be looking for particular things and as a consequence will be much less likely to be distracted and mischievous. They will also come away with much more information.

Bumping up our own knowledge of a topic has paid off handsomely, and we strongly recommend that teachers explore topics on their own as well as with the children. Increasing one's own knowledge of topics makes class discussions richer. A teacher whose knowledge of a topic is extensive is in a good position to recommend appropriate books to children and guide them as they explore different aspects of the subject. The more a teacher knows, the more options he or she can provide to children of varying abilities and interests.

Finally, we have learned a great deal from each other as we work together on these projects. While we design teaching activities that are suited to our individual teaching styles and to the children we have in our own classrooms, we plan projects together and share many of each other's ideas for projects.

Frequently, children from the three classes join together for group activities such as read-alouds. Our program has benefited enormously from the collaboration of three teachers, and working together has lightened the load for each of us. Apart from that, it has been great fun working on these projects.

Although we visit the fish hatchery every year, our projects are not always as elaborate as the ones we have described in this chapter. In any year, we will give more attention to one topic over another so that we aren't exploring the same topics as extensively each year. Since it takes quite a lot of preparation to cover a theme extensively, we try to vary the topics from year to year so that one year we will delve into a topic, another we'll dip into it. In truth, covering a topic thoroughly is not as much hard work as it sounds. Looking for new materials and reading recently published adult and children's books takes time, but it's such a pleasant and rewarding activity that we don't even think of it as work. The hardest part is the day-to-day business of managing over twenty first graders, all at different stages of various projects, all wanting attention at the same time. But given how much the children learn from these projects and how enthusiastic they are about this approach to learning, we would never go back to just teaching from the textbook.

REFERENCES

Arnosky, J. (1982). *Freshwater fish and fishing: A guide for beginners.* New York: Scholastic.
[*Describes the parts of a typical fish, then goes on to show how to fish for sunfish, perch and pike, catfish and carp. Excellent illustrations.*]

Cole, J., & Wexler, J. (1987). *A fish hatches.* New York: William Morrow.
[*This book describes the development of a trout from egg to adult, illustrated with detailed photographs and drawings. The descriptions are informative and very interesting.*]

Creative Educational Society. (1973). *Fishes we know.* Chicago, IL: Children's Press.
[*Simply written, clear description of trout, their mating habits, and different kinds of trout.*]

Decker, D. J., Howard, R. A., & Everhart, W. H. (1978). Identifying New York's salmon and trout. *Conservation Circular, 16*(4), 1–11.
[*This is an excellent source for identifying the various strains of trout.*]

Fichter, G. S., & Francis, P. (1965). *A guide to fresh and salt-water fishing.* New York: Golden Press.

[Small encyclopedia about fish and fishing. Has good illustrations of the various strains of trout.]

Field Enterprises Educational Corporation. (1973). *Childcraft: How and why library*, (Vol. 5). Chicago: Field Enterprises Educational Corporation.
[This is an informative series that has an excellent section devoted to fish.]

Fischer, V. K. (1967). *One way is down—a book about gravity*. Boston: Little Brown.
[A book with excellent illustrations that explains the concept of gravity to young readers.]

Heacox, C. E. (1974). *The compleat brown trout*. New York: Winchester Press.
[A comprehensive, in-depth study of the brown trout. Has excellent illustrations. Sections on habitat, breeding, eating, etc.]

Held, J. (1976). *Fabian the fish-boy*. New York: Addison-Wesley.
[A story about a boy who wanted to be a fish. He rescues fish from the catch, and they in turn help him become a fish. In the end, he turns back into a boy, on the condition that his father no longer fishes. Beautifully illustrated.]

Langan, D., Braico, J., & Spissinger, J. (1990). New York's Adirondack's heritage strain brook trout. *The Conservationist/NYSDEC*, 45(5), 32–33.
[Describes the various trout "strains" (variations) in the Adirondacks. Includes Honnedaga, Horn Lake, Tamarack, Windfall, Dix, Nate, Stink, and the Little Tupper—all variations on the native brook trout.]

Lionni, L. (1963). *Swimmy*. New York: Pantheon.
[Beautifully illustrated, this book tells the story of "Swimmy," a black fish who escapes being eaten by a large fish and eventually teaches a shoal of small fish to swim in the formation of a large fish, so they too can escape being eaten.]

Lionni, L. (1970). *Fish is fish*. New York: Pantheon.
[The frog tells the fish about the world above the sea, but the fish has a hard time visualizing it.]

McClane, A. J. (Ed.). (1974). *McClane's new standard fishing encyclopedia and international angling guide*. New York: Holt, Rinehart and Winston.
[A gold mine of information about types of trout, their habitats, spawning, and survival. It also has information on trout in the Adirondack region.]

McCullough, R., & Stegemann, E. (1991). The trout of New York. *The Conservationist/NYSDEC*, 45(5), 24–31.
[Describes the various kinds of trout found in New York state. Clear text, superb color illustrations.]

New York State Department of Environmental Conservation. (n. d.). *Educator's Guide*. Albany, New York: New York State Department of Environmental Conservation.
[*Sourcebook of materials and services for environmental studies in New York.*]

Sabin, F. (1982). *Wonders of the pond*. Mahwah, NJ: Troll Associates.
[*Describes the many varieties of plants and animals, including fish, that live in a pond.*]

Say, A. (1988). *A river dream*. Boston: Houghton Mifflin.
[*While sick in bed, a young boy opens a box from his uncle and embarks on a fantastical fishing trip.*]

Schwiebert, E. (1984). *Trout, Volumes 1 & 2*. New York: E. P. Dutton.
[*A massive, authoritative sourcebook on trout. Has sections on the evolution of fly-fishing, American species of trout and grayling, physiology, habitat and behavior, and fishing for trout. *]

Shoemaker, M. E. (1941). *My fish friends*. DuBois, PA: Gray Printing Co.
[*Reprint of an old pamphlet describing various fish. Superb illustrations.*]

Thomas, A. (1980). *Fishing is for me*. Minneapolis: Lerner.
[*Two young boys share their fishing experiences.*]

Warren County Department of Public Works. (1990). *The Warren County fish hatchery self-guided tour*. Warrensburg, New York: Warren County Department of Public Works, Parks and Recreation Division.
[*This pamphlet is intended to help visitors find their way around the fish hatchery, but it also has excellent information about various aspects of the trout's life cycle.*]

Wildsmith, B. (1968). *Fishes*. New York: Watts.
[*Picture book about a variety of fish including trout.*]

Wylie, J. (1983). *A big fish story*. New York: Children's Press.
[*A story about a child who describes the fish he caught. Each time he's asked, its size increases. This book is really about the concept of size and the vocabulary to describe size.*]

Chapter 3

Indian Land: A Second Grade Theme
Colleen McNall

In my first year teaching second grade, I was nervous about what I should be doing in Social Studies. The second grade social studies curriculum comprised mainly a large unit on Native Americans and several smaller units on topics such as citizenship, holidays, safety, and maps and globes. To accompany each of the units, the school district provided bundles of guides, unit packets, and dittos. I studied these carefully, and two things struck me immediately about them. The first was that there really wasn't enough time in the year to give each of these topics adequate attention, especially given how little time was available for social studies in the first place. The second was that the materials provided by the district were, to put it kindly, a tad out of date. What especially caught my attention was the almost total absence of any literature in the unit. Since the Native American unit was not scheduled to be taught until January, I decided to put it on hold until the holiday vacation while I coped with other more pressing things.

The more I thought about the Native American unit, the more I realized that it provided a golden opportunity to bring the unit up to date (just adding literature to it would be a demanding task); but I began to think of other possibilities, too. The unit as it stood provided few opportunities for children to integrate language arts with content area learning; it also wasn't that challenging for the kinds of children that typically I have in my class. Children simply did a series of teacher-constructed activities that didn't engage them as learners, respect what they already knew, or challenge them to explore new and worthwhile information about the topic.

ENLARGING MY OWN KNOWLEDGE

The first thing I needed to do was to enlarge my own knowledge of Native Americans so that I could better understand what it was that I wanted the children to explore. I started with the district's curriculum guide. The Native American unit was organized around the five major regions: Northeast, Northwest, Southeast, Southwest, and Great Plains. The unit taught each region in a similar way: first, the region's geography was studied, then family life

127

(focusing primarily on the roles of each family member), and finally miscellaneous topics such as shelter, dependence on animals, tools, food, clothing, religion, and legends. All of these topics seemed appropriate and worthwhile for second graders to study, but what troubled me was how fragmented and isolated each of these were from one another. Part of this stemmed from the nature of the activities themselves—a series of short, isolated activities.

But the more I looked through these materials, the more it occurred to me that what undergirded the entire unit was the attachment—perhaps affinity is a better word—that Native Americans have to the land itself. Once having been drawn in this direction, I abandoned geography, family structure, and isolated subtopics such as tools and religion as the organizing theme, and began to reorganize it around the concept of land. I found one major source, a recent book on Native Americans (Collins, 1991) that provided detailed descriptions of the various tribes throughout North America and was organized by the five regions. This book not only reinforced the notion of land as an organizing framework, but it also added enormously to my knowledge of the different tribes, their customs, religious beliefs, houses, arts and crafts, and so on. This book is beautifully illustrated with drawings and photographs and is rich in detail. Its illustrations are so good that second graders could learn from them even though much of the text is too difficult for them. I found another source, tucked away in a box at the back of my school library; it was a teacher's guide prepared by the American Museum of Natural History (American Museum of Natural History, n. d.). In addition to providing more information about food, clothing, housing, tools, and weapons of tribes from the Eastern Woodlands and Plains, this book emphasized the adaptations made by the Indians to their environments in order to survive. There was a common thread running through the literature on Native Americans, namely the extreme importance of the land to Indian survival. Everything the Indians accomplish throughout their lives is made possible by nature. The Indians are well aware of what they consider a wonderful gift, and in return, they treat the earth with great respect. They know how to preserve the land, the air, and the water, notions that we are just beginning to take seriously once more. This is why I chose land as the organizing framework for this unit.

The second thing I needed to do was to find literature suitable for the unit. The district had provided copies of a series of nonfiction trade books entitled *New True Books* (Osinski, 1984; Tomchek, 1987). Each book in the series took a different tribe and described their origins, religious beliefs and customs, their houses, and their daily life. They provided much important information in a manner that second graders could easily understand, but they were woefully inadequate as the sole sources of information for the children. Not only did I want to expose the children to a wide range of literature (fiction and nonfiction) on early Native Americans, but also I wanted them to encounter both traditional and current literature relating to Native Americans. Finally, I wanted to be sure that even the brightest child in the class would be challenged by the material I provided, and frankly, the *New True Books* would need to be supplemented in order for this to be accomplished.

PLANNING THE THEME

My original plan was to set aside six to eight weeks for the unit. I needed this amount of time for children to read a number of full-length books and to cover the topic in greater depth than was possible in the original curriculum. I thought it would make sense to divide the unit into seven weeks, with a week devoted to each of the following topics: geography, shelter, food, tools, trade, legends, and a week devoted to an Indian festival. My intention was that Indian affinity with the land would be the glue that held each of these subtopics together; we would also study each of these subtopics as they related to specific tribes. In each of the six weeks, I wanted the children to be immersed in literature (reading it aloud, reading it on their own, and discussing what was read), in writing (personal responses to reading, taking notes, and writing stories), and in arts and crafts (drawing, making models, weaving, cooking). Through all of these activities, I hoped that the children would significantly enlarge their knowledge of Native Americans in a way that wasn't possible by simply studying a "text" or doing innumerable worksheets.

As I started to get the unit ready for the children, it became clear that I wouldn't be able to study Indian tribes from each of the regions separately because there wasn't enough literature on each of the tribes that dealt specifically with each of the subtopics. I decided to keep the original subtopics but study them from the perspective of whatever Native Americans we had suitable literature on. Not having enough literature forced me to make other changes, too. Originally, I had planned to have enough books on each of the subtopics for all the children to be studying the same topic at the same time. Because there weren't enough books available, I had to compromise and have children studying different subtopics at the same time. This turned out to have a silver lining because they were learning from each other.

In the end, I decided that I would focus in my daily read-aloud to the children on each region in turn, but the children, in their daily independent reading, would be reading books on Native Americans from all of the regions and related to all the subtopics. So while I focused on each of the regions in turn, the children's reading would be broadly focused. By the end of the unit, both the children and I would have covered all the regions, and all the subtopics (geography, shelter, food, tools, trade, and legends), but we would get there by slightly different routes.

I also decided that six to eight weeks was too long for this theme, and planned on a three-week theme.

CARRYING OUT THE THEME: THE FIRST YEAR

I started the theme by discussing with the children the importance of land to Indians. I asked them about the different ways that Indians may have used the land, and why they thought the land was so important to the Indians. We then constructed a web on chart paper, laying out the subtopics of geography, shelter, food, tools, trade, and legends. This exercise gave me an idea of what the children already knew about Native Americans, but it also helped us create a plan for organizing the theme's activities.

After this, I explained to the children how we were going to explore this theme. I told them there were Indians in many different regions of the country, and that in each of these regions there were big differences in climate, terrain, and available resources that affected the Indians' way of life. I also explained which Indian tribes came from each of the regions (for example, Navajo and Apaches from the Southwest, Mohawk and Algonquin from the Northeast), because in many of the books, tribes are referred to without saying where they came from. I said that we were going to be reading many different books about Indians; some of these I would read to them, and some they would be reading on their own.

Each week, we focused on a different aspect of the theme. We started with geography, then moved on to shelter, food, tools, trade, and legends. During reading time, each child selected a book to read and then wrote about that book in his or her journal, focusing on the topic of the week. Later in the day, students could share what they had read. We also did some class projects. These varied according to the topic we were studying. For example, during the geography week, we did things like making maps; during the shelter week, we made models of Indian buildings. At the end of the theme, the children wrote a longer piece on any aspect of the theme they chose, including poetry, stories (legends, recalled or invented), and so on. As a finale, we held a Native American "festival," to show their families what we had been doing throughout the theme.

Reflections on the First Year

Although the theme went well—the children certainly enjoyed it and learned a lot—I wasn't completely satisfied with it. One of the things that concerned me was that I wasn't sufficiently sure about what I wanted the children to learn. Another was that I think I gave the children too much responsibility for acquiring the information. Also, I had difficulty getting the children focused on their topics, probably because I wasn't familiar enough with the material (I hadn't even finished reading all the children's books). Still, for a theme that was hastily assembled, it went much better than I thought it would, and I started thinking about how I might improve it for the second year. I had spent a great deal of time in the first year enlarging my own knowledge of Indians, and I felt comfortable about that; by the end of the first year, I had caught up with my reading of the children's books. Something I learned from this reading was that many of the books on Indian legends were written at a level that most second graders would find too difficult, and so I dropped legends as a major subtopic, but I included books on legends that I felt were accessible to second graders and could be included in other subtopics.

The overall approach to the theme (breaking it up into different subtopics such as geography, shelter, food, etc.) worked well. What I needed to do now was to make it flow better.

CARRYING OUT THE THEME: THE SECOND YEAR

Day 1. I started the theme in the same way I started before, by talking about the importance of the land to the Indians. I told the children how Indians honored and greatly respected the land. I then asked the children why they thought this was so. Some responses:

"They want animals to live so they have something to eat."

"Land is like their home. They don't want it to be wrecked."

"Indians needed to respect the land. If they threw things all over, they would have a mess. Then they would have to move, but they would just mess up there, too. Soon there would be no place left for them to live."

"All their food came from the land."

I then told the children that in all the books they'd be reading throughout the theme, there's one common thread uniting all the different books: *the land was very important to the Indians.* This theme would come up again and again as they read. I then read *Brother Eagle, Sister Sky* (Chief Seattle, 1991). This book is an account of one chief's words when Indian land was being given to the white man; the chief expresses how precious and sacred the earth is and how it should be treated as such by all people. This book sends a very powerful message to all readers and listeners.

Next we made a class web, tying our theme to the various subtopics (see Figure 3–1).

Later that day, I described the five regions we would be studying. I gave the children the names of the North American regions: Northeast Woodlands, Southeast Woodlands, Great Plains, Southwest, Northwest Indians. Since the children were already familiar with directional terms, they were able to locate the regions on an outline map of North America. I gave the children additional information about tribal names. This is crucial because regions are not directly stated in most of the books children would be reading, and tribes are generally mentioned without reference to the areas they come from. I also showed the children how to locate a tribal name and identify its region on a map of North America. This map, which turned out to be very helpful throughout the theme, had tribal names printed on it and the regions in which they lived.

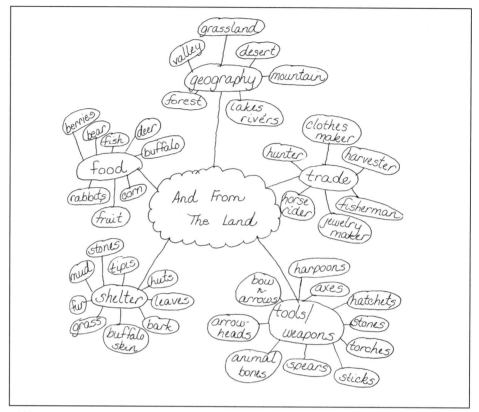

FIGURE 3–1. Class Web on "Indian Land."

Day 2. I met with the children on the rug to read a story. I wanted to carefully model the wealth of information a reader can learn from a single book. I wanted the children to observe my behavior as I closely examined the book. I decided to share with them *Annie and the Old One* (Miles, 1971). This is not only a very touching story about a relationship between a young girl and her dying grandmother, but it also provides lots of detailed information relating to Navajo lifestyle. (It's essential at the beginning of the story when a reference is made to the tribal name, to locate this tribe on the map. For this story, we discovered it was about the Southwest Indians.) A reader learns about the climate and geography of this Southwest region, as well as about the shelter, food, and trade of the Navajo tribe. While reading the text, we would periodically stop and discuss new things we learned. Later the same day, the children made maps depicting the five regions we were going to explore. After being given an outline of North America, the children color coded it and made a key to accompany their map.

Day 3. I read *Where the Buffaloes Begin* (Baker, 1981) to the children. I wanted to stress to the children things they might learn about the geography of an area

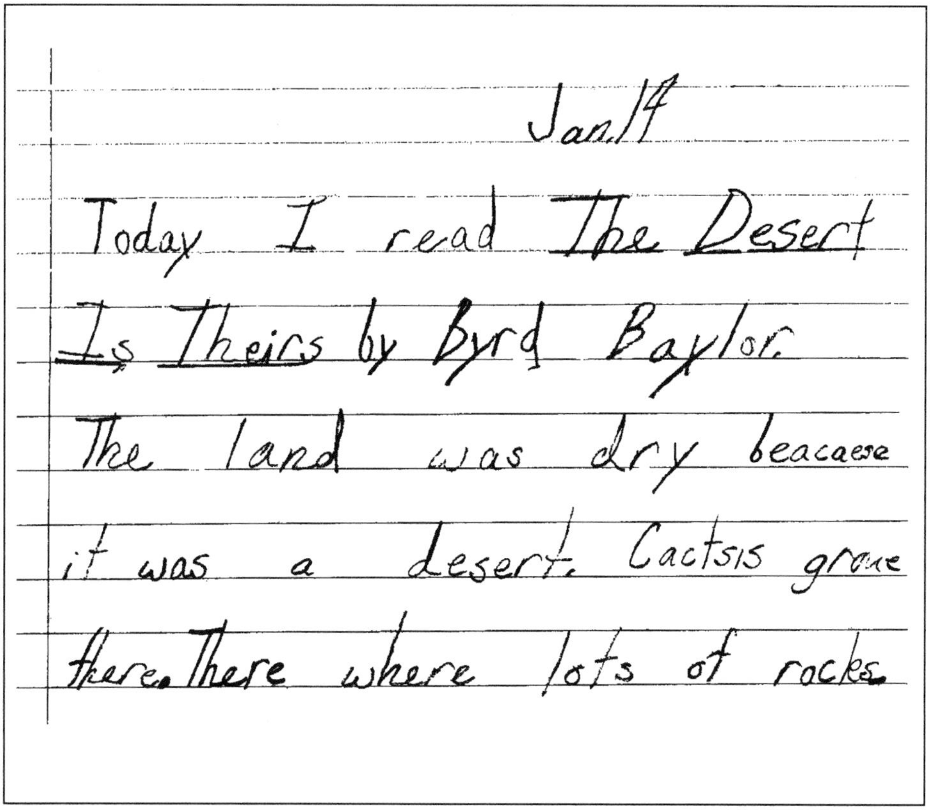
Jan 14

Today I read The Desert Is Theirs by Byrd Baylor. The land was dry beacaese it was a desert. Cactsis grove there. There where lots of rocks.

FIGURE 3–2. Laura's Journal Entry on The Desert is Theirs.

by looking very closely at the illustrations. Stephen Gammell's drawings illustrate the vast grasslands of the Great Plains region.

From the collection of children's books on Indians, I selected ten titles to read and learn about the geography of all the different regions:

People of the Breaking Day (Sewall, 1990)
In My Mother's House (Clark, 1941)
The Desert People (Clark, 1962)
Where the Buffaloes Begin (Baker, 1981)
The Desert is Theirs (Baylor, 1975)
Annie and the Old One (Miles, 1971)
North American Indians (Gorsline & Gorsline, 1977)
The Indian and his Pueblo (Floethe, 1960)
Indians of the Eastern Woodlands (Bains, 1985a)
A New True Book: Indians (Martini, 1982)

After reading one of these stories, the children made entries in their reading response journals (see Figures 3–2 and 3–3). I had modeled the format I wanted the children to use after reading *Where the Buffaloes Begin.*

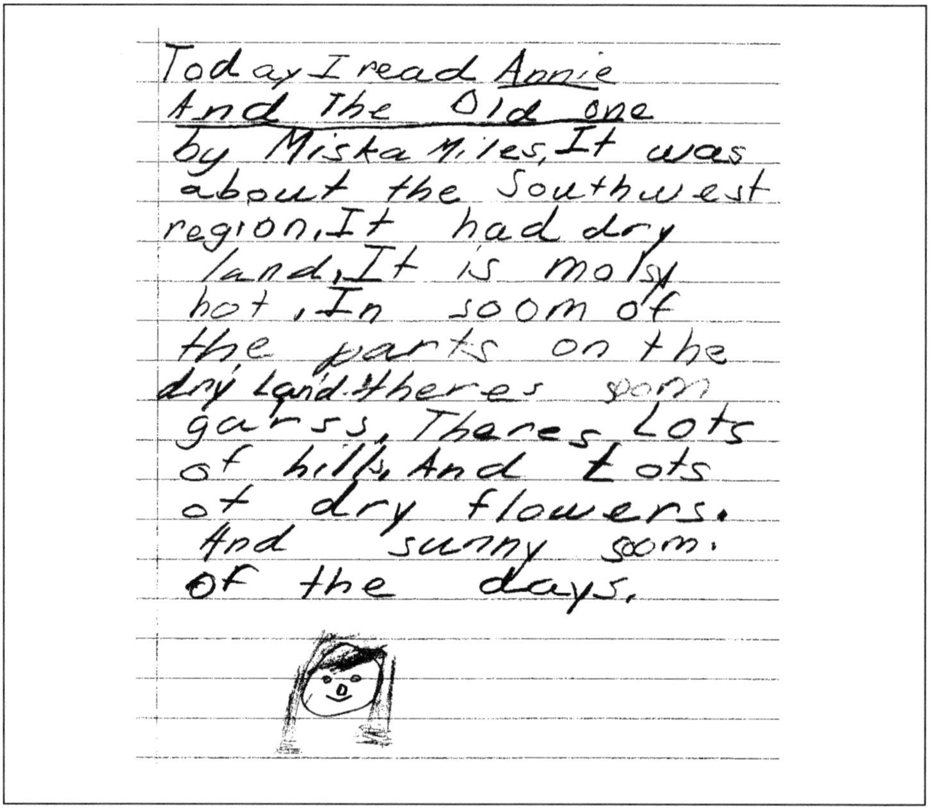

Today I read Annie
And The Old one
by Miska Miles, It was
about the Southwest
region, It had dry
land, It is molsy
hot, In soom of
the parts on the
dry Land theres soom
garss, Thares Lots
of hills, And Lots
of dry flowers.
And sunny soom.
of the days.

FIGURE 3–3. Alex's Journal on Annie and the Old One.

Later in the day I had the children gather on the rug to share ideas learned about the geography of the five regions. Students were given the opportunity to read from their journal entries. Together we made a class chart (see Figure 3–4).

Besides considering land formations, another goal was to reflect on different weather patterns, for the climate greatly impacts the Indians' struggle for survival. Since many of my students have traveled throughout the United States, our discussion went quite smoothly. We used our Indian region map and a map outlining the states to help us better understand weather across the different regions. We added this information to our geography chart.

Day 4. Our day began with a whole-group reading of *Blue-Wings-Flying* (DeHuff, 1986). Before we started this selection, I had the children look at the illustration on the title page. Using the material we learned the day before about geography, the class was able to identify the setting of this story. After reading the story together, we discussed the importance the Indian culture placed on the naming of a child. Several children commented that names were often related to something in the world. They were made aware of this point by reading several

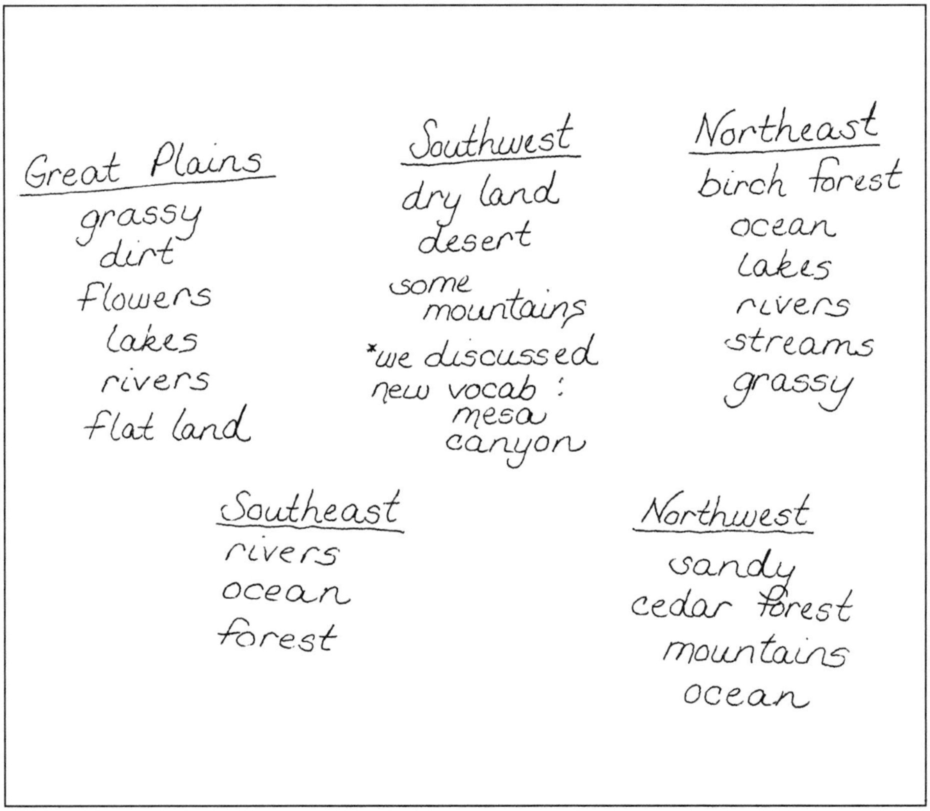

Great Plains
grassy
dirt
flowers
lakes
rivers
flat land

Southwest
dry land
desert
some
  mountains
*we discussed
new vocab :
   mesa
   canyon

Northeast
birch forest
ocean
lakes
rivers
streams
grassy

Southeast
rivers
ocean
forest

Northwest
sandy
cedar forest
mountains
ocean

FIGURE 3–4. *Class Chart on Geography of the Five Regions.*

of the books in the theme. (For example: *Blue-Wings-Flying, Little Wolf, Stone Fox, Boy-Strength-Of-Blue-Horses, Singing Rains*).

Later in the day I read *Knots On A Counting Rope* (Martin & Archambault, 1987), a story of a grandfather's explanation of who his grandson is, with a special emphasis on the significance of naming this new baby boy. After reading this story, I had the children pick a Native American name—a name that would reflect a special characteristic about themselves and that would show something that makes them different or special from anyone else. I told the class that often Native American names reflected some special ability, deed, or characteristic. To help stir some of their own thoughts and give them some direction, I told them a name I would give myself (Teacher-of-Small-Children). I told them I chose a name I thought described something special about me.

After sharing my name, I asked the children for some possible names they may have for themselves. Here are a few ideas from the class: Gray-Squirrel, White-Skin-Comic-Reader, Princess-of-Wild-Horses, Long-Haired-Dancer. One boy had read that some names were decided upon by the first thing the father saw as he left the place where the child was born. For this reason, he felt an appropriate name for himself would be Traffic-Jam-of-the-City!

Once ideas started to flow, the children went back to their seats to write their new Native American names in their journals. I asked them to write why they chose this particular name. We then decorated a feather with our names and shared our entries (see Figure 3–5).

Day 5. We began a new subtopic centered on Native American homes. The children selected and read a book from the unit and completed a blueprint. On the blueprint, the children were asked to name the type of housing, materials used to make the house, and any special features of this home (see Figure 3–6). At this time, some of the children realized their book didn't contain enough information, while others needed additional details about their shelter. I suggested they get assistance from other children reading about the same topic. This activity took an extended period of time to complete.

Day 6. We shared information on the various types of Indian shelters that we learned about the day before. We made a class chart containing these contributions (see Figure 3–7). The children used details from their blueprints to describe the housing. It was a great discussion, with the children talking at length about the details they had read in their books.

Day 7. We read the poem "Dancing Teepees" (O'John, 1989). We expanded on some aspects of teepees started the day before. We talked about how the teepee had to be warm in the winter against the cold, and cool in the summer against the heat. The children were already aware that the teepees had to be moved easily to follow the buffalo. I shared with the children from my own personal research that women were in charge of making, carrying, and putting up the teepees. The snugness and comfort of the teepee reflected the woman's ability as a housekeeper. We also discussed the designs placed on the outside of this home. I showed the class various symbols and their corresponding meaning to the Native American people. The children then made teepees with cloth, paints, sticks, and so on (see Figure 3–8).

Days 8, 9. For the next few days, I wanted the children to become acquainted with materials found in the Indian shelters. To do this, I invited them to do an independent research project, and gave them the following set of directions:

> Please read a story from our Native American unit. Look for information about the *insides* of different homes. Place any bits of information under the correct shelter. Be sure to tell *what* it is made of and *how* it is used by the family.

Before the children began reading for their project, I wanted to help them organize their journals so they could easily jot down ideas. Together we wrote the different types of homes on top of an individual piece of paper in our journals. By leaving an entire piece of paper blank for each home, this provided lots of room to add information. They also wouldn't run into organizational

FIGURE 3–5.
Megan's
"Indian"
Name, and the
Reasons Why
She Chose It.

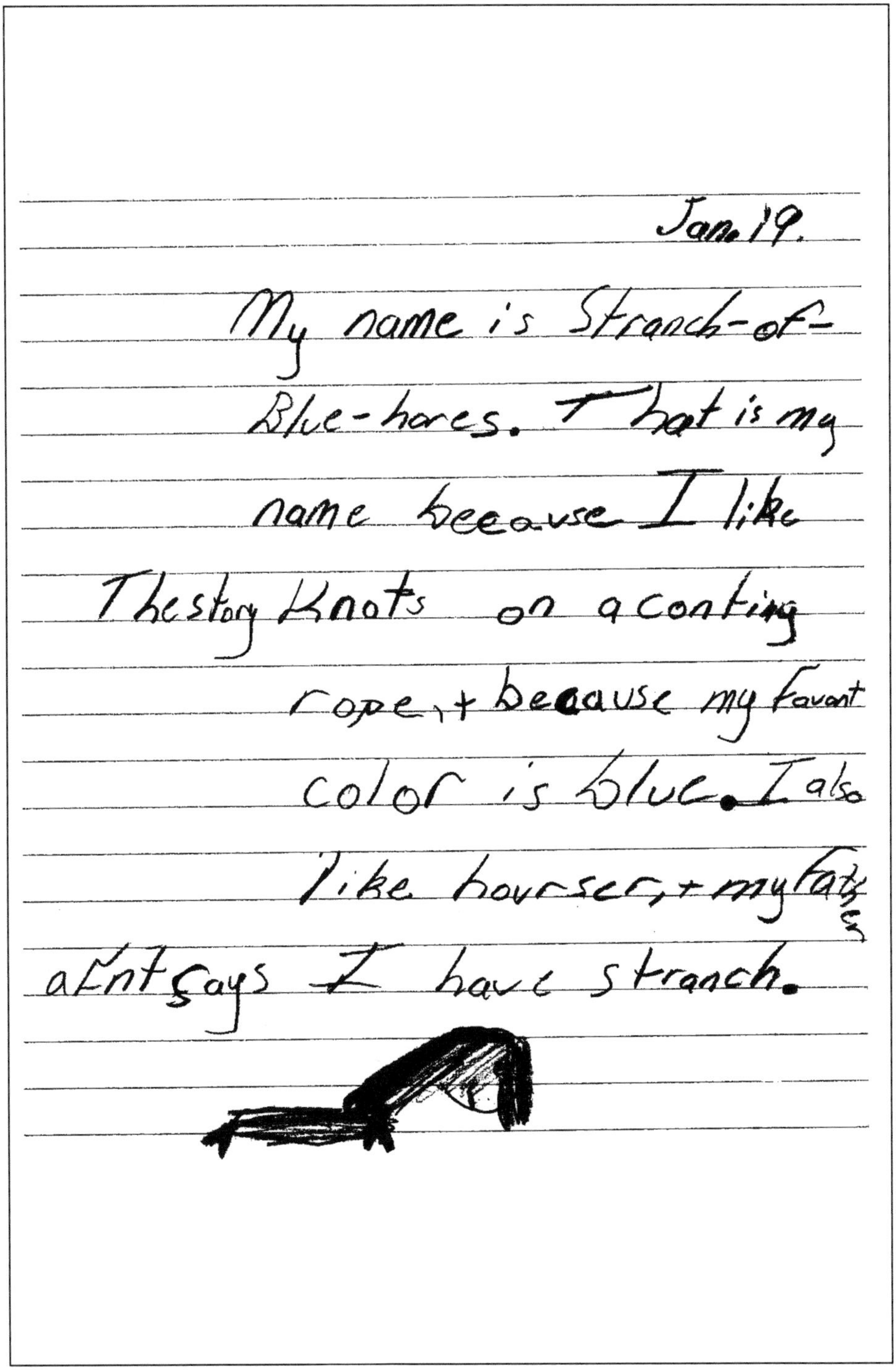

Jan. 19.

My name is Stranch-of-
Blue-hores. That is my
name beeause I like
The story Knots on a conting
rope, + beeause my favont
color is blue. I also
like hourser, + my fatz
aEnt says I have stranch.

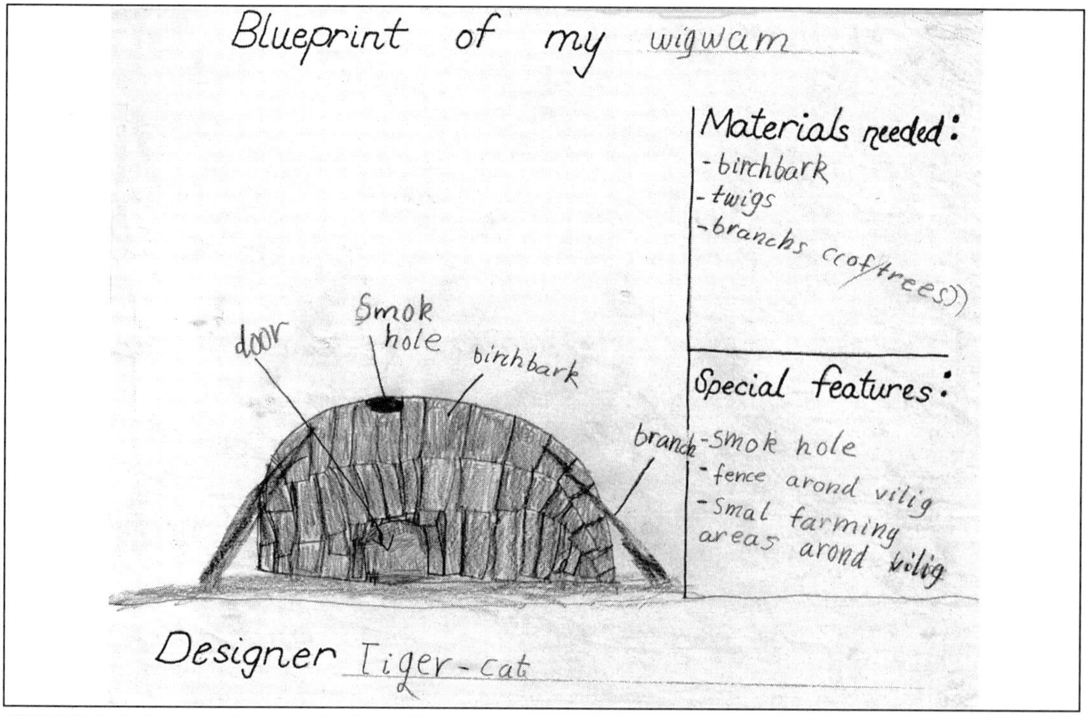

FIGURE 3–6. Emma's Blueprint For Her Wigwam.

problems when they changed from one shelter to the next. I then proceeded to quickly demonstrate how to write down notes:

Wigwam
- one room
- no windows
- fire in center
- smoke hole

Finally, the children were prepared to start their reading for the day. This activity lasted through the next day.

Day 10. After providing sufficient time for independent projects, I needed to decide how we could share what we had learned. The problem was how to manage presentations when children had so much to share. While skimming through their notes, I noticed most children had collected more information on one particular home. I decided to break the children into seven groups and have each group combine what they had learned about that one home. Each group was to use a sheet of chart paper and markers to combine their findings on one type of shelter and present them (see Figure 3–9).

Later in the day, we shared the results. Since I wanted to be sure to include all aspects of the home every child had discovered, I also allowed feedback from the class. After the group presented their sheet, the children looked through

FIGURE 3–7.
Class Chart on
Various Types
of Indian
Shelters.

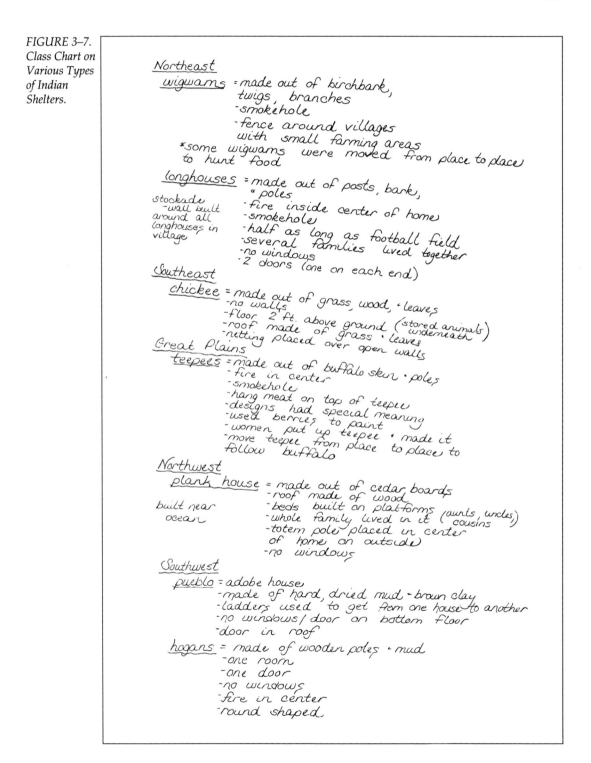

<u>Northeast</u>
  <u>wigwams</u> = made out of birchbark,
              twigs, branches
              -smokehole
              -fence around villages
              with small farming areas
     *some wigwams were moved from place to place
     to hunt food

  <u>longhouses</u> = made out of posts, bark,
                 " poles
stockade   -fire inside center of home
-wall built   -smokehole
around all   -half as long as football field
longhouses in -several families lived together
village   -no windows
              -2 doors (one on each end)

<u>Southeast</u>
  <u>chickee</u> = made out of grass, wood, · leaves
             -no walls
             -floor 2 ft. above ground (stored animals underneath)
             -roof made of grass · leaves
             -netting placed over open walls

<u>Great Plains</u>
  <u>teepees</u> = made out of buffalo skin · poles
             - fire in center
             -smokehole
             -hang meat on top of teepee
             -designs had special meaning
             -used berries to paint
             - women put up teepee · made it
             -move teepee from place to place to
             follow buffalo

<u>Northwest</u>
  <u>plank house</u> = made out of cedar boards
                 -roof made of wood
built near   -beds built on platforms
ocean   -whole family lived in it (aunts, uncles, cousins)
                -totem pole placed in center
                of home on outside
                -no windows

<u>Southwest</u>
  <u>pueblo</u> = adobe house
             -made of hard, dried mud · brown clay
             -ladders used to get from one house to another
             -no windows/door on bottom floor
             -door in roof

  <u>hogans</u> = made of wooden poles · mud
              -one room
              -one door
              -no windows
              -fire in center
              -round shaped

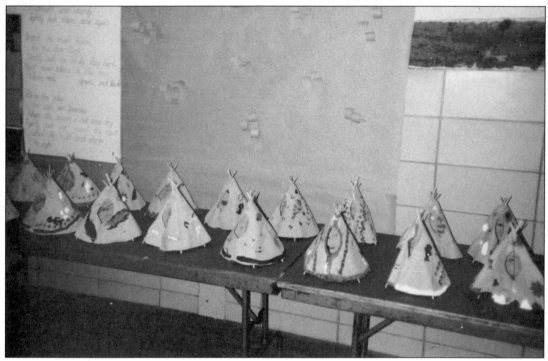

FIGURE 3–8. Photograph of Children's "Teepees."

their own notes on the shelter. If anyone had a different idea not yet recorded on the sheet, we would add it.

Day 11. We started the day by discussing how the Native Americans believed the earth was sacred or holy ground. Some of the children had read that Native Americans would take from the land only what was absolutely needed. Megan told us, from her reading, that before the Native Americans would kill an animal, or even chop down a tree, they would ask for forgiveness from the thing they were taking. I discussed with the class how the environment affected the homes they lived in.

We also started a new subtopic—family responsibilities, trades, and tools. Before examining the Native American way of life, I wanted the children to become more aware of responsibilities of family members in today's world. I assigned each child a family member role (mother, father, son, daughter) then I had the children write about their "job" and their "tools" in their response journals (see Figures 3–10 and 3–11).

Day 12. We looked at jobs and tools needed by a Native American family in the Northeast region. I guided the class in setting up their journal page similar to the one done the previous day. Once the children had set up their paper, they brought their journals and pencils over to the rug, and I read to them from *People of the Breaking Day* (Sewall, 1990). As I read, the children were to jot down

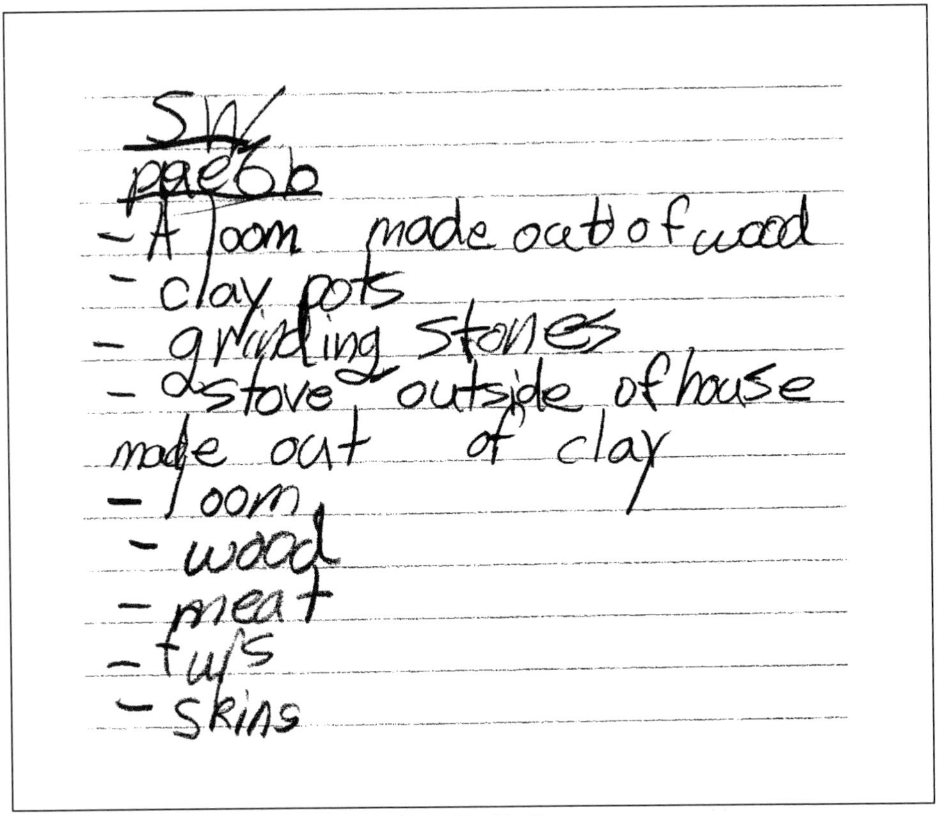
SW
paebb
- A loom made out of wood
- clay pots
- grinding stones
- stove outside of house
made out of clay
- loom
- wood
- meat
- furs
- skins

FIGURE 3–9. Emily's Notes on the Southwest Pueblo Home.

the jobs and tools of each family member, as discussed in the story. I wish that I had multiple copies of this section of the book, so the children could read with partners, and work at a more comfortable pace.

Day 13. Using the information recorded about jobs and tools of a mom, dad, daughter, or son in the present day and that of a Native American family, we discussed similarities and differences in lifestyles. The children then made Venn diagrams to illustrate these comparisons (see Figure 3–12).

Day 14. I wanted to continue addressing trades associated with family members. I read *The Sunflower Garden* (Udry, 1969). After sharing this story, I modeled the writing of a response. I especially wanted to draw attention to the method of recording information. Once again, I didn't want them to write sentences. My goal was for the children to use an easy technique to express their ideas.

I now gave the children time to start on their independent research of trades and tools of family members.

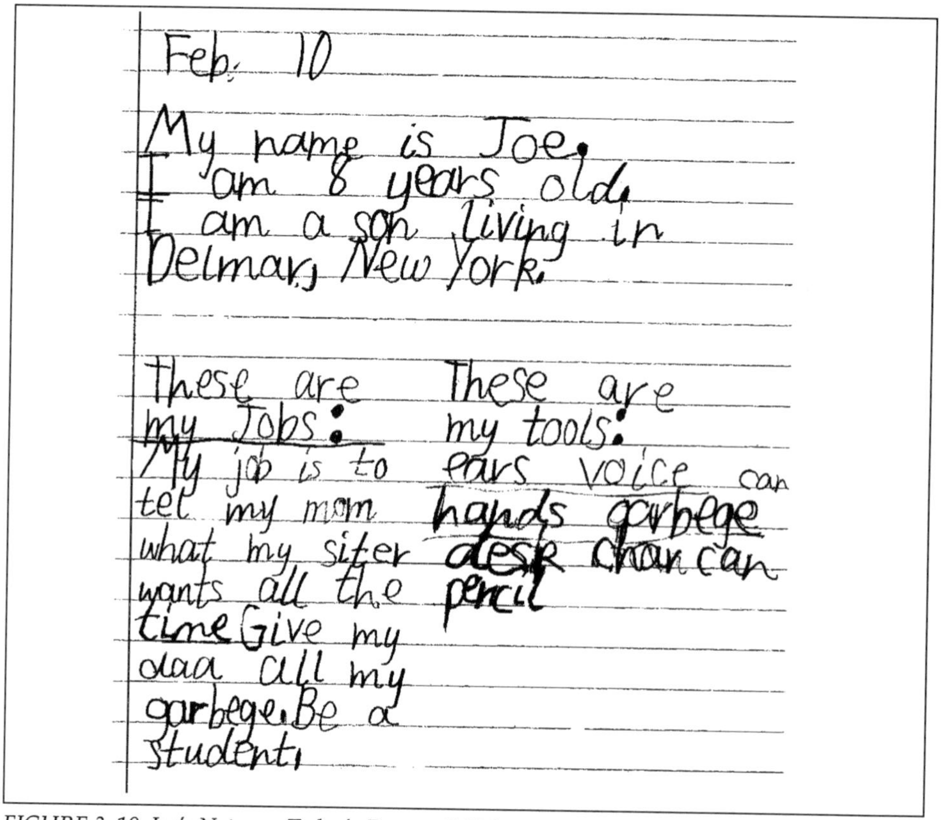

Feb. 10

My name is Joe.
I am 8 years old.
I am a son living in
Delmar, New York.

These are   These are
my jobs: my tools:
My job is to   ears voice can
tel my mom   hands garbege
what my siter   desk chair can
wants all the   pencil
time Give my
dad all my
garbege. Be a
Student.

FIGURE 3–10. *Joe's Notes on Today's Responsibilities.*

In the afternoon the children did a weaving project. Weaving was a common job among all North American regions. Together we retold the story of *Annie and the Old One* (Miles, 1971), a book I had read to the children earlier and one they had read independently. We looked at the weaving loom, and the sequence of steps involved in weaving. The class then began weaving miniature rugs, using looms made out of cardboard, and yarn for the rugs. This task takes quite a long time, so while they were weaving, I read to them *The Sign of the Beaver* (Speare, 1983).

Day 15. During their independent research time the previous day, I noticed the children were becoming overly anxious if they read a book and it didn't contain any information on the topic they were exploring. Some of the children were becoming quite frustrated. I told them that they shouldn't expect all books on Native Americans to have information about trades and tools, and that they shouldn't worry if a book doesn't. I think this came as somewhat of a relief to them.

Today I read *Dancing Drum* (Cohlene, 1990b). In all of Teri Cohlene's books, information is provided on a specific tribe at the back of the book. The children

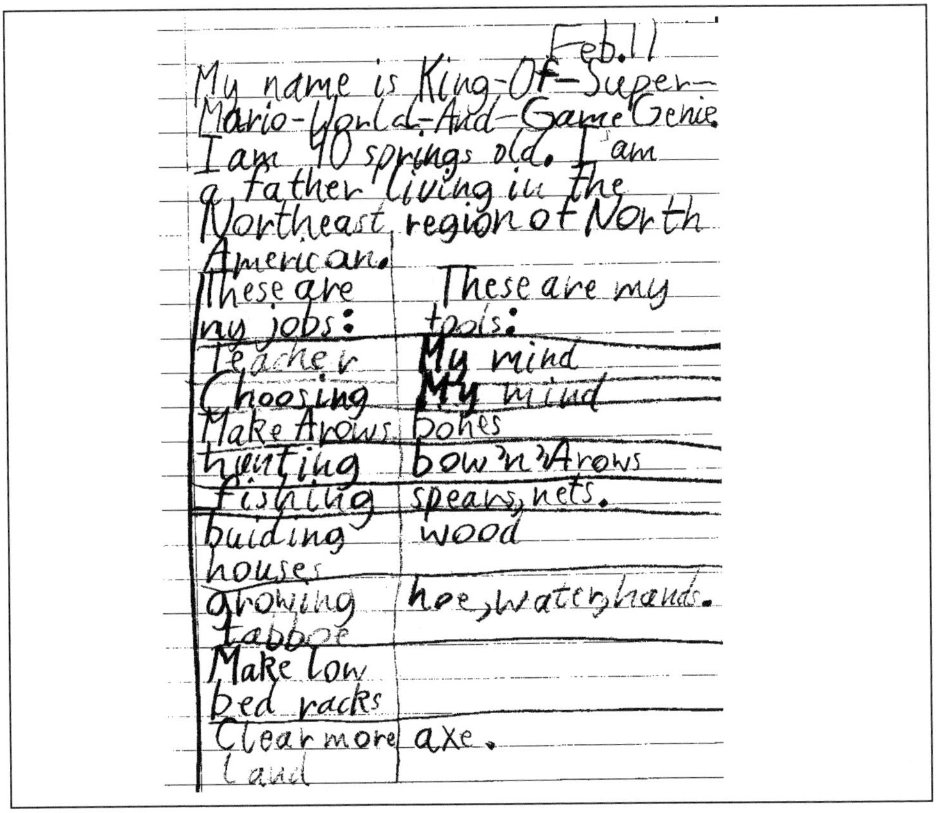

Feb. 11
My name is King-Of-Super-Mario-World-And-Game Genie. I am 40 springs old. I am a father living in the Northeast region of North American.

These are my jobs:	These are my tools:
Teacher	My mind
Choosing	My mind
Make Arows	bones
hunting	bow'n'Arows
fishing	spears, nets.
buiding houses	wood
growing tabboe	hoe, water, hands.
Make low bed racks	
Clear more Land	axe.

FIGURE 3–11. Ryan's Notes on Indian's Responsibilities.

loved listening to this legend. I reminded the children of the information at the back of the story. We read through this section to see if any details were given about trades or tools. I shared the information provided by the author, and once again I modeled how to record it.

Day 16. The children completed and shared their research projects on responsibilities, trades, and tools.

In the afternoon, I read *When Clay Sings* (Baylor, 1972), and we made clay pots, a job done by Indians in all the regions. (The pottery of the Pueblo women was the most famous. The shapes of the bowls varied depending on the maker. Coiled bowls were smoothed inside and out, dried in the sun, and painted in bright colors. The pottery was used as drinking and eating containers, and for cooking, storage, and carrying.) The class made small clay pots using a flour mixture since we couldn't obtain clay.

Day 17. We started the final topic, food. I gave the children a blank map of the regions, and I invited them to draw on the map the different kinds of food typically found in the different regions, using their books as sources for this information.

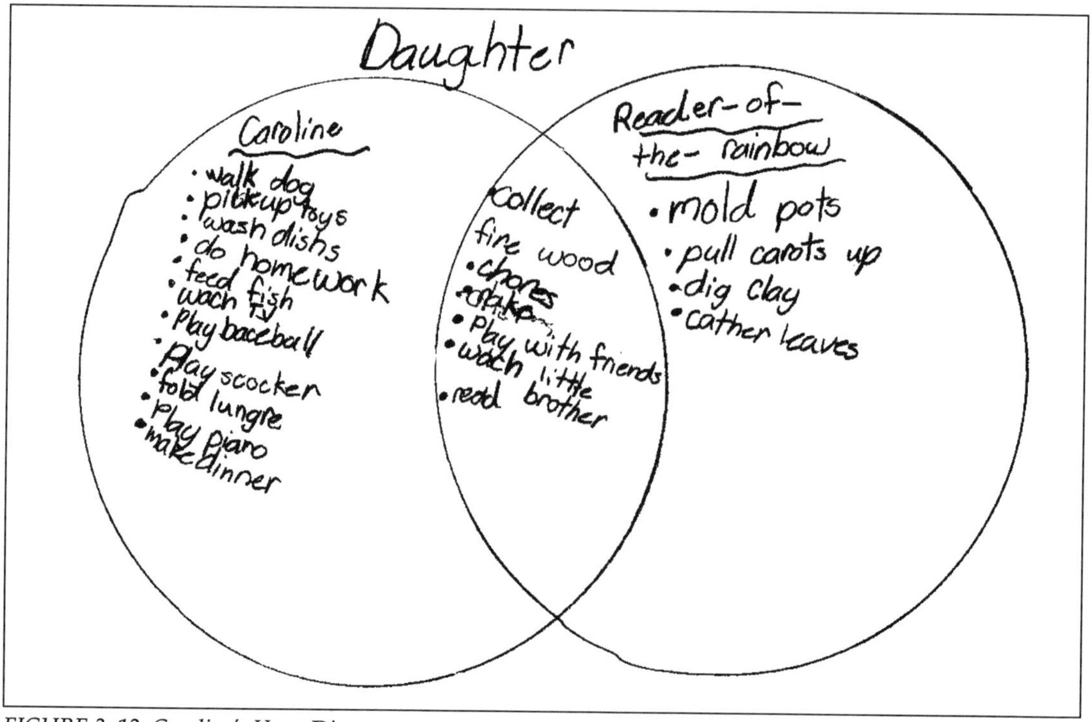

FIGURE 3–12. Caroline's Venn Diagram.

Day 18. We shared the maps containing information on the different foods and where they would typically be found. We ended the day with a potlatch, a Northwest Indian celebration, which involves preparing and eating a stew whose ingredients are corn, beans, and a broth. It was quite an experience. For children with modern eating tastes, the combination proved a little too primitive for them!

Day 19. We talked about how maple sugaring was discovered, which is an Iroquois legend. Because we worked on this theme in early spring, we took a quick field trip to Five Rivers, a nearby environmental center, where the children could see maple sugaring in action.

REFLECTIONS ON THE THEME

This is a challenging theme, especially if one wants children to engage in real literature and come to grips with some fairly sophisticated notions about Native Americans. While there is a growing body of children's literature devoted to the legends and lifestyles of Indians, not all of it is easy for second graders to read and understand. Some of the vocabulary is especially difficult for some youngsters who are emerging readers and who have limited knowledge of this important topic. Even though I knew some of the material was difficult for some of my students, I didn't want to deny them the experience of reading it, so I had to make some accommodations. One thing I did was to tape some of the more challenging books and then to encourage children to listen to them while following along in the text. This technique worked extremely well, and I'll use it again with difficult material.

I haven't said anything about the teaching of reading and writing skills in the description of the theme above because the main objective was to enlarge children's knowledge of Native Americans, not to teach skills directly. However, there are a number of skills woven into the activities. For example, I taught vocabulary within the context of the read-alouds and shared readings; I helped children with comprehension and vocabulary in the books they read on their own; I also took time to model appropriate strategies for finding information in books (study skills). When the children wrote, I helped them with their composing, revising, and editing skills. My district requires me to teach spelling as a separate subject area, but I was able to incorporate spelling words from the Indian Land theme materials into the spelling program. I was surprised how many new words there were in the theme's subtopics that could be used in the spelling program (see Figure 3–13).

I set out to teach children about the importance Indians attached to the land, and I'm sure they came away from this theme with a much better understanding of this concept, because so many of the books we read during this theme articulated this message in one way or another. Whenever this topic came up in read-alouds, in children's independent reading, or in any of the discussions we had, I made sure to emphasize this point. Each time we came across a phrase or sentence that expressed or captured the Indian affinity with the land, I made sentence-strips out of them (and so did the children, after they saw me doing it), and attached them to a model of the earth made by the children with their handprints all over. It would have been difficult to emerge from this theme without having repeated exposure to this "central idea."

Because the children were engaged in a number of activities and projects in which they had to choose a topic and explore it on their own, I found that even second graders can become responsible, independent learners, and they could share their knowledge with their classmates. I think sometimes we underestimate what children of this age are capable of doing on their own and with peers.

One of the problems I had was that there really weren't enough books available for the theme. Each time we explored a subtopic, we had to use books that had information on several topics. What this meant was that we had to use the same books over and over again for information on the different subtopics. If I had more books, I could use different books for different subtopics, and all of them would be fresh for the children. I've noticed that each year more and more books are published on Native Americans, and so the situation will improve each year I do this theme.

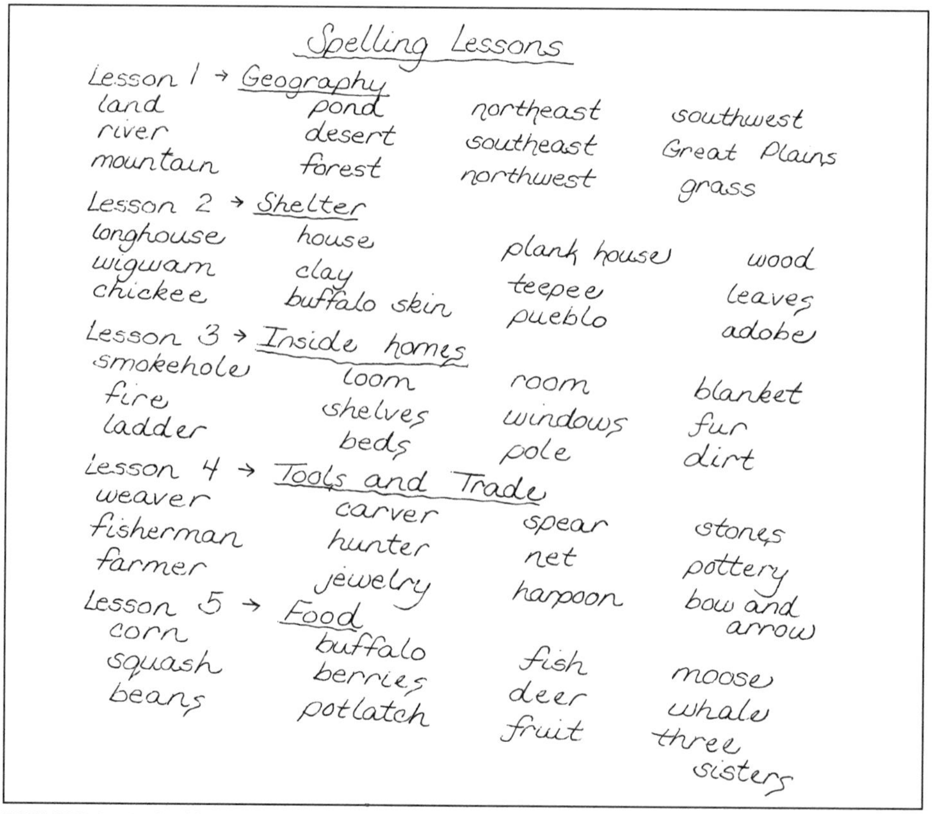

Spelling Lessons

Lesson 1 → Geography
land pond northeast southwest
river desert southeast Great Plains
mountain forest northwest grass

Lesson 2 → Shelter
longhouse house plank house wood
wigwam clay teepee leaves
chickee buffalo skin pueblo adobe

Lesson 3 → Inside homes
smokehole loom room blanket
fire shelves windows fur
ladder beds pole dirt

Lesson 4 → Tools and Trade
weaver carver spear stones
fisherman hunter net pottery
farmer jewelry harpoon bow and arrow

Lesson 5 → Food
corn buffalo fish moose
squash berries deer whale
beans potlatch fruit three sisters

FIGURE 3–13. Spelling Words from "Indian Land" Theme.

I have now done this theme twice, and I plan on making it a regular feature of my second grade curriculum. The activities seem to work well with the children, and the books, even though there aren't enough of them, excite the children, teach them worthwhile knowledge about Indians, and lead them into interesting topics for independent research.

REFERENCES

Teacher Resources

American Museum of Natural History. (n. d.). *Teacher's Guide: Eastern Woodlands & Plains Indians*. New York: American Museum of Natural History.

Collins, R. (Ed.). (1991). *The Native Americans: The indigenous people of North America*. New York: Salamander Books.

Osinski, A. (1984). *The Sioux*. Chicago: Children's Press.

Tomchek, A. H. (1987). *The Hopi*. Chicago: Children's Press.

Sources for Classroom Use

Accorsi, W. (1992). *My name is Pocahontas*. New York: Harper & Row.
   [*An Indian princess meets John Smith and travels to England.*]

Aliki. (1976). *Corn is maize*. New York: Harper & Row.
   [*Describes the cultivation of corn and the many uses of corn by the Indians.*]

Bains, R. (1985a). *Indians of the eastern woodlands*. Mahwah, NJ: Troll Associates.
   [*An easy-to-read book about the lifestyle of the woodland Indians.*]

Bains, R. (1985b). *Indians of the west*. Mahwah, NJ: Troll Associates.
   [*Describes different lifestyles of tribes living in various parts of the West.*]

Baker, B. (1962). *Little Runner of the longhouse*. New York: Harper Collins.
   [*Little Runner wants to participate in the New Year's celebrations with the older boys from the tribe.*]

Baker, O. (1981). *Where the buffaloes begin*. New York: Puffin Books.
   [*Beautifully told story of the origins of the buffaloes. Stephen Gammell's illustrations are exceptional.*]

Baylor, B. (1972). *When clay sings*. New York: Charles Scribner's Sons.
   [*Children find pieces of pottery with designs made from long ago. They think about the lives of earlier Indian tribes.*]

Baylor, B. *(1975). The desert is theirs*. New York: Macmillan.
   [*Describes the characteristics of the desert and its plant, animal, and human life.*]

Baylor, B. (1976). *Hawk, I'm your brother*. New York: Macmillan.
   [*An Indian boy captures a hawk that he hopes will help him learn to fly.*]

Benchley, N. (1964). *Red Fox and his canoe*. New York: Harper & Row.
   [*Red Fox and his father build a larger canoe for Red Fox's fishing trip.*]

Boegehold, B. (1990). *A horse called Starfire*. New York: Bantam Books.
   [*While on a hunting trip, an Indian boy and his father encounter a new strange new creature, a horse.*]

Bulla, C. R. (1954). *Squanto, friend of the pilgrims*. New York: Scholastic.
[*Squanto leaves with the Englishmen on a journey to their land. After spending years in London, Squanto finally returns home, but many things have changed in the New World.*]

Cherry, L. (1992). *A river ran wild*. New York: Harcourt, Brace, Jovanovich.
[*A history of the Nashua River with special emphasis on respect given it by the Indians and its later destruction by humankind.*]

Chief Seattle. (1991). *Brother eagle, sister sky*. New York: Dial Books.
[*Tells how the earth and the creatures on it are special and sacred to Indian people, as they should be to all people.*]

Clark, A. N. (1941). *In my mother's house*. New York: Puffin Books.
[*A young Indian describes the way of life for the people of the Southwest region.*]

Clark, A. N. (1955). *The little Indian pottery maker*. Los Angeles: Melmont.
[*Description of Southwest Indian way of life.*]

Clark, A. N. (1962). *The desert people*. New York: Viking Press.
[*A book about the Papago Indians.*]

Clark, A. N. (1988). *Little herder in autumn*. Santa Fe: Ancient City Press.
[*In verse, this book reveals the way of life of the Navajo people. Stories are also provided using the Navajo alphabet.*]

Clymer, E. (1971). *The spider, the cave, and the pottery bowl*. New York: Dell.
[*Kate and her little brother, Johnny, spend the summer on the Mesa with Grandmother. Something is wrong with Gramma, and together Kate and Johnny find the remedy for her problem.*]

Cohen, C. L. (1990). *The mud pony*. New York: Scholastic.
[*A boy longs for a pony of his own.*]

Cohlene, T. (1990a). *Clamshell boy*. Mahwah, NJ: Watermill Press.
[*Clamshell by rescues a group of children from the Wild Basket Woman.*]

Cohlene, T. (1990b). *Dancing Drum*. Mahwah, NJ: Watermill Press.
[*Cherokee legend in which Dancing Drum tries to make Grandmother Sun smile on the people again.*]

Cohlene, T. (1990c). *Ka-ha-si and the loon*. Mahwah, NJ: Watermill Press.
[*Legend of Ka-ha-si who rescues his people in time of desperate need.*]

Cohlene, T. (1990d). *Little firefly*. Mahwah, NJ: Watermill Press.
    [*Algonquin legend of how a young girl becomes the bride of a hunter.*]

Cohlene, T. (1990e). *Quillworker*. Mahwah, NJ: Watermill Press.
    [*A Cheyenne legend explaining the origin of the stars.*]

Cohlene, T. (1990f). *Turquoise boy*. Mahwah, NJ: Watermill Press.
    [*A Navajo Indian legend in which Turquoise boy looks for something that will make his people's lives easier.*]

DeHuff, E. W. (1986). *Blue-wings-flying*. Boston: Houghton Mifflin.
    [*Blue-Wings-Flying has a new baby sister and a name must be chosen. He would like his suggested name to be the one decided on for his sister.*]

De Paola, T. (1983). *The legend of the bluebonnet*. New York: G. P. Putnam's
    [*A Comanche Indian legend of how a girl's sacrifice brought the flower called the bluebonnet to Texas.*]

Esbensen, B. (1988). *The star maiden*. Boston: Little, Brown.
    [*A legend explaining the origin of water lilies.*]

Fleischer, J. (1979). *Sitting Bull*. Mahwah, NJ: Troll Associates.
    [*The life of a young Indian boy who becomes a strong and courageous warrior.*]

Fleischer, J. (1979). *Tecumseh Shawnee, war chief*. Mahwah, NJ: Troll Associates.
    [*A biography of an Indian's fight to defend his people.*]

Floethe, L. L. (1960). *The Indian and his pueblo*. New York: Scribner.
    [*This book is about Indians of North America and Mexico.*]

Fritz, J. (1982). *The good giants and the bad pukwudgies*. New York: G. P. Putnam's.
    [*The legend describing the formation of the Cape Cod area.*]

Fritz, J. (1983). *The double life of Pocahontas*. New York: The Trumpet Club.
    [*A biography of the famous American Indian princess and the role she played in two different cultures.*]

Gardiner, J. R. (1980). *Stone fox*. New York: Harper & Row.
    [*A little boy hopes to pay the back taxes on his grandfather's farm with the money won from a dog sled race he is entering.*]

Goble, P. (1978). *The girl who loved wild horses*. New York: Macmillan.
    [*An Indian girl prefers to live among wild horses where she is happy.*]

Goble, P. (1980). *The gift of the sacred dog.* New York: Macmillan.
[*An Indian boy prays to the Great Spirit for help for his hungry people. The spirit sends the Sacred Dog horses, which let the tribe hunt for buffalo.*]

Goble, P. (1984). *Buffalo woman.* New York: Macmillan.
[*A hunter marries a female buffalo in the form of a beautiful maiden.*]

Goble, P. (1985). *The great race.* New York: Macmillan.
[*A contest is held between the people and the buffalo to determine which is superior.*]

Goble, P. (1988a). *Her seven brothers.* New York: Bradbury Press.
[*A Cheyenne legend explaining the presence of the Big Dipper.*]

Goble, P. (1988b). *Iktomi and the boulder.* New York: The Trumpet Club.
[*Iktomi enters into a terrible predicament with a boulder.*]

Goble, P. (1989). *Iktomi and the berries.* New York: Orchard Books.
[*Describes Iktomi's attempts to pick berries.*]

Goble, P. (1992). *Love flute.* New York: Bradbury Press.
[*A gift to a shy man from the birds and animals helps him express his love to a beautiful girl.*]

Gorsline, M., & Gorsline, D. (1977). *North American Indians.* New York: Random House.
[*Describes the survival of various Indian tribes in North America.*]

Hoff, S. (1961). *Little Chief.* New York: Harper & Row.
[*Little Chief searches for someone to play with.*]

Knight, J. (1982). *Blue Feather's vision.* Mahwah, NJ: Troll Associates.
[*An elderly Indian chief fears that the white man will destroy the Indian way of life.*]

Krensky, S. (1991). *Children of the earth and sky.* New York: Scholastic.
[*Five stories about Native American children from various regions.*]

Lopez, A. (1972). *Celebration.* Littleton, MA: Sundance Publishers.
[*Paintings of various Indian dances celebrated by different North American tribes.*]

MacGill-Callahan, S. (1991). *And still the turtle watched.* New York: Dial Books.
[*A turtle carved in a rock by the Indian people observes many changes in humankind throughout the years.*]

Martin, B., & Archambault, J. (1987). *Knots on a counting rope.* New York: The Trumpet Club.
[*Grandfather and boy together tell the story of the boy's life.*]

Martini, T. (1982). *A new true book: Indians.* Chicago: Children's Press.
[*Describes how Indians throughout various regions lived and how their lives were influenced by the environment.*]

McDermott, G. (1974). *Arrow to the sun.* New York: Puffin Books.
[*A Pueblo Indian myth that explains how the spirit of the Lord of the Sun was brought to the world of humans.*]

McGovern, A. (1972). *If you lived with the Sioux Indians.* New York: Scholastic.
[*Responses to questions about the way of life of the Sioux tribe.*]

Medearis, A. (1991). *Dancing with the Indians.* New York: Holiday House.
[*A black family attends a Seminole Indian celebration.*]

Miles, M. (1971). *Annie and the old one.* Boston: Little, Brown.
[*Annie comes to accept her grandmother's death.*]

O'John, C. (1989). Dancing teepees. In V. Driving Hawk Snave (Ed.). *Dancing teepees: Poems of American Indian youth.* New York: Holiday House.
[*An illustrated collection of poems from the oral tradition of Native Americans.*]

Ortiz, S. (1977). *The people shall continue.* San Francisco: Children's Book Press.
[*The Indians struggle for survival throughout history in dealing with the earth, with one another, and finally with the white man.*]

Parish, P. (1962). *Good hunting, Blue Sky.* New York: Harper Collins.
[*Blue Sky, a young Indian boy, goes hunting.*]

Payne, E. (1965). *Meet the North American Indians.* New York: Random House.
[*Describes how North American Indians were living at the time Columbus arrived at America.*]

Perrine, M. (1986). *Nannabah's friend.* Boston: Houghton Mifflin.
[*Nannabah is asked to take the sheep to the canyon alone.*]

Pine, T. (1957). *The Indians knew.* New York: Scholastic.
[*Comparison of what we know today with what the Indians knew years ago.*]

Red Hawk, R. (1988). *A, B, Cs the American Indian way.* Newcastle, CA: Sierra Oaks Publishing.
[*An introduction to various Indian topics.*]

Rowland, D. (1989). *The story of Sacajawea.* New York: Dell.
[*A biography of an Indian girl who is separated from her family and taken by warriors to be a slave. She was also the guide for the Lewis and Clark expedition.*]

SanSouci, R. (1978). *The legend of Scarface.* New York: The Trumpet Club.
[*The adventures of Scarface, a young boy who sets out on a journey to meet the sun, whose blessing he needs in order to marry.*]

Sewall, M. (1990). *People of the breaking day.* New York: Macmillan.
[*Describes the lifestyle of the woodland tribes inhabiting the Northwest region.*]

Siberell, A. (1982). *Whale in the sky.* New York: E. P. Dutton.
[*A Northwest Indian legend telling how a story is carved into a totem pole.*]

Speare, E. G. (1983). *The sign of the beaver.* New York: Dell.
[*A story about a boy who survives in the Maine wilderness. He's rescued by an Indian chief and his grandson, Attean.*]

Udry, J. M. (1969). *The sunflower garden.* New York: Harvey House.
[*A young Indian girl named Pipsa earns great respect from her father, her brother, and people in her village.*]

Van Lann, N. (1989). *Rainbow crow.* New York: Alfred A Knopf.
[*A legend explaining why animals hibernate during the winter.*]

Warren, E. (1975). *I can read about Indians.* Mahwah, NJ: Troll Associates.
[*Describes the lifestyles of North American Indians.*]

Chapter 4

Human Body: A Third Grade Theme

Pam Brumbaugh

OCTOBER 13

I've been floundering for two weeks now trying to decide on a topic for a theme. I first considered plants. I have a house full of plants and have several in my classroom. When I teach the plant unit in the spring, the children enjoy it. That's why I chose not to use it for my theme. There were several other topics that I considered: Space, New York, Schenectady, Nutrition, the Earth, Pets, Wild Animals, a Foreign Country, Ocean Life, Careers, and the Environment. I finally decided to focus on the Human Body for this theme. I have been interested in genetics since I took a class about it in college. This would be a good way to learn more about the systems of the body and help me to teach health and science in a better way to my third grade class. I don't know if I will include all of them, but I will begin with the muscular, skeletal, nervous, respiratory, digestive, and circulatory systems.

OCTOBER 16

I noticed several different children reading *The Magic School Bus* (Cole, 1989) about the human body (from my own personal library). This is a book that I will put on a reading list for the theme.

OCTOBER 20

I went to the library in Clifton Park. They have a good variety of books to use for this theme. I took out five books so that I can begin to learn more. Four of the books are from *Encyclopedia of Health* (Garell & Snyder, 1988), a collection of health books. The fifth book is called *The Human Brain* (Kettelkamp, 1986). I started reading it and although it is informative, I found it quite boring.

OCTOBER 21

I've been thinking about how I would organize this theme in a classroom. If I taught the six systems I've been considering, I would probably try to spend a week on each system. After yesterday's trip to the library, I'm thinking about doing fewer than six systems—maybe skipping the muscular and nervous systems. I'll decide after I've spent more time at the libraries.

Chapter two of *The Human Body: An Overview* (Kittredge, 1990) discussed the nervous system. I read about the nerves and parts of the brain—things I knew long ago, but had forgotten. I was amazed by the variety of substances our bodies release under different circumstances. This book is more interesting than the one I started to read yesterday. I would keep this book in the classroom during the entire unit since it covers all of the systems I was considering, in addition to others. It combines the muscular and skeletal systems to form the musculoskeletal system. Depending on how much information there is in these areas and how they can be taught together, I might combine them as well.

After reading the chapters on the respiratory and circulatory systems, and drawing pictures of the systems to help me, I see that they relate to each other. If I don't teach them together, circulatory should follow respiratory in the order of study.

OCTOBER 22

Our school nurse learned of my theme and brought in her book, *Textbook of Anatomy and Physiology* (Kimber, 1972). While it was on my desk, several children commented on the picture of veins and arteries on the cover. I was happy that I could share my new knowledge of how the veins, heart, and arteries are connected.

I read about the digestive system tonight and realized that the urinary and endocrine systems should be included with that system. I think that including all three of these systems would make the theme too lengthy. Therefore, I've decided to remove the digestive system from my theme, leaving the musculoskeletal, circulatory, respiratory, and nervous systems. My concern at this time is that the theme might be too long if I include these four systems, but I am encouraged to keep these because they fit together so well and I want my students to know how they interact.

OCTOBER 25

I read about the musculoskeletal system and was especially interested in the haversian canals (the canals in the bones that contain the blood vessels and nerves). I had known these were found in bones, but I hadn't known very much about them.

As I read about this system I became more certain that the four systems include too much information for this one unit. I think I'll cut the nervous system from the theme and keep the other three, spending about one week on each system. Certain facts about the nervous system will necessarily arise, but I don't think it's necessary to include the whole system in the theme.

As I finished reading *The Human Body: An Overview* (Kittredge, 1990) I noticed a glossary, a list for further reading, and a list of addresses to write for more information. These will aid in planning the theme and teaching it. The addresses also offer a way of including letter writing into the study of these body systems.

OCTOBER 27

I spent several hours at the Shenendehowa Public Library today. I did more reading about the musculoskeletal, circulatory, and respiratory systems in "adult" books. I also found a dozen books that I could use to teach this theme. I copied a page from each and noted useful information about the book on the back of the pages (see Figure 4–1).

Five of the books I found dealt primarily with the musculoskeletal system. Three dealt mainly with the circulatory system. The remaining four discussed all three systems that I am planning to teach. Of these four books, two were simple, one was average reading for third grade, and one was more difficult. While I'd have liked to have located some books that specifically dealt with the respiratory system, I was happy that I had books that discussed each of these systems on a variety of reading levels. I plan to visit the Schenectady Library next.

OCTOBER 28

I read about the skeletal system in *Textbook of Anatomy and Physiology* (Kimber, 1972). It discussed all the bones of the body and which ones change or fuse throughout life. It also told about how different bones fit together, why they fit the way they do, and why each bone is shaped as it is (extra strength, flexibility, etc.). I honestly did not remember many of the bones's names after I finished reading it all, but I would use this book as a reference for myself and the students when teaching this theme.

I also read about the circulatory system in the same book. After reading the names of blood parts, the names of diseases and their symptoms make more sense to me. For example, white blood cells are called leukocytes, which are directly connected to leukemia, a disease characterized by an increase in white blood cells.

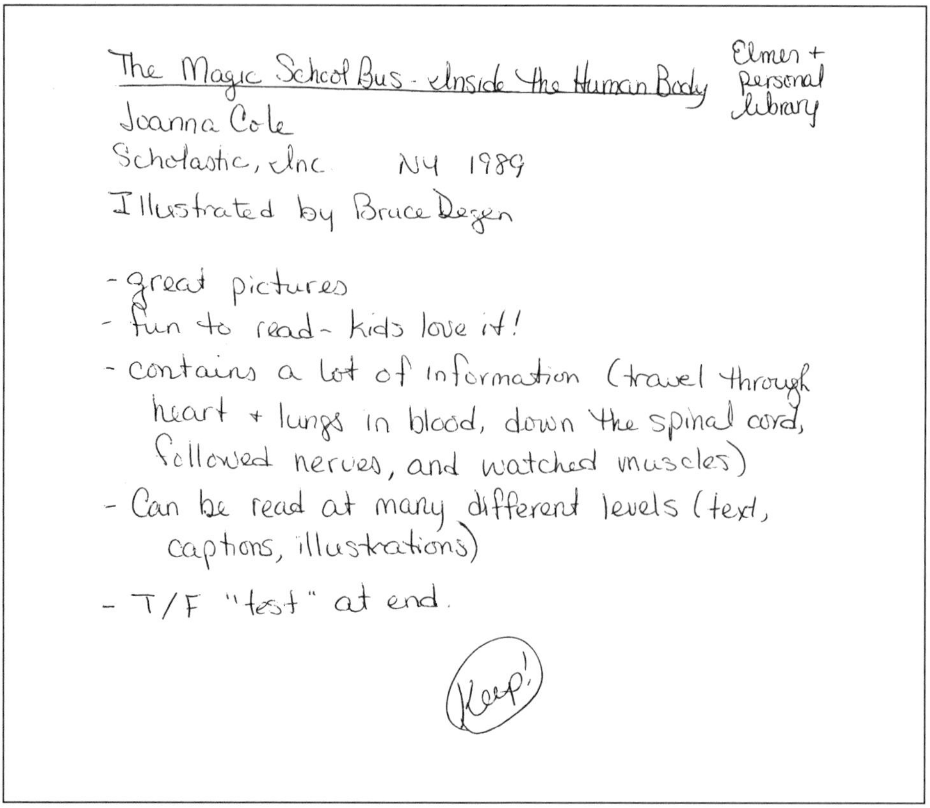

The Magic School Bus - Inside the Human Body   Elmer +
Joanna Cole   Personal
Scholastic, Inc.   NY 1989   library
Illustrated by Bruce Degen

- great pictures
- fun to read - kids love it!
- contains a lot of information (travel through
    heart + lungs in blood, down the spinal cord,
    followed nerves, and watched muscles)
- Can be read at many different levels (text,
    captions, illustrations)
- T/F "test" at end.

        (Keep!)

FIGURE 4–1. Teacher Notes on The Magic School Bus.

Also included in this reading was a diagram of the heart, veins, and arteries. I was pleased to note that it is quite similar to the one I drew in my notes on October 21 when I first read about the circulatory system.

OCTOBER 30

I spent an hour in the school library today. I found a few books, but the majority on this topic were older books—1950s, '60s, and early '70s. There was one book from the '80s, *The Magic School Bus* (Cole, 1989), which I already knew about.

This library wasn't as helpful as the Shenendehowa Library, but if I taught this theme at school, it would be convenient to get books for use in the classroom. Between the two libraries, I think I have a fairly good selection of books to use for this theme.

I'd like to note here that the Scotia-Glenville Museum has a show called "The Inside Story." This show deals with the musculoskeletal system. The teacher brings several visual aids including a complete human skeleton, X-rays, and cut-out skeletons that are put together by the students. I have had the museum visit my classroom for the past two years, and my classes have not only enjoyed it, but they have learned a lot from the experience.

OCTOBER 31

Looking over the pages I've copied from the books as I waited for more trick-or-treaters, I counted the number of books I had for each category. I would like to find more books involving the respiratory system, and I also need more books to choose from for read-aloud. I'll visit the Schenectady Public Library this weekend.

NOVEMBER 1

I received my class book order from *Scholastic* today and enclosed was my book, *The Skeleton Inside You* (Balestrino, 1990). It's a good addition to my book list.

I've also been thinking about activities to fit in with this theme. I began listing activities that would include all three systems involved in this theme and would also include as many academic areas as possible. While the list is off to a good start, I would like to list more activities than we could possibly do in three weeks so I can choose each time I use this theme.

NOVEMBER 3

I spent several hours at the Schenectady Public Library today finding books on the three systems and people who are known for their work with them. The librarians were very helpful and I found several good books on these topics. Many books on these subjects listed on the computerized card catalogue were not in the library today. I feel that I have enough titles listed to teach the theme, but I'm happy to know that there are others in the library if I need them later.

I learned many things about the three body systems, and I enjoyed reading about the people who discovered "common knowledge of today." I am surprised that there are so many good books on this topic.

GETTING THE THEME ORGANIZED

I now had a large number of books to use in the theme, and I needed to decide which I wanted to use for read-alouds, which for guided/shared reading, and which for independent reading. As I organized the books, I realized that some of them belonged in more than one category. For example, several books that I planned for read-alouds would also be made available for individual students to read and possibly for guided/shared reading as well.

When I xeroxed sample pages from each of the books, I made notes on them as well as recording bibliographic information. These notes would help me to choose which books would be most useful for my current students.

I also started thinking about the activities and projects I thought my students might enjoy doing. I made a list of some of the possibilities:

Visitors/Field Trips:

- Invite the Scotia-Glenville Museum for "The Inside Story."
- Visit the museum for the "Dinosaurs Alive" program.
- Visit the x-ray department at a local hospital.
- Invite someone from the Red Cross to discuss blood collection, matching, storage, and so on.
- Ask the Schenectady County Medical Auxiliary to bring in "Smoking Sam" (a model of the lungs that shows what happens when a cigarette is smoked).

Read about, discuss, and do projects on:

- William Harvey (English physician who discovered how blood circulates, and who explained heart valves, pulse, and pulmonary circulation).
- Ellie Metchnikoff (Russian biologist who originated the theory of why blood gathers at a wound. Nobel Prize winner in 1908).
- Karl Landsteiner (Discovered the main types of blood and made transfusions safe. Worked with rhesus factor. Nobel Prize winner in 1930).
- Effects of smoking on breathing.
- How bones grow and heal.
- Bleeding as a treatment for sickness.
- Artificial limbs or body parts.
- The use and study of the human body (skeleton) in art.

Activities:

- Make charts showing how and when the number of bones in the body change.
- Create exercises using various muscles.
- Calculate the number of cells that die/are produced/are used each day.
- Draw body systems and color code them.
- Write to addresses given in books for further information.
- Create a table of the number of bones different animals have in their bodies.

- Make skeleton models using pipe cleaners, twist ties, and Bonz dog snacks.
- Have children take their respiration and pulse, then exercise for two minutes, take respiration and pulse again; children then rest for sixty seconds and take readings again; continue until readings are at the original levels.
- Draw and label pictures of five different animals. Explain how they breathe.
- Research how bones were used in the past (e.g., Native Americans used them as needles).
- Write a diary for a finger explaining how your cut heals.
- Visit a chiropractor's office.
- Put splints on children's arms and legs at the joints; have the children try to walk, sit, eat, write, and do other common activities.

GATHERING THE MATERIALS

With the theme planned, I now needed to visit the libraries again and collect the materials for my class of twenty-seven third grade children. I was able to borrow many of the books I had listed on the original bibliography, but the list was altered for two reasons. First, some of the books I had planned to borrow were not available when I returned, so I chose some other books to substitute for them. Second, one of the libraries limits the number of children's books individuals may borrow. With the help of my sister's card, I was able to borrow most of the books that I needed from that library.

Before taking these books to the classroom, I took them home and became familiar with them. This made it much easier to guide children toward specific books that would be helpful for their projects. Also, I needed to choose specific books to be used as read-aloud books. I chose books representing each system for this purpose.

STARTING THE THEME

Finally, I took the books to school. They were in a large canvas bag by my desk for most of the day and several children spied them and questioned me about them. Their curiosity was great.

Toward the middle of the afternoon, I invited the class to sit on the green rug. There, I read *The Magic School Bus* (Cole, 1989) to them. Some of the children had already read this book and enjoyed pointing out amusing pictures or side comments. I had chosen this book because, due to the way it was written, it can be geared toward different levels. A wonderful discussion followed the story, which helped children to become even more interested.

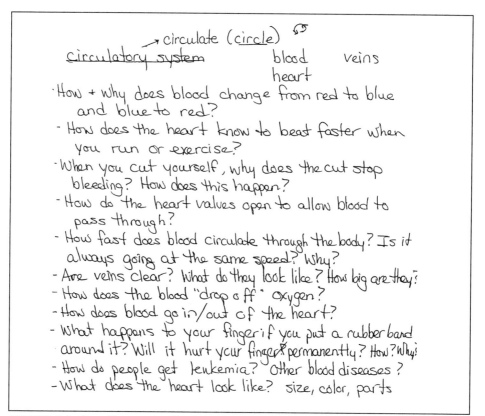

circulate (circle)
Circulatory system   blood   veins
                                      heart
· How + why does blood change from red to blue
    and blue to red?
- How does the heart know to beat faster when
    you run or exercise?
- When you cut yourself, why does the cut stop
    bleeding? How does this happen?
- How do the heart values open to allow blood to
    pass through?
- How fast does blood circulate through the body? Is it
    always going at the same speed? Why?
- Are veins clear? What do they look like? How big are they?
- How does the blood "drop off" oxygen?
- How does blood go in/out of the heart?
- What happens to your finger if you put a rubber band
    around it? Will it hurt your finger permanently? How? Why?
- How do people get leukemia? Other blood diseases?
- What does the heart look like? size, color, parts

FIGURE 4–2. Class Chart on the Circulatory System.

During this discussion, I deliberately mentioned each of the three systems (circulatory, respiratory, musculoskeletal) included in the theme. The class had participated in the Scotia-Glenville Museum's "The Inside Story" class earlier in the year, so they felt quite comfortable with the musculoskeletal system. None of the children knew what was included in the other systems, so we briefly discussed the words *circulate* and *respiration*. We also discussed which organs were involved with each system.

Next, I brought out three pieces of chart paper and labeled each with a body system. On the chart paper we listed what was included in each system (see Figures 4–2 and 4–3). We then listed questions we would like to find answers to, and categorized them on the chart paper. I helped children define or expand questions as needed.

For example, "What does the heart do?" needed to be narrowed down, whereas "What color are the lungs?" is too narrow a question for the project. If questions were too broad, the children might have had a problem finding information because they often expected to find answers in a few sentences in one section of a book. Conversely, if children were to use very narrow questions

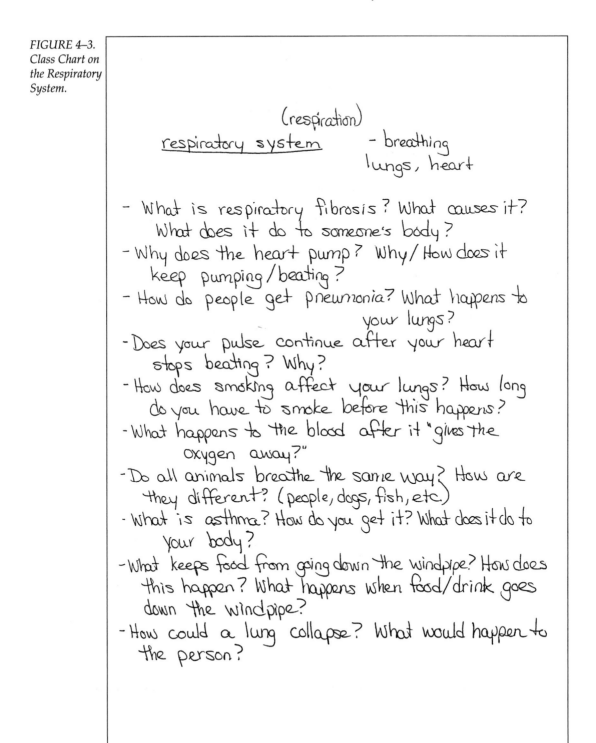

(respiration)

respiratory system   - breathing
                            lungs, heart

- What is respiratory fibrosis? What causes it?
  What does it do to someone's body?
- Why does the heart pump? Why/How does it
  keep pumping/beating?
- How do people get pneumonia? What happens to
  your lungs?
- Does your pulse continue after your heart
  stops beating? Why?
- How does smoking affect your lungs? How long
  do you have to smoke before this happens?
- What happens to the blood after it "gives the
  oxygen away?"
- Do all animals breathe the same way? How are
  they different? (people, dogs, fish, etc.)
- What is asthma? How do you get it? What does it do to
  your body?
- What keeps food from going down the windpipe? How does
  this happen? What happens when food/drink goes
  down the windpipe?
- How could a lung collapse? What would happen to
  the person?

for their project, many would tend to answer one or two questions that might not be logically connected and would consider the project complete. By defining the questions at this time, these problems could be avoided.

The next day I introduced the books briefly and explained which were easy, medium, and difficult reading. I also noted which books had photographs, colored pictures, or drawings. I asked the children to guess which body system(s) would be included in each book by looking at the title and pictures on the book covers. I explained how the index or contents in certain books would help them to locate specific topics easily. The class was extremely anxious to use the books on their own and they spent the next half hour with them. Many children located answers to some of the questions we had listed, while others were engrossed by pictures. I encouraged those who found answers to jot them down. These would be useful later.

Individual Projects

After the children had enough time to familiarize themselves with the books and systems, I asked them to choose the system that interested them the most and decide on a way to show others what they had learned. The next day I met with students individually to listen to their project ideas. Some children had difficulty deciding on a project. In these situations, the child and I would discuss the child's "favorite system" and why it was their favorite. From there we determined some questions the child had about that system and how the child could present that information.

I liked holding conferences with the children before they began their projects. It gave me the opportunity to talk with each child and find out what they already knew and what they wanted to learn. Meeting also allowed me to hear the children's ideas for their projects. Most students planned projects that were challenging and interesting, and that could be completed within the allotted time. Some children planned elaborate projects that could not possibly be completed in school, so we discussed either paring down the project or finding ways the original idea could be worked on outside of school. A few students needed their projects to be made more challenging and were able to expand on their plans during the meeting. By holding individual conferences, appropriate goals were set for each student.

I scheduled between forty-five and ninety minutes three times each week for the theme. Most days, I started by reading aloud to the class. We would then discuss any questions children had about their research. The children enjoyed this time because it gave them an opportunity to share their expertise of the books and materials they had already used. For example, when one student said he was having a hard time finding information on the causes of pneumonia, several other children quickly suggested books that would help him.

Following this, individuals worked on projects in addition to watching movies and filmstrips and sharing books. Most children read these theme books during free reading time and for enjoyment throughout the day when assignments were completed. One problem some students encountered was writing projects in their own words. It was not difficult to recognize when projects were copied from books. When this happened, the student and I would discuss ways to paraphrase the information. One way of doing this was for the child to explain the project aloud to the teacher or a classmate without looking at the report notes. They could also explain the report into a tape recorder and use that to help them write the project in their own words.

Listing questions on chart paper before the children started their individual projects was a great help to some children, but it hindered others. The majority of the class used groups of questions to focus on one particular area of a system. Other children were either limited by the questions or they had difficulty narrowing their research by grouping the questions. Some children felt that they could only use information that directly answered questions listed on the chart paper. Even though they found information in sources that related to the topic they were exploring, they were reluctant to use it because they didn't think it applied to the specific question they had raised. Others found answers for questions but couldn't organize material from different places. For example, if the question was: "How many bones are in the human body?" and if information relating to this question wasn't given directly in a source (i.e., the number of bones in the hands and legs were discussed in one chapter, but major bones in other parts of the body were given in another), then some children couldn't put the two pieces of information together. Because listing the questions wasn't helpful to all students, I will continue to brainstorm questions with the class when teaching this theme.

Figures 4–4 and 4–5 illustrate two examples of projects done by my students. Both Amy and Courtney chose to research the respiratory system, but their reports are quite different in style and content.

REFLECTIONS ON THE THEME

When teaching this theme in the future, there are a number of changes I'll make. When doing questions on the chart, I will update the list of questions every few days with the children. This could help students to share information they had already found and together form additional questions. It will also help to "unglue" students from the idea that only specific questions can be researched. By working as a class we could also continue to organize the new questions on our charts to aid the children's research.

The most important change I will make when teaching this theme again is to help the children take notes and use them better. Keeping information in folders or using small notebooks could help to eliminate misplaced notes. Also, I would duplicate forms for students to keep in their folders or notebooks, which would

FIGURE 4–4.
Amy's
Explanation of
How People
Breathe.

Person Breathing

Lungs

How do people breathe
You inhale through your nose
and exhale through your mouth.
Your lungs do all the work. Your
lungs are an organ in your body
that make you breathe. Well
inorder for your lungs to be safe
there has to be somthing to
protect the lungs. Well there is! It is
called the ribcage. Well were not
talking about the ribcage so lets get
back to breathing. Now if we didn't
have our lungs we would die
so you see lungs are very important.

FIGURE 4–5.
Courtney's
Report on the
Respiratory
System.

The Respiratory System
What Could Go Wrong?

Breathing is one of the body's automatic functions. It happens without us having to think about it. A first glance it seems fairly simple; air goes into your lungs and then comes out again. But breathing is much more complicated than apears to the eye.

Your lungs are strong, hard-working organs, but even so they are able to be crippled of defense. Over time cigarette smoke crippled the lungs defense system. It is estimated that 83% of all lung cancers are smoking related.

In emphysema, the lungs produce large amounts of excess mucus and the alviolie get baggy, losing their springiness or elasticity.

The air around us isn't suitable to go directly into our delicate lungs. It is often to dry, usually to cold or hot, and almost alway to dirty. But the respiritory system has several sprotective devices.

The pharynx (throat) is a passage-way for food as well as air. Air entering you food passage does not cause major problems, but food entering your windpipe would cause trouble.

Respiritory System Disorder
Bacteria, the most common species of Streptococcus and Hemphilus, may effect any part of the Respiritory System, causing diseases such as: Sinusitis, Bronchitis, Pharyngitis, Strep Throat, Tonsilitis, and Whooping Cough. All of this information comes to one sentence: Take care of your lungs and they will take care of you.

help them to organize their questions and answers. This could make organization of information into the project less difficult.

After receiving the projects, I was impressed by how much the children had learned, not only about science but also about the books housed in the libraries and how to find information in them. The projects, for the most part, were of better quality and were more comprehensive than I had expected. I had never used this technique to teach my class before, but I will be using it quite often now that I have seen the benefits. It does require some additional teacher preparation (visiting libraries, choosing books and materials, familiarizing yourself with the library materials), but the results make it worthwhile. By using this teaching technique, my students learned science, reading, writing, organization, and communications skills. They not only improved these skills, but they enjoyed learning.

REFERENCES

Professional Sources

Garell, D. C., & Snyder, S. H. (Eds.). (1988). *Encyclopedia of health.* New York: Chelsea House.

Kettlekamp, L. (1986). *The human brain.* Hillsdale, NJ: Enslow.

Kimber, D. C. (1972). *Textbook of anatomy and physiology* (16th ed.). New York: Macmillan.

Kittredge, M. (1990). *The human body: An overview.* New York: Chelsea House Publishers.

Read-Aloud

Balestrino, P. (1990). *The skeleton inside you.* New York: Scholastic.
[Color pictures and diagrams. Simple/average text.]

Barnard, C. (1983). *Junior body machine.* New York: Crown Publishers, Inc.
[Excellent pictures and diagrams. Reading not easy, but well explained. Interesting facts listed throughout.]

Bertol, R. (1970). *Charles Drew.* New York: Thomas Y. Crowell Company.
[Good story and information. Pictures, easy reading.]

Bruun, R., & Bruun, B. (1982). *The human body: your body and how it works.* New York: Random House.
  [Large colored, labeled diagrams. Index. Excellent information.]

Education Reading Service. (1971). *My super book of the human body.* New York: Education Reading Service.
  [Large color pictures. Average text. Covers all three theme systems and more.]

Facklam, M., & Facklam, H. (1987). *Spare parts for people.* New York: Harcourt Brace Jovanovich.
  [Good book with pictures and diagrams. Average reading.]

Grey, V. (1982). *The chemist who lost his head.* New York: Coward, McCann & Geoghegan.
  [Book with pictures. Good story and information. Above average reading.]

McGowen, T. (1988). *The circulatory system: from Harvey to the artificial heart.* New York: Franklin Watts.
  [History of science and discovery about blood. Index. Slightly difficult.]

Nolen, W. (1971). *Spare parts for the human body.* New York: Random House.
  [Book with pictures and diagrams. Average reading.]

Weart, E. L. (1964). *The story of your respiratory system.* New York: Coward, McCann & Geoghegan.
  [Glossary and index. Good labeled diagrams. Follows the path of air through the body.]

Shared/Guided Reading

Asimov, I. (1986). *How did we find out about blood?* New York: Walker and Company.
  [Traces the development of scientific knowledge about the functions of blood in the body. Has excellent illustrations.]

Avraham, R. (1989). *The circulatory system.* New York: Chelsea House Publishers.
  [Good pictures. Further Reading list, glossary, index. Somewhat difficult reading, explained well.]

Bornancin, B. (1983). *Know your own body.* London: Burke Books.
  [Good pictures and diagrams. Covers many body systems. Slightly difficult reading.]

Caselli, G. (1987). *The human body and how it works.* New York: Grosset & Dunlap.
   [Glossary and index. Outstanding pictures, diagrams, and explanation.]

Goldsmith, I. (1975). *Anatomy for children.* New York: Sterling Publishing Co.
   *[Good book with pictures and diagrams. Slightly difficult text. Covers all three
   systems.]*

Grey, V. (1982). *The chemist who lost his head.* New York: Coward, McCann &
   Geoghegan.
   [Book with pictures. Good story and information. Above average reading.]

Holland, P. V. (1987). *Blood transfusions: benefits and risks.* Washington, D.C.: U.S.
   Department of Health and Human Services.
   [Color pictures. Good information. Questions and answers at end.]

Marr, J. S. (1971). *A breath of fresh air and a breath of smoke.* New York: M. Evans
   and Co.
   [Good pictures and text.]

Parker, S. (1982). *The lungs and breathing.* London: Franklin Watts.
   [Color pictures, index, glossary. Discusses aspects of breathing, smoking, voice, etc.]

Schneider, L. (1958). *Lifeline: the story of your circulatory system.* New York:
   Harcourt, Brace & World.
   *[Book with labeled diagrams. Excellent, complete information. Slightly difficult
   reading.]*

Weart, E. L. (1964). *The story of your respiratory system.* New York: Coward,
   McCann & Geoghegan.
   [Good labeled diagrams. Follows the path of air through the body.]

Weart, E. L. (1966). *The story of your bones.* New York: Coward, McCann &
   Geoghegan.
   [Pictures, glossary, index.]

Independent Reading

Allen, G., & Denslow, J. (1970). *Bones.* New York: Franklin Watts.
   [Good pictures, easy reading. Encourages reader to participate.]

Asimov, I. (1986). *How did we find out about blood?* New York: Walker and
   Company.
   *[Traces the development of scientific knowledge about the functions of blood in the
   body. Has excellent illustrations.]*

Avraham, R. (1989). *The circulatory system*. New York: Chelsea House Publishers.
   [Good pictures. Further Reading list, glossary, and index. Somewhat difficult reading, good explanations.]

Balestrino, P. (1990). *The skeleton inside you*. New York: Scholastic.
   [Thirty-two pages. Color pictures and diagrams. Simple/average text.]

Barnard, C. (1983). *Junior body machine*. New York: Crown Publishers.
   [Excellent pictures and diagrams. Reading not easy, but well explained. Interesting facts listed throughout.]

Bertol, R. (1970). *Charles Drew*. New York: Thomas Y. Crowell.
   [Good story and information. Pictures, easy reading.]

Branley, F. M. (1967). *Oxygen keeps you alive*. New York: Thomas Y. Crowell.
   [Color drawings. Easy/average text. Discusses how oxygen is used by a variety of animals.]

Broekel, R. (1974). *Your skeleton and skin*. Chicago: Children's Press.
   [Color pictures. Glossary and index. Easy text.]

Bruun, R. D., & Bruun, B. (1982). *The human body: your body and how it works*. New York: Random House.
   [Large, color, labeled diagrams. Excellent information.]

Burstein, J. (1977). *Slim Goodbody: the inside story*. New York: McGraw-Hill Book Company.
   [Told in rhyme. Fairly easy reading. Includes simple experiments.]

Caselli, G. (1987). *The human body and how it works*. New York: Grosset & Dunlap.
   [Outstanding pictures, diagrams, and explanations.]

Children's Press. (1978). *Young people's science encyclopedia*. Chicago: Children's Press.
   [Includes information on William Henry.]

Cole, J. (1985). *Cuts, breaks, bruises, and burns*. New York: Thomas Y. Crowell.
   [Grades two through six. Good pictures, diagrams, and explanations.]

Cole, J. (1987). *The human body: How we evolved*. New York: William Morrow & Company, Inc.
   [A superb book on the evolution of the human body.]

Cole, J. (1989). *The magic school bus: Inside the human body*. New York: Scholastic.
   [Great pictures and information. Fun to read. True/false "test" at the end.]

Daly, K. N. (1980). *Body works*. New York: Doubleday.
[*A dictionary of the human body, how it works, and some of the things that affect it.*]

Drew, D. (1992). *Body facts*. Crystal Lake, IL: Rigby.
[*A small, well-illustrated book with useful information on the human body.*]

Drew, D. (1992). *Body maps*. Crystal Lake, IL: Rigby.
[*This book shows the different parts of the body. Very useful resource for student projects.*]

Dunbar, R. E. (1984). *The heart and circulatory system*. New York: Franklin Watts.
[*Book with pictures. Difficult reading.*]

Education Reading Service. (1971). *My super book of the human body*. New York: Education Reading Service.
[*Large color pictures. Average text. Covers all three theme systems and more.*]

Elgin, K. (1971). *The human body: the skeleton*. New York: Franklin Watts.
[*Labeled diagrams. Skull-to-feet, bone-by bone.*]

Facklam, M., & Facklam, H. (1987). *Spare parts for people*. New York: Harcourt Brace Jovanovich.
[*Good book with pictures and diagrams. Average reading.*]

Gallant. R. A. (1971). *Me and my bones*. New York: Doubleday.
[*Very good book with pictures. Fairly easy text. Good information.*]

Grey, V. (1982). *The chemist who lost his head*. New York: Coward, McCann & Geoghegan.
[*Book with pictures. Good story and information. Above average reading.*]

The Grolier Society, Inc. (1963). *The book of popular science*. New York: Grolier Society.
[*Information on Harvey, Metchnikoff, and Landsteiner.*]

Holland, P. V. (1987). *Blood transfusions: benefits and risks*. U.S. Department of Health and Human Services.
[*Color pictures. Good information. Questions and answers at end.*]

Lauber, P. (1962). *Your body and how it works*. New York: Random House.
[*Good pictures and diagrams. Covers all three systems.*]

MacLeod, S., Skelton, M., & Stringer, J. (1993). *Body business*. Crystal Lake, IL: Rigby.
[*A well-illustrated book that describes how various parts of the body work.*]

MacLeod, S., Skelton, M., & Stringer, J. (1993). *The body machine.* Crystal Lake, IL: Rigby.
[*This book describes how various parts of the body work together—for example, how bones and muscles interact, how the heart and digestive system operate. Excellent illustrations.*]

Marr, J. S. (1971). *A breath of fresh air and a breath of smoke.* New York: M. Evans.
[*Good pictures and text.*]

McGowen, T. (1988). *The circulatory system: From Harvey to the artificial heart.* New York: Franklin Watts.
[*History of science and discoveries about blood. Index. Slightly difficult.*]

McMinn, R. M. H., & Hutchins, R. T. (1977). *Color atlas of human anatomy.* New York: Year Book Medical Publishers.
[*Color pictures of anatomy and bones. Good reference.*]

Nolen, W. A. (1971). *Spare parts for the human body.* New York: Random House.
[*Book with pictures and diagrams. Average reading.*]

Parker, S. (1982). *The lungs and breathing.* London: Franklin Watts.
[*Color pictures. Discusses aspects of breathing, smoking, voice, etc.*]

Raintree Publishers. (1981). *Let's discover you and your body.* Milwaukee: Raintree.
[*Easy reading. Color pictures. Includes projects.*]

Schneider, L. (1958). *Lifeline: The story of your circulatory system.* New York: Harcourt, Brace & World.
[*Book with labeled diagrams. Excellent complete information. Slightly difficult reading.*]

Schuman, B. N. (1965). *The human skeleton.* New York: Atheneum.
[*Excellent book with diagrams. Index. Good information.*]

Showers, P. (1967). *A drop of blood.* New York: Thomas Y. Crowell.
[*Illustrated book about blood.*]

Turner, E. F., & Fenton, C. L. (1961). *Inside you and me.* New York: The John Day Company.
[*Pictures. Easy text. Covers all three systems.*]

Weart, E. L. (1964). *The story of your respiratory system.* New York: Coward, McCann & Geoghegan.
[*Good, labeled diagrams. Follows the path of air through the body.*]

Zim, H. S. (1959). *Your heart and how it works.* New York: William Morrow. [Labeled book with pictures. Average text difficulty.]

Zim, H. S. (1968). *Blood.* New York: William Morrow. [Technical, but average reading.]

Additional Titles

Baldwin, D., & Lister, C. (1984). *The structure of your body.* New York: The Bookwright Press.

Brandreth, G. (1979). *This is your body.* New York: Sterling Publishing Co.

Elgin, K. (1968). *Read about the hand.* New York: Franklin Watts.

Elting, M. (1986). *The Macmillan book of the human body.* New York: Macmillan.

Freeman, D. (1984). *Beautiful bodies.* New York: Peter Bedrick Books.

Jackson, G. (1984). *Medicine.* New York: Franklin Watts.

Kittredge, M. (1989). *The respiratory system.* New York: Chelsea House Publishers.

Lambert, M. (1988). *The lungs and breathing.* Englewood Cliffs, NJ: Silver Burdett Press.

National Geographic Society. (1982). *Your wonderful body.* Washington, D.C.: National Geographic Society.

O'Neill, C. (1988). *How and why: a kid's book about the body.* New York: Consumer's Union.

Silverstein, A., & Silverstein, V. B. (1983). *Heartbeats: your body, your heart.* New York: J. B. Lippincott.

Whitfiels, P., & Whitfiels, R. (1988). *Why do our bodies stop growing?* New York: Viking Kestrel.

Wilson, M. (1972). *The human body: why and how it works.* New York: Western Publishing Company.

Chapter 5

Architecture of Kinderhook, New York: A Third and Fourth Grade Theme

Janice Fingar and Donna Beaudry

The people of Kinderhook love their village. They take pride in the birthplace of President Martin Van Buren and embrace *The Legend of Sleepy Hollow*. Its tree-lined streets, its Dutch, Colonial, Federal, and Georgian homes, and its rich history have attracted home buyers who are intensely involved in restoration, maintenance, and research of their homes. The character and charm of the village invite any newcomer to explore and find out more. It was with the same sense of admiration and excitement that we began to plan a unit of study in local history. Although we have self-contained classes (Donna has third grade, Janice fourth grade), we regularly work together on language arts projects, which encompass not only reading and writing but also content areas. We got started on this project through our involvement in the Capital Region Institute for the Arts in Education; the focus of the children's literature grant for the year we did this project was research. We were looking for a project that would allow us to have the third and fourth graders work together, and researching our local village seemed like an ideal way to accomplish this. We thought both third and fourth graders could handle describing buildings, investigating building histories, mapping, and perhaps modeling a section of the village.

PREPARING THE THEME

Before going ahead with the project, we needed to assure ourselves that we could get access to a sufficient number of buildings in the village and that there was enough historical and architectural information available on each of them. We also wanted to be sure that the students would have access to people who could help them in their research, so we went on a walking tour with Robert Monthie, village historian, and Ralph Duck, author of *Kinderhook and Its People 1914–1984*. They enthusiastically shared information and anecdotes about specific buildings in the village, and they offered to conduct guided walking tours and slide presentations to the students during the project itself. They also said they would be willing to be interviewed by the students.

We then visited the Columbia County Historical Society in our village. We examined maps of Kinderhook from 1914 and browsed though the society's collection. We found some interesting books on local history: Ellis's (1878) *History of Columbia County, New York*, Collier's (1914) *A History of Old Kinderhook*, and Duck's (1985) *Kinderhook and Its People, 1914–1984*. The staff said they would welcome small groups of students to come to the historical society for study.

Finally, we contacted Mr. Allen Thomas, President of the National Union Bank and lifelong Kinderhook resident, and Sharon Palmer, coordinator of educational programs from the Historical Society. They were very interested and supportive of our project and offered to make themselves available to students for interviews and tours. It was clear to us by then that there were enough buildings, with a reasonable amount of information about each (although some of this information would not be easy to retrieve), and there were plenty of knowledgeable people willing to work on the project.

The next step was to select specific buildings for the project. As we continued to read and review sources, a number of important and interesting sites started to surface. There were more than enough sites to use for the project, so we narrowed down the choices by selecting buildings on the basis of age, access, availability of information, and function. For example, we decided to limit the study area to approximately a quarter mile in all directions from the village square so that all buildings were within walking distance of the school. This area included our school building, the village square, and a number of important historical buildings (see Figure 5–1).

We decided to assign community buildings to third graders as a tie-in to their social studies curriculum and to assign historic homes to fourth graders as a tie-in to local history. After assessing all the information available on each of the buildings, we chose the following community and historic buildings:

- Post Office, built in 1862 as a bank.
- Village Hall, brick building, built in 1874.
- National Union Bank, Federal style building with Ionic columns, built in 1858.
- Lou's Market, a small village grocery, built circa 1873.
- The Treasure Shop, former knitting company that is now a gift shop, built in 1880.
- Kinderhook Memorial Library, built in 1932.
- Martin Van Buren School, built in 1929 as a W.P.A. project.
- James Vanderpoel House, a Federal 1810 home currently maintained by the Columbia County Historical Society and open for tours.
- Van Schaack Mansion, a "Victorianized" Federal home and first law school in New York State.
- Burgoyne Mansion, a Georgian style mansion where British General John Burgoyne stayed as a prisoner of war after the Battle of Saratoga.

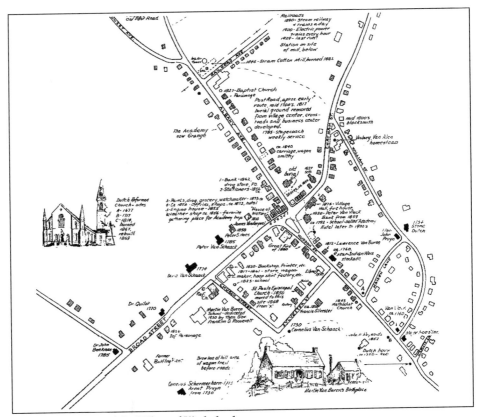

FIGURE 5–1. *Map of the Village of Kinderhook.*

- Mr. Thomas's residence, a Dutch Colonial built in the late 1700s.
- Dutch Colonial 1766 house.
- Benedict Arnold House, a Dutch home built in 1770 where Benedict Arnold stayed en route to New York City after the Battle of Saratoga.
- The Columbia Academy, a preparatory school attended by Martin Van Buren.

CARRYING OUT THE THEME

Our original plan was to have small groups of students research selected buildings and do three tasks: write about the building's history and architecture, draw a picture of the building, and build a scale model. We would complete the project by constructing a replica of the historical sites as a class activity.

To get the project started, we asked Mr. Monthie and Mr. Duck to present a slide show to the students. Mr. Monthie has a large collection of slides made from old postcards and old books, and he shared these with the students.

A few days later, we took a walking tour around the village with all the students; Mr. Monthie and Mr. Duck acted as guides.

The next stage in the project involved spending two afternoons in front of the James Vanderpoel House observing and drawing. Each student was responsible for his own drawing. This house is owned by the Columbia County Historical Society and is open to the public. We did this exercise partly to familiarize students with the unusual task of drawing a building, but partly also to teach them how to behave on others' property; later in the project, they would be examining and drawing private homes, and appropriate behavior was crucial. Many students were extremely frustrated by these initial drawings; they found perspectives especially difficult to draw. We returned to the Vanderpoel House several times, showing students the placement of windows, textures of roof and wall surfaces, trim, moldings, and foundation materials. As they drew and redrew, their perspective improved, and details appeared in subsequent drawings. The students increased their observation skills and raised their expectations. They began to understand the amount of work and care required in a study of this type. These insights would be useful when they began work on their own building.

Having set the stage for our unit, we held a brainstorming/organizational class. The purpose of this meeting was to compile a list of sites to be investigated, to list questions that students would like to answer, and to decide where and how they would go about finding their answers.

Students had a large number of questions. For example, what did the building look like, what materials were used in its construction, what shape was the roof, were there were any additions or alterations, what was the history of the building, what its uses were and are, were there any stories about the house, did any special people live there. Very quickly, the chalkboard was covered with questions and ideas generated by the students.

Next, we grouped similar types of questions together. For example, questions about materials and appearance were delegated to one group, questions about people went in another group, and questions about a building's history were organized together. An additional category, "other," was included to accommodate interesting and unusual findings.

We next encouraged students to think about how they would find out answers to their various questions. This was an important step in making students aware of the way researchers work. They suggested books, interviews, and observations as possible ways of finding information and hypothesized connections between their questions and sources.

Finally, we divided the students into groups and allowed them to pick from the list of available sites. As all buildings had to be included, once a building had been assigned, it was removed from the list.

We asked each group to do the following tasks: (1) find out as much as they could about their building, using all of the available sources, including interviewing Robert Monthie and Ralph Duck; (2) draw their building; and

(3) make a scale model. After completing these tasks, each group was to write a report on what they had learned, which was to include the drawing. The scale model was to become part of a class project later.

The first task was for students to find out as much as they could to answer the questions they raised. We knew from the outset that there were limited written sources for the students to read, and what was available had been written for adults, not children. This didn't deter us, for several reasons. First, the material was all there was on this topic, but what was there was genuine. We didn't think it made sense to abandon the topic merely because there wasn't an abundance of material available. Professional researchers frequently find themselves in situations where the material is limited. Why should student researchers only research topics where the materials are abundant? Second, we have always instilled in our students the notion that if the expectations are there, the means for fulfilling them will follow. We expected students to gain information from these limited sources, and they did. In any event, we would be there to help the students if they ran into difficulties.

There were four major written sources for the project. Captain Frank Ellis wrote his *History of Columbia County, New York* in 1878 as the centennial history of the county. It includes the history of the townships in Columbia County and focuses on special or historic buildings in each; some of the buildings to be researched in the project are included in Ellis's book. The text is difficult to read and understand but is a primary source. Edward A. Collier's (1914) *A History of Old Kinderhook* details the history of the village from its beginnings in 1609 to 1914. This book is easier to follow because the format follows a street by street approach and includes several pictures. Mr. Duck's book, *Kinderhook and Its People, 1914–1984*, continues the village's history from where Collier leaves off. This is the easiest for students to handle because of its language and format; they also have the benefit of the author's presence. Some students found useful information in a pamphlet, *The Village of Kinderhook 1609–1976*, published by the Village Bicentennial Committee as a walking tour guide.

People were very important as sources of information for students. Mr. Robert Monthie, village and town historian, was on hand throughout our project. His interest and expertise were evident to the students, and they came to view him as their personal reference. Mr. Monthie thoroughly enjoyed the students' enthusiasm for his anecdotes and for his historical and architectural knowledge. Mr. Ralph Duck, lifelong Kinderhook resident, was also generous with his time and expertise. The students enjoyed his talks, especially his stories about the construction of Martin Van Buren School. Sharon Palmer, the school's program coordinator (now, Director) of the Columbia County Historical Society, gave a tour of the interior and exterior of the James Vanderpoel House and answered questions. Mr. Monthie and Mr. Duck met with small groups to help answer the questions students had about their buildings. These interviews not only helped the students gather important information on their chosen buildings, but had some pleasant and unplanned side-effects, too. First, the students gained valuable experience with interview techniques. Second, they had a chance to interact meaningfully with older people in the community. Third, they gained from these encounters an understanding and appreciation of how people acquire information for their own use and how they do other things with their lives than simply work or rest.

Students had an opportunity to meet and learn from other residents of Kinderhook. Mr. Allen Thomas (President, National Union Bank, Kinderhook) was interviewed by the students, and Mrs. Thomas welcomed a small group into her home. Both were invaluable resources for the student researchers.

The second task was to draw the building. Each student in the group made a preliminary sketch of their building but eventually settled on one "artist" to do the final version. Because we had small groups of students going to selected buildings throughout the village, we arranged for parent volunteers to accompany students to individual buildings. So that they could recall details later, students either took or were supplied with photographs of their buildings and these were used extensively.

The drawings of individual buildings were much better from the start, students having had some practice with the James Vanderpoel House. Even so, many of these drawings went through several sketches before the final version. Again, students' drawing abilities improved considerably through the project.

The third task was to make a scale model. We started by having the students assemble some cut-and-fold houses, using an approach suggested by Goodman and Goodman (1988). We weren't sure how exactly we were going to make the scale models, but we thought that if students could master the cut-and-fold approach, they might be able to adapt it to the houses they were studying. But we soon ran into problems. One was that the cut-and-fold houses had to be cut out with Exacto knives, a task that required more precision cutting than most of the students could handle: we didn't have any accidents, but two very nervous teachers couldn't take the stress for more than a day, and so we abandoned that idea. Another problem was that the students' own drawings of buildings did not lend themselves to being transformed into models. We reluctantly abandoned the scale models, and the class project based on them. (Later, we learned that starting with a scaled drawing of the building's foundation and using foamboard to build the walls, ceilings, and roofs is a much better technique, and when we do this project again, there will be scale models.)

EXAMPLES OF STUDENT PROJECTS

The "Van Schaack" group had selected their building because the school librarian had read a ghost story (von Behr, 1986) about the mansion. They were excited to see a haunted house story about a place in Kinderhook published in a collection of scary stories. They used the list of questions copied from the board as a guide to gathering information. This group was very organized and worked

FIGURE 5–2. Students' First Drawing of the Van Schaack Mansion.

well together. During the first week they discovered that their ghost story was set in another location, and that there were two homesteads that had been called the Van Schaack mansion. They read, took notes, studied pictures, and consulted the dictionary as needed. They included an explanation of a mansard roof that they considered necessary for their audience. They noted changes in the building and landscaping in illustrations from Collier and Ellis and the home as it stands today. A newspaper article appeared by chance in a local newspaper that described Peter Van Schaack's support of the British during the Revolutionary War. In many ways they were natural researchers. One student wrote, and the others looked on and told him what to write. They were not satisfied with their first drawing (see Figure 5–2), and they asked a parent to take them back to their site so they could redraw it.

The final drawing is very faithful to the details of the original house (see Figure 5–3). Their final report contains information about Peter Van Schaack, architectural features of the mansion, and some personal commentary.

Other groups needed more guidance in using sources and composing. There was a tendency to use information from notes in the order that they were recorded. We helped some students organize their notes under various headings, recognize duplicate information, and investigate unanswered questions. Some students did not pull their weight in their groups and were very upsetting to other group members. Students were more accepting of members who followed closely what was happening even if they did not actually contribute greatly to the report. Other students were not as successful in using previous knowledge or finding related information. For example, the fourth graders had toured the Van Allen House, a restored Dutch house built in 1737. It was similar in many ways to the 1766 house being researched by one group. They did not use this information even though it was suggested by their teacher. They seemed to be relying heavily on their printed sources and had difficulty including some of their own observations and knowledge.

The report on Mr. and Mrs. Thomas's Dutch Colonial (see Figure 5–4) primarily relates this group's reaction to visiting the house and talking with Mr. and Mrs. Thomas. Although the house is scarcely mentioned in Collier's and Duck's books, Mr. Thomas shared all that he knew with them. The remainder of the report highlights Mrs. Thomas's guided tour. The students were obviously impressed.

A third grade group was successful in combining information from observing, reading, and interviewing. The building the group chose was in the process of changing from the Post Office to a realty business and was featured in a local newspaper article. Although their piece lacks organization, it shows evidence of citing sources and describing their building. It is a good example of recording information in the same order that it occurred in their notes (see Figure 5–5).

REFLECTIONS ON THE THEME

We were very pleased with our students' involvement in this project. As with any field experience, there were strong attitudinal changes. They now view the village from a different perspective and understand the concept of and the need for the preservation of historic districts. Using building histories to learn historical information was a new approach to learning for students. But they didn't see their research as work, and they became proud owners of their information. They experienced recorded history in the context of things, like buildings, they could see. The Battle of Saratoga was now linked to stories of General Burgoyne and Benedict Arnold, real people who had been in their village. They encountered references to slavery and the Underground Railroad and contrasted Kinderhook Village with Valatie, a nearby village known for its mills. They learned some of the language of architecture. They grew in their understanding of the concept of changes that take place in communities over time.

Students also experienced the process of research. Writing skills, note-taking, and using several sources were all necessary to get answers to their questions. They noted sources of information in their reports.

FIGURE 5–3.
Final Drawing
and Report on
the Van
Schaack
Mansion.

Van Schaack Mansion

The Van Schaack Mansion was built in 1785 by Peter Van Schaack. It has been here for 204 years. The house was part of his father's large estate. It is a white house with a rectangular shape and used to have a fence and many trees around it. Originally it resembled a large Georgian house with a hip roof, but in the nineteenth century a mansard roof and other Victorian trimmings were added. A mansard roof is a sloped roof in which the lower part curves out and usually contains dormer windows while the upper slope is nearly flat.

The house has been called by many names after its owners. It has been known as the James Mix House, the Van Schaack Mansion, the Frisbee-Mix House, and the William A. Harder place. Many generations have lived in this house. It is now the Reilly residence. The house is nice, but we think they went overboard with the Victorian trimmings and that makes it a pain to draw.

Peter Van Schaack was a well respected lawyer who started the first law school in New York State in his Kinderhook home. His nickname was the "Great Lawyer". He helped rewrite the Colonial Laws. Van Schaack was loyal to the British during the Revolutionary War and left to live in England. He later returns to the United States with the help of his close friend, John Jay, the first Supreme Court Judge. If Van Schaack had not left the country, he might have held any political office he wanted. He died on September 17, 1832. Later on people wanted to make the mansion a museum for law papers and other important stuff.

Joey Dybas   Daniel Helenius
Scott Graham   Chris Valentine

FIGURE 5–4. Final Drawing and Report on Mr. Thomas's House.

Mr. Thomas' House

We had an interview with Mr. Thomas and he said his house is one of the oldest homes in the village; it was built in the 1700's. We asked him to tell us about his house, and he said that when he took the porches off the house he saw brick instead of insulation in some of the walls. It was used as a stockade to which villagers retreated during Indian attacks. When the Kinderhook Hotel was full, they would send people over there for the night. This house used to be a two family house and has very few electrical outlets.

After the Thomas' bought the house, they put on an addition. The front door on the house has two parts. You can open the top and the bottom. From the outside it doesn't appear to be a Dutch door but from the inside it does. The house has five fireplaces in it. There is a polar bear rug hanging in the dining room. Mr. Thomas shot it in Canada. It almost looks alive. Mrs. Thomas collects sleigh beds and has about four of them. She would get them at auctions. Mrs. Thomas also has two chairs for which her mother and she made needlepoint seats. We were invited to go there and we had a good time.

Megan Barford
Sabrina Eaton
Denise Murray

FIGURE 5–5.
Final
Drawing and
Report on the
Post Office.

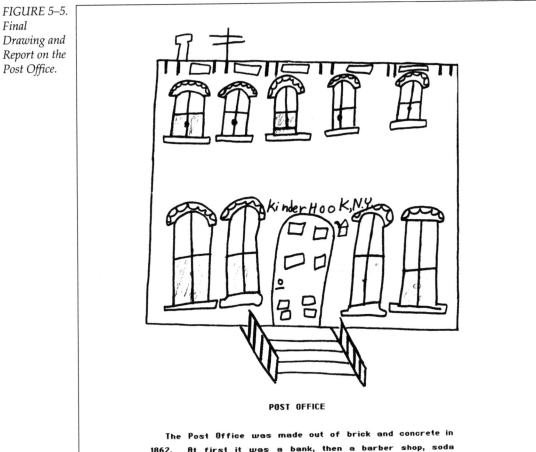

POST OFFICE

The Post Office was made out of brick and concrete in 1862. At first it was a bank, then a barber shop, soda shop, grocery store, and of course the Post Office. The Post Office is two stories tall and stands about 24 feet high. Mr. Duck told our group that the Post Office has been there since 1949 and had been used for the same purpose in the 1920's and 30's. There has been an apartment on the top floor. Mr. Duck also said that there used to be two entrances. In April, 1989 the Post Office moved next door to the National Union Bank. This building is going to be a real estate office. During work on the building, they found cement in the ceiling which was probably there when the building was used as a bank in the late 1800's.

Amanda Burt
Katie Donnelly
Jackie Engel
Annie Felix

Students learned how closely they needed to observe details. Final drawings are evidence of what students learned about scale and drawings. At times we were overwhelmed with watching our students cope with so many new tasks and experiences. Groups would get bogged down or lose information and have to search through notes or books again. Descriptions taken from their drawings had to be composed. They had difficulty understanding some references and couldn't put information into their own words. References described two different Post Offices; there were two Van Schaack homesteads. Some groups enjoyed these mysteries and pressed on; others were frustrated by these ambiguities or simply failed to notice them. Combining and organizing information was a challenge. In the end, some opted to leave out things that they couldn't quite grasp. We noticed a big difference between the third grader's and fourth grader's ability to draft reports. However, when we review what the students wrote, we feel much more positive about the information that our students actually included.

The students had the opportunity to work with some outstanding people in the project. Mr. Monthie and Mr. Duck were model observers and recorders of history. The close friendship, respect, and common interest of these older men was obvious. Our classes were impressed with the fact that someone would make the study of local history an enduring pastime and love. They heard the historians make a date to dig along a hedgerow at the village cemetery in search of a marker for a grave that belonged to a thief who had been executed in the early 1900s, and were fascinated by it. Sharon Palmer and Mr. and Mrs. Thomas also showed enthusiasm for learning and interest in helping our students learn. The Columbia County Historical Society was welcoming and helpful. Our students were fortunate to have had such experiences, which will make an indelible impression on some of the students.

Interviewing did present a particular problem. Students relied heavily on prepared questions, and they did not frame new questions based on the responses they were given. They also had difficulty listening and writing at the same time—they hadn't developed the skill to listen and then record. Fortunately tape recordings were made, and students could listen to their interviews again.

A research project like this that has students actively involved is great for public relations. Students were visible in the village; they talked about what they were learning at the dinner table. They pointed out their buildings and architectural features when they drove by with their families. Students were sleuths in the cemetery, finding familiar family names from the past on memorial stones, and making rubbings on rice paper of Van Allen, Vanderpoel, Van Schaack, and President Van Buren. It doesn't hurt, especially in times like these when schools budgets are the cause of such stress between town and gown, to do projects that bring the school and residents together to work on projects that the community takes pride in.

We had planned to include a scale model of the village as part of this project. We have already described why it didn't work, but we have since taken two workshops with Kathlyn Hatch, an architectural historian; she's going to offer a construction class the next time we do this project.

We have increased the amount of nonfiction materials that we introduce to students and have available in our classrooms. We have new information about brick bonds and house styles to share with our students.

We have decided to do this full-scale project every three or four years and undertake smaller units on architecture in between. In one of these smaller units we introduced architectural terms; students then made booklets that included drawings and definitions and identified examples of architectural features on our school building. Their list of terms was very specific and extensive, and students learned the technical language very easily. After this introduction students were ready to participate in a scavenger hunt. The task was to find examples of architectural features on real buildings in a specified area. They also had field experience in recognizing styles of buildings and, using some of their background information (brick bonds, location of garages), in speculating on ages of buildings. Students also drew apples from the side (elevation), top (aerial), and cutaway (plan), in order to "think like an architect." They built structures from marshmallows and toothpicks to explore span and load bearing. In these activities, students applied their knowledge and developed skills in observation and problem solving.

Architecture is an exciting field study for any level and lends itself to a variety of visual representations. A final project one year was a "Doors of Kinderhook" poster inspired by the well known "Doors of…" poster series. Students selected a photograph of a door from a large selection and carried it with them on a walking tour to match the real door in the village. They carefully drew their door to a predetermined size. They traced over their pencil drawings with black fine line markers and washed them with water color. We compiled three posters: one for third grade, one for fourth grade, and a black and white best of the third and fourth grades. We are currently seeking funding to have the combined "Doors of Kinderhook" poster printed. Another project required students to use their knowledge of architecture as inspiration for an architectural quilt. Students focused on one small pattern or feature that appealed to them as they looked at buildings on a walking tour. They sketched as many designs as they could as a record to be used for work in the classroom later. Selecting from their designs, students used a specific pattern to design an eight-by-eight-inch quilt square. Patterns were enlarged, repeated, or embellished. In the final quilt their designs were outlined using dimensional fabric paints on muslin. Brick bonds, column capitals, porch brackets, and keystones were sources for block designs.

Our village is the perfect study area for architectural projects. Every building is within walking distance of our school. The area's rich history provides interesting topics for research. We believe a similar project is possible in other settings where students might explore anything from industry, immigration, community services to agriculture. Both students and teachers will find this hands-on approach to history exciting and worthwhile.

REFERENCES

Abhau, M., Copeland, R., & Greenberger, G. (Eds.). (1986). *Architecture in education*. Philadelphia: Foundation for Architecture.
[Activities for architecture across curriculum areas.]

Bicentennial Committee. (1981). *The village of Kinderhook, 1609–1976*. Kinderhook, NY: Village of Kinderhook.
[Historical information and guided walking tour.]

Blumenson, J. J. G. (1981). *Identifying American architecture*. New York: W. W. Norton.
[Pictorial guide to American architectural styles. Good reference book.]

Bower Studios. (n. d.). *Archiblocks*. Vergennes, VT: Bower Studios Corporation.
[Wooden miniature reproductions of architectural features (columns, fences, etc.). Excellent for designing and drawing buildings. Comes in various styles—Gothic, Greek, Victorian, Santa Fe, Roman.]

Clinton, S. (1986). *I can be an architect*. New York: Henry Holt and Company.
[Describes work and training of an architect. Easy reading.]

Collier, E. A. (1914). *A history of old Kinderhook*. New York: G. P. Putnam's Sons & Knickerbocker Press.
[Earliest history of Kinderhook we can find.]

D'Alelio, J. (1989). *I know that building!* Washington DC: The Preservation Press.
[Activities and games, varied and unique.]

Demi. (1991). *The artist and the architect*. New York: Henry Holt and Company.
[Picture book of a Chinese folktale.]

Duck, R. S. (1985). *Kinderhook and its people, 1914–1984*. Kinderhook, NY: Ralph S. Duck.
[History of the village and town; brings Collier's book up to date.]

Ellis, Cptn. F. (1878). *History of Columbia County, New York*. Philadelphia: Everts and Ensign.
[*Centennial history, includes townships and biographical sketches.*]

Goodman, J., & Goodman, D. L. (1988). Salthouse house model. *Cobblestone, 9*(8), 16–17.
[*Instructions for making a cut-and-fold model of a salthouse.*]

Isaacson, P. M. (1988). *Round buildings, square buildings, and buildings that wiggle like a fish*. New York: A. Knopf.
[*Architectural styles throughout the world. Clear text, color photographs.*]

Kassabaum, D. (1981). Good old houses. In *Neighborhood: A book of historic houses to color and cut out*. Ann Arbor, MI: Educational Designs.
[*Puzzle game, using historic American architectural features.*]

Kassabaum, D. (1982). *Main Street*. Ann Arbor, MI: Educational Designs.
[*Puzzle, using architectural features.*]

Korab, B. (1985). *Archabet: An architectural alphabet*. Washington, DC: National Trust for Historic Preservation.
[*Architectural features, beautifully photographed.*]

Maddex, D. (1986). *Architects make zigzags*. Washington, DC: The Preservation Press.
[*An architectural alphabet book.*]

Mullins, L. C. (Ed.). (1987). *Architectural treasures of early America*. Harrisburg, PA: National Historical Society.
[*Reference book, richly illustrated.*]

Smith, K. B. (1989). *Hudson heritage*. Cold Spring, NY: Salmagundi Press.
[*A collection of superb drawings of buildings in the Hudson Valley, each briefly described.*]

von Behr, H. (1986). *Ghosts in residence*. Utica, NY: North Country Books.
[*Eyewitness accounts of supernatural happenings.*]

Waters, F. (Ed.). (1969). *Architecture*. London: Macdonald Educational.
[*Reference book written for younger students.*]

Winters, N. B. (1986). *Architecture is elementary*. Salt Lake City: Gibbs Smith.
[*Activities in visual thinking and architecture, lessons supported with detailed drawings.*]

 *Chapter 6*

Whales: A Fourth and Fifth Grade Theme

Mary Capobianco

Recently I agreed to teach a fourth and fifth grade self-contained combination class. It was particularly challenging, not only because I had never taught a multi-age class before, but also because I would be dealing with a new science curriculum.

In our district, the science curriculum is decided by a science committee. In the fourth grade science curriculum, students study rocks and minerals, ecosystems, mammals, and digestive systems. In the fifth grade, students study weather, chemistry, respiratory systems, and the "Voyage of the Mimi." For the fourth and fifth grade combination class it was decided that the science curriculum would comprise units on rocks and minerals, ecosystems, and whales. Since some fourth graders in this combination class might be going to a self-contained fifth grade next year, I had to be careful that what I taught about whales in the combination class would not be repeated in the fifth grade class when students studied the "Voyage of the Mimi." Other fourth graders could be staying in my class next year as fifth graders; for them, I would need either to develop different topics or to pursue the same topic from a different direction. I need to develop units that take into account what children already know and modify existing units to challenge children to go beyond what they already know. Having never taught a unit on whales, I knew I had my work cut out for me.

In beginning any theme, I always organize my information before I begin working with the students. I had already developed a plan for organizing themes. This plan has two major components: first, I gather my information and sources, then the children and I work through the project together (see Figure 6–1).

GATHERING INFORMATION

I gather information about a topic from a variety of sources, some that are obvious and easily accessible (for example, my school library), others that are

189

FIGURE 6–1.
Plan for
Organizing
Themes.

Stage	Description of Activities
Gathering Information	*Immediate sources* (school library, media center, colleagues, children, and parents)
	Outside sources (public library, colleges, foundations, interest groups, museums)
Doing the Theme	*Taking inventory* (gathering knowledge children already possess, seeking questions they want to answer)
	Selecting topics (inventorying students' interests, helping them develop categories or topics)
	Presenting information (teacher presents an overview of the topic, discusses technical aspects of investigating a topic)
	Individual projects (students working alone or in groups on self-chosen topics)
	Final presentations (students choose appropriate formats for presenting their topics; coaching in presentation techniques)
Assessment	Assessing what students have gained from the theme, what they liked about it

less evident and sometimes more of a challenge to uncover. One of the exciting aspects of gathering information from a variety of sources is that one discovery often leads to another: what starts out as predictable uncovers entirely new possibilities. I begin gathering information in my school. My sources include the school library/media center, and my colleagues.

School Library/Media Center

I started my research on whales by making a trip to the school library. I asked the librarian if she would gather all the books and articles that she had pertaining to whales. She gave me a list of children's books relating to whales. She also gave me a list of audio-visual materials.

I carefully reviewed these materials to see what was appropriate for the project. I have learned that what sounds like a wonderful documentary on a particular subject often turns out to be too long, too boring, too difficult, or sometimes inaudible. I learned this the hard way when I showed a film on mammals. The jacket promised to cover all the information I wanted to share. However, it wasn't long into the film that I realized the announcer was speaking with a heavy English accent. Most of the children were unable to understand him, and they quickly lost interest. I had to stop the film in the middle. Had I previewed the film I would have discovered the problem right away. Previewing a film also lets me mark areas of particular interest and take my own research notes. I can then check the students' notes to see how well they listen for important information. In viewing an older film, students need to know that numbers that were correct in the past may no longer be true in the 1990s. In these cases, I have the students predict the new numbers.

Colleagues

I usually post a note in the faculty room, informing colleagues of my class projects. Recently, we were working on a local history unit. I asked teachers if they had any information on early Dutch settlers. The speech teacher, who works part-time, heard about my project, and turned up one day at the end of class with her arms filled with books, paper houses, and a six-foot child-drawn map of early Albany in the 1600s. She had worked with a small group of high school students researching the early Dutch as part of Albany's bicentennial celebrations. Until this, I never even knew about her interest in this topic; we rarely had an opportunity to meet, let alone discuss curriculum.

Another time I did a unit on Mexico. I found out that the art teacher had gone to Mexico to study the early Mayan architecture. The physical education teacher had also been there to parasail off mountains. Both colleagues brought back hundreds of photographs. I was able to show my class the contrast between the old and the new Mexico (including some of Mexico's ancient architecture) and the mountainous terrain versus the fertile basins.

I posted a note in the teacher's room for the whales research project. One colleague gave me a National Geographic videotape on whales; another gave me a tattered box of *National Geographic* magazines dating back to 1984 that had been in her basement. By going through these magazines, I was able to copy several articles dealing with whales for the children to use as sources, including:

"New Light on the Singing Whales" (Nicklin, 1982); "An Incredible Feasting of Whales" (Giddings, 1984); "Narwhal Hunters of Greenland" (Silis, 1984); "The Whales Called 'Killer'" (Hoyt, 1984); "Narwhal: Unicorn of the Arctic Seas" (Ford & Ford, 1986); and "Gray Whales at Play in Baja's San Ignacio Lagoon" (Swartz & Jones, 1987).

Outside Sources

Besides the sources immediately at hand, I also try to explore sources beyond my school and colleagues. I look for materials in local public libraries and in the collections of colleges, museums, foundations, television stations, educational centers, and private individuals. I also seek out individuals who have a special interest and knowledge of the topic and who may be willing to come and share what they know with my students.

Public Library

I always investigate materials in the local Public Library. With a data search, I was able to get a list of over one hundred articles dealing with the topic of whales and covering several categories (e.g., diseases, behavior, communication, evolution). This list was particularly helpful, not only in helping students choose topics for individual research projects but also in providing specific references for students to access (see Figure 6–2).

My local public library offers a service to teachers whereby they will hold on reserve topic-related books while a class is studying a particular unit. Teachers simply fill out a form and leave it with the children's librarian. This can be done for a single theme or for a year's worth of themes. While she was with the Bethlehem Public Library (she is now our school librarian), Mrs. Iris Bartkowski also let me bring my class to the library, and she offered a walking tour of the library to show children the catalogs, reference materials, and indexes. This helps the children spend their own time in the library more productively.

The library's media center loans filmstrips, audiotapes, and videotapes. The center had travel videotapes on Cape Cod and Baja, California that included segments on whale watching and whale migration.

Other Outside Sources

In New York State there is a network of Bureaus of Cooperative Educational Services (BOCES), which provide a variety of services to schools, teachers, and students. I obtained a catalog of BOCES video materials for classroom viewing, which included several items relating to whales.

There are a number of colleges and universities in the Albany area that have experts in various fields and diverse collections of books, journals, and artifacts. Unlike public libraries that regularly reach out to schools, college faculty do not typically work directly with elementary classroom teachers, and their expertise has to be sought out. Normally, what I do is call the particular department of a college that seems closest to the topic I am studying in my classroom. For example, when I did a theme on Northeast Indians, I contacted Professor Dean Snow in the Anthropology Department at the State University of New York at Albany for specific information on totem poles. Dean Snow told me that the Northeast Indians did not construct totem poles. However, in my New York State social studies text book, there was a picture of a totem pole constructed by Northeastern Indians. After tracking down the source at the New York City Museum of Indian Affairs, I learned that the picture in question was simply a

```
1.      A grave tale; do whale remains help life spread on
        the deep-sea floor? by John Horgan il v262 Scientific
        American Jan '90 p18(2)
        52K1605
            LIBRARY SUBSCRIBES TO JOURNAL

Heading:    WHALES
            -Communication systems

1.      Cosmic babble. (sonar measurement of whale and
        porpoise communication) by John Futterman il v15 Omni
        April '93 p79(1)
        68B1994
            ABSTRACT AVAILABLE, LIBRARY SUBSCRIBES TO JOURNAL

Heading:    WHALES
            -Environmental aspects

1.      Giants of the seas. (whales) by Mike Van Stappen
        il v20 Backpacker Dec '92 p32(2)
        67B3977
            ABSTRACT AVAILABLE, LIBRARY SUBSCRIBES TO JOURNAL

2.      The expanding human threat. (effect of pollution
        on whales) by Betsy Carpenter il v113 U.S. News &
        World Report July 13 '92 p64(1)
        65C1161
            ABSTRACT AVAILABLE, LIBRARY SUBSCRIBES TO JOURNAL

3.      Gentle giants. (whales) by Bruce Oboe il v110
        Canadian Geographic Dec-Jan '90 p22(9)
            LIBRARY SUBSCRIBES TO JOURNAL
```

FIGURE 6–2. *Computer Listing of Sources on Whales.*

carved stick. If I hadn't contacted Professor Dean Snow, both my students and I would still believe that the Northeast Indians constructed totem poles.

Unfortunately for the theme on whales, local colleges and universities in the Albany area were not productive sources because very little research on whales takes place in any of them (the major research institutions are, naturally, located closer to the sea). However, I was able to contact an area college that just happened to be hosting an art show, *Mammals of the World.* Although I wasn't able to arrange a field trip to this particular exhibition, it would have been a worthwhile activity because it viewed the topic of mammals from such a different perspective.

Museums and cultural centers maintain the most comprehensive and publicly accessible collections of materials for most projects done in elementary classrooms. We are lucky to have within driving distance New York State's Museum and Cultural Center, the Albany Institute of History and Art, The Rennselaer Junior Museum, the Scotia-Glenville Traveling Museum, The Schenectady Planetarium, and the Quackenbush House, to name just a few. All of these museums and centers have programs for children that follow the New

York State science and social studies curricula, and most of them have outreach programs that come to schools, often at no charge. In an era of tightening school budgets, these outreach programs make an excellent alternative to costly field trips.

For the theme on whales, I contacted the New York State Museum in Albany and was able to schedule a visit to the *Giants of the Deep* exhibit, a traveling collection of life-size models of whales, sharks, and other sea creatures. The museum also offers a guided tour that includes a study of a life-size skeleton of a baleen whale.

Finally, I take advantage of people in my local community who have experience and interest in particular topics. My local public library publishes a list of local interest groups, and they have a copy of the *Encyclopedia of Associations* (Gale Research, 1987), that lists a number of organizations associated with whales. When I did a theme on ecosystems, I contacted a member of a local gardening club for information on plants that grow well in our area. For the whale theme, I was able to find a group of community members who were interested in the study of endangered species. Although our schedules could not be coordinated and I wasn't able to have a member of this group visit the classroom during the whale theme, I do plan on having such a visit the next time.

TEACHING THE THEME

There are several stages I go through in every theme we explore: the first stage is what I call taking an inventory. This includes gathering the information the children already possess, and listing the questions the children want to answer. The second stage involves helping children select their topics. This includes developing categories or topics and inventorying students' interests. In the next stage, I present information to the children and make materials available to them. I also show them how to gather information and how to organize and present it, and we do class activities to enlarge everyone's knowledge of the topic. Then, the children explore their topics on their own. Finally, we conclude the project with presentations.

Taking An Inventory

Gathering the Knowledge the Children Already Possess

When I feel I have gathered sufficient information and lists of available sources, I start the unit by finding out what the children already know. I send notes home informing parents of the theme we are about to begin. I encourage parents to discuss the new project with their child and encourage the children to bring in all they have at home on the subject that they would be willing to share.

For the whale theme, one of my students brought in a wonderful book by the staff of Allied Whale at the College of the Atlantic in Bar Harbor, Maine. The book is entitled *Finbacks and Friends: Adopt-a-Whale Program* (Katona, 1990). As a direct result of the information in this booklet, the class voted to adopt a class whale.

Other students brought in stuffed whales, dolphins, posters, and books, even recordings of whales singing. One child brought in a family VCR recording of their family on a Cape Cod whale watch.

Sometimes I find a parent who has a particular interest in the subject we are researching. One year during an Indian unit, a grandparent volunteered to visit the classroom and share his Indian jewelry collection. He had lived and taught English on a Native American Reservation in Arizona. During the whale project, I had a parent who had recorded their family on a whale watching trip off Cape Cod. They were willing to share the tape as well as their experience with the class.

I begin by asking the children what knowledge they have about the subject, and I write down the information they give me on the chalkboard. I am always amazed at the amount of background information children bring into a new topic. Soon, the chalkboard is covered with the collective information they share.

Seeking the Questions the Students Want to Answer

I ask the children to write down in their journals and discuss with one another what they want to know about the topic. For example, Renata had a number of questions she still wanted answered after the class had brainstormed the topic (see Figure 6–3).

By involving the children as a source of information, I hope to spark their interest and their natural curiosity to know more. Once they are interested, they usually cannot wait to begin. Motivation is a very important factor in any research project.

Selecting Topics

Developing Categories or Topics

Next, we take the information that we've written on the chalkboard, and we organize it into major headings. With the whale theme, we combined all the pieces of information into five major categories: Whales as Mammals, Baleen and Toothed Whales, Specific Types of Whales, Whales as Endangered Species, and Hunting the Whales.

Next, I divided a piece of paper into six squares and placed one of the headings in each of the squares. Then I asked students to look at their questions and see which category they addressed. This exercise helped the

① What type or kind of whale is the smartest?

② How do whales jump out of the water?

③ Why `                                        `?

④ Why does the Narwhale have a twisted tooth?

⑤ How did Baleen evolve?

⑥ Explain the evolution of whales

⑦ Why do some whales have Dorsal fins & others don't?

⑧ What is the age of whales?

⑨ Why do whales sing?

⑩ What number of teeth do whales have?

⑪ What covers a whales body & why?

⑫ How big can a whales throat extend?

⑬ What are all the uses of a dead whale?

⑭ What are the major differences in whales?

⑮ What is the average number of babies a female whale has?

A baby whale can survive a long cold journey. -The whale can make a whirlpool. Beluga has such creamy white skin.

FIGURE 6-3. Renata's Questions About Whales.

students to discover where their interests lay and in what categories they had the most questions.

Inventorying Students' Interests

Next, I meet with each student. I review the questions they want answered and try to discover where their greatest interest lies. I try to encourage them to find the answers to the questions they find most interesting. When students do not formulate their own questions, they will not seek answers. In this process, the students begin to uncover subtopics to their topics. For example, students began breaking down the topic "Whales as Mammals" into smaller units: parts of the whale, intelligence of the whale, ways whales communicate, sounds of the whales, echo locations, beaching, migration, and so on.

At this point of the project, most of the students have selected a topic they want to pursue as an individual research project. Before they start their inquiries, however, I like to take some time and present broad information on the topic.

Presenting Information

There are two major activities in this stage. I present an overview of the topic so that the students have a sense of the whole before they begin exploring the parts. I also devote some time to the technical aspects of investigating a topic, such as how to read for information, how to reword paragraphs, and how to keep notes and reference sources. Once I've done this for one project, all I have to do is review these suggestions as we begin another project. Then I have the students work these through in small groups.

For the whale theme, I began presenting information on whales by showing the National Geographic film *All Whales are Mammals* (National Geographic Society, n. d.) one day, and the Smithsonian film *Magnificent Whales and Other Marine Mammals* (Smithsonian Institute, 1988) on another day. Both these films present an overview of the topic, and demonstrate to students how large, how powerful, and how provocative this topic is. What I'm really trying to do here is to excite the children and entice them into the topic. I want children to explore an aspect of this topic not because they've been assigned it, but because they have the desire and enthusiasm to know more. By exposing children to the breadth of the topic of whales, I am also helping them see how their individual questions relate to the topic as a whole.

For example, by watching these two films, a child whose questions are about endangered species of whales will see that the survival of these mammals depends on various factors such as pollution, international fishing practices, even divine acts. As they watched each film, I had the children take notes in their science journals and suggested they put question marks in the margins to indicate questions they had about specific information presented in the films (see Figure 6–4).

After each film was over, I broke students up into four small groups to share their notes. I listen in on each group to see what the children felt was significant in the films. Then each group shares with the class what it learned from the film. Children can add to their own notes any information they gained from either their group's discussion or the class sharing. Even though I have taken detailed notes on these films before showing them to the children, I rarely have to add anything myself to these discussions because the children, either on their own or working cooperatively, have already identified the major points of the films.

Presenting this overview of whales may prompt children to rethink or refocus the areas of interest they have previously developed. This is really no different from the recursive process that professional researchers use as they develop and refine their questions, and it is healthy for children to realize that their questions can be redefined as they uncover new information.

Fourth and fifth graders have some experience taking notes from books, but they have rarely if ever taken notes from other media. Before I show the films, I explain what is different about taking notes from film as opposed to written material (for example, text in books can be re-read over and over again, but the

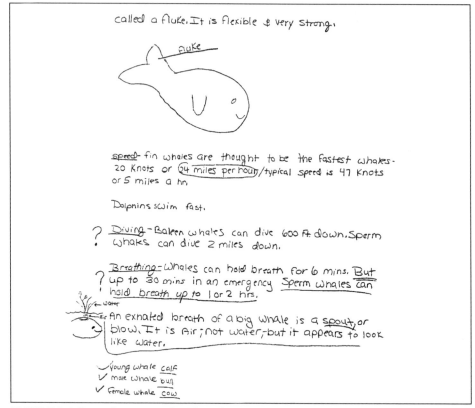

called a fluke. It is flexible & very strong.

fluke

speed - fin whales are thought to be the fastest whales.
20 Knots or 24 miles per hour/typical speed is 47 Knots
or 5 miles a hr.

Dolphins swim fast.

? Diving - Baleen whales can dive 600 ft down. Sperm
Whales can dive 2 miles down.

? Breathing - Whales can hold breath for 6 mins. But
up to 30 mins in an emergency. Sperm whales can
hold breath up to 1 or 2 hrs.
← water
Air An exhaled breath of a big whale is a spout, or
blow. It is Air; not water; but it appears to look
like water.

Young whale calf
Male whale bull
Female whale cow

FIGURE 6–4. Renata's Notes on the Film All Whales Are Mammals.

"text" in film is not only linear, it's also mostly oral, not written; another difference is that in film, the content is partially conveyed in pictures and partially in the narration). I offer suggestions for taking notes (e.g., jotting down words and phrases rather than trying to transcribe the narration; sketching rather than trying to write a description; listening for clues such as numbers or dates that signal something interesting to follow; not worrying about spelling or handwriting), and let them know ahead of time that they will be sharing their notes, so if something is missed, it isn't gone forever. At least one person in the group is likely to have recorded it, and anyway, the children can always view the film again. The goal here is not to have a set of perfect written notes to be graded, but rather to have children experience the process of extracting information from a source. Although the primary purpose of viewing these films is to broaden children's knowledge of the topic and to entice them into it, they are also improving their ability to translate information from one medium to another, to learn from each other, and to extract from other people's information what's important to them.

I generally follow the showing of films with a presentation about written materials. From the books I have in the classroom, I select one that deals with the overall topic of whales (e.g., Royston, 1989), and I show the children how they can find information about their specific questions, even though the book covers a wide variety of topics. I work through an example or two using the book as a model, pointing out how the table of contents, chapter headings, or the index helps locate the answers to particular questions. I do this exercise several times, using both general books (e.g., Palmer, 1988), and books that deal with specific topics (e.g., Cook & Wisner, 1973). Next, I put out on the tables all the materials I have on whales and let each group familiarize themselves with them. I don't insist that students take notes at this point; rather, they are previewing the materials to see what's available on their subtopics.

A third technique for bringing information to the students is to invite a guest speaker to the classroom. I have learned (the hard way) that not all subject matter experts are good speakers, and some of them really don't know how to relate to children, so I make sure that I talk with potential guests ahead of time and check with colleagues on how they are with children. I also let the guest know what we have been studying so that they come prepared with a talk that relates to our topic and which can stimulate the students into further learning. It helps, too, if the students have thought about questions they want the guest to address. For the talk itself, I ask students to have their journals ready to take notes, and I usually videotape the talk if the guest permits it, so we can make it available to the students to review later. These tapes serve as excellent reference material for subsequent years if a speaker is not able to make a return visit.

When we were studying Shakespeare and his works as part of a poetry unit, I invited into the classroom a high school English teacher who teaches drama. He came with six high school students who had studied drama under him and who were currently performing in a drama production at the high school. After his presentation, he broke my students into groups, each led by one of his students, and had them work on different scenes from Shakespearean plays. The exercise was so successful that the high school students volunteered to come back for at least twelve more working sessions, which culminated in a schoolwide performance.

For the study on whales, I invited a high school biology teacher to our classroom. Over the years he has taken groups of high school students on overnight whale watching expeditions, so his insights into both whales and whale-watching were particularly relevant to the students' questions.

While these films, books, and guests bring whales into the classroom, they aren't that effective in getting students to reach beyond the classroom for information. I therefore spend some time encouraging students to seek information from outside sources. I ask the children where they think we might locate these sources and how we might go about contacting them. Students usually will suggest looking in the bibliographies of the classroom books on whales. I also share with them some suggestions I have for possible leads. For example, my local public library puts out a pamphlet called *Community Contacts* in which the names and addresses of a large number of local organizations and chapters of national organizations are listed. There are no whale-related organizations, but there are several that are concerned with environmental issues and endangered species from whom valuable information might be sought. A better source is the *Encyclopedia of Associations* (Gale Research, 1987); it lists such organizations as Save the Whales, the Whaling Museum Society, the Center for Coastal Studies, and the Pacific Whale Foundation, and it gives addresses, telephone numbers, and a brief description of the aims of each organization. Armed with these leads, we set off on our search.

To obtain information from these external sources, one of the vehicles that works well for fourth and fifth graders is writing letters. For example, Erin wrote to the American Cetacean Society for information about their magazine, *Whalewatcher*, but she really wanted to know if the profits from the magazine are devoted to saving whales. Alexis wanted to know if *Whalewatcher* was printed on recyclable paper. In the back of book *Finback and Friends: Adopt-a-Whale Program* (Katona, 1990) that Bethany brought to school, there was a reference to an organization that shows people how to "adopt" a whale, so we decided to write for more information and as a result got onto a mailing list for environment concerns. We received several flyers and newsletters on the topic of sea mammals.

Frequently one letter-writing activity leads to another. One of flyers we received from a mailing list was about Japanese whale-hunting; its descriptions so moved the students that they wrote to the Japanese Embassy about their concerns for whales (see Figure 6–5).

During a theme on ecosystems, my fourth graders wrote to the New York State Environmental Conservation (NYENCON) to get information about the habitat of the loon. NYENCON sent the children detailed descriptions of loon habitats, maps, environmental posters, and a list of current proposals before the state legislature. The students were urged to write their legislators to urge passage of a bill to protect the habitat of the loon. The students drafted a petition, collected signatures from the community, and presented the petition to the New York Legislature, along with their own letters and a specially-commissioned protest song written by the students in collaboration with Chris Holder, an accomplished local singer/storyteller. Although the legislation ultimately did not pass, the students received a letter from Governor Cuomo, thanking them for their support and encouraging them to continue their involvement. From one simple letter asking for information about loons came an entire project that taught the children about an important issue in environmental protection, how bills become law, and about democracy in action.

A technique that we've only started to use in the past year or so is having students retrieve information from PRODIGY, an on-line database our school

FIGURE 6–5.
*Alexis's Letter
to the Japanese
Embassy.*

> Japanese Embassy
>
> 299 Park Avenue
> New York, New York
>
> Dear Sir:
>
> Why kill the whales? They have done noth-
> ing to harm us and we have found substitutes for
> all things that come from the whale. On top of
> that whales are loving. No one has been killed
> by any kind of whale except for in accidents.
>
> I didn't tell you yet- I think that whales
> should be killable. But in your country you are
> over doing it. You are killing too many whales.
> They may even become extinct!
>
> Belive me, Im not writing this letter for
> nothing- So please honor the 1996 moratorium
> whales' hunts.
>
> I honor whales,
>
> Alexis Grant

subscribes to. The students sign on, navigate to PRODIGY's encyclopedia database, search for a topic, and then download information. We didn't have access to PRODIGY at the time we did this theme, but if we study the topic of whales again, we'll be sure to use this resource. It has already proved itself to be valuable for other themes, including Canada and mammals.

Another technique I like to use whenever possible is to take the class to the source. When students study rocks and minerals in the fourth grade curriculum, it is more meaningful to visit Howe Caverns than to see obscure pictures in a book. In May, 1990, I took my fourth graders on a field trip to Cherry Hill, an historic 1800 family home in Albany. It would not have been possible for a child to have written such detailed descriptions of nineteenth century furniture had he not been able to observe it closely and write about what he had actually seen. Field trips also allow students to form their own opinions about what they see, rather than having to rely on the judgments and perspectives of writers, artists, and photographers.

For the whale unit, the students took a field trip to the Boston Aquarium. For many students, this trip was the first time they had come closer to a dolphin than photographs in a book, and the experience of close observation was unforgettable.

INDIVIDUAL PROJECTS

In this stage, the students work independently on their projects and in small groups. For a period of two weeks, I devote two hours a day to this activity (taken from my reading, writing, and social studies time). So that students can work with a minimum of distractions, I try to make sure that all the materials they need are at hand. I bring a library cart full of school library books and other materials into the classroom, and I also make available materials brought in by parents, fellow teachers, and the students themselves. These are the primary sources the children will be using to find answers to the questions that they have raised in their journals. The students are free to work on their own or in small groups. This is not a quiet time—everyone is busily engaged in their research, reading books, talking with me and other students, helping each other, and sharing what they have learned. Each child is responsible for an individual project at the end of the unit, so students will ultimately be accountable for gathering their own information; however, I encourage students to work together on their research and give each other the benefits of individual talents. For example, one child did a project on Japanese tuna fishing and its relation to whales. The child's final presentation involved creating a videotape depicting a debate between fishermen and environmentalists. The student wrote the dialog but needed the assistance of other students to serve as actors in the debate. She still was responsible for her own project, however, and for the quality of the information in it. Children often help each other by illustrating reports. I encourage this sharing of talent, even though ultimately the project is the sole responsibility of the child who created it.

These individual projects last over a month. Even after the formal research time is over, I allow students to continue their projects during social studies, giving them additional forty-minute periods to complete their work. It is important that time be allowed in the classroom for research. Too often, research projects done at home are parent initiated and parent controlled. Students should be actively seeking the answers to their own questions. Also, if research projects have to be done only at home, children whose parents aren't able to give them unlimited support are penalized through no fault of their own. By allowing students classroom time for research, I can also monitor the way they find information. If needed, I can do mini-lessons in table of contents, index, topic headings, etc. Also, if I'm right there with the students, I can assist them with paraphrasing, highlighting important facts, and outlining information.

I can also monitor student progress. If they are working on their projects in the classroom for an extended period, students pace themselves and engage in sustained inquiries, rather than waiting until the deadline and doing a "night before quick copy." Students will begin to behave like researchers who need extended amounts of time for their inquiries. Also, when students work in the same room together on their projects, they see each other's progress and products, and this alleviates many of the anxieties that are associated with projects done secretly at home and then brought in at the last moment. This is especially problematic when one suspects that parents have designed, carried out, and word-processed the child's project.

Finally, if we allow children plenty of time in school to do their projects, it sends a powerful message about how we value their research efforts. Projects simply assigned and collected after a month are frequently seen as a chore and a punishment, and children attach more importance to getting them in on time and escaping punishment for not meeting the deadline than they do to the substance of the project. By spending time on projects in class, children become involved in them and are much more willing to spend additional time on them at home.

Final Presentations

It is very important for the students to know how they are going to present the results of their individual projects. In some cases, a written report may be enough. However there are many more alternatives available for the children to present their information.

Students can role-play characters from the past to present; write nonfiction reports; write fictional newspapers, diaries, travel logs, journals; tape commercials, news reports, debates; build dioramas, displays, models; make videotapes; create songs, poems, picture books; demonstrate crafts, hobbies, experiments, and so on.

My advice to students is that they think about the way they will present their project while they are doing the project, not as an afterthought. Knowing how they're going to present a project often helps shape the direction of the research. For example, if a child is exploring different kinds of whales, then he might be drawn to a presentation format that is visual and offers the audience sharp contrasts between the various kinds. On the other hand, examining the pros and cons of whaling might lend itself to a debate format or a dramatic presentation. I don't insist that children present their projects in one format or another, but I do conference with them about the suitability of a given format with a particular topic. I want them to learn how to make a match between the way they have investigated their topic and the way they are going to share it with their classmates. There should be a connection between the content and the presentation.

All too often, children do projects and then present them without receiving any assistance in making the transition from exploring a topic to presenting it. This is especially difficult if we have encouraged children to decide how they want to present their research, and if they don't have to follow a rigid presentation format. In addition to suggesting that they match the content and form of their topic to the content and form of the presentation, I assist children with techniques for accomplishing this. For example, if a child decided to create a newspaper devoted to the topic of whales, they need to know something about the structure and format of a newspaper, what headlines are, what sections a newspaper typically has, how a news story is written, and so on. If a child decided to make a videotape, he'll need to know quite a bit about the technical aspects of videotaping (holding the camera steady, editing, close-ups versus long shots, etc.), scripting, and how dialog best works in front of a camera. It isn't enough to simply tell children the rules for assembling a newspaper or a video. What needs to be done is modeling for the child, giving feedback on first attempts, and generally coaching so that the child's efforts with a particular presentation format are guided and supported.

In the whale theme, the children's presentations were varied and creative, ranging from the more traditional research report and dioramas, to graphs and posters, video presentations, audiotapes of whale "songs" with a running commentary, whale dictionaries, whale newspapers, debates, "news" reports, dramatizations, whaling journals, and realistic fiction writing.

I allotted about a week and a half for the presentations inside the classroom, scheduling about four to five per day. Each presentation lasted about twenty minutes, and I encouraged response and discussion following each of the presentations. It's important for me that children don't merely recite their presentations in front of a quiet, passive audience, but rather involve everyone in the class in sharing their research findings. Because children have decided on the method of presentation and are encouraged to present their work in a variety of ways, we don't run into the problem of an endless series of similar presentations, nor do children "dread" the public exposure of their work. In fact, they look forward to presenting it. Also, since we have all shared to some extent in the creation of the projects and in the preparation of the presentation, these culminating activities are truly a celebration of our efforts.

I like to invite to these presentations people who have assisted the children during the theme. Whenever possible, I also give students the opportunity to share their projects with other classes. Sometimes, I videotape the presentations for use at parent meetings or open house, or I simply set up a VCR in the hallway or main lobby and let it run all day so that visitors can watch segments of the students' presentations. Sometimes I set up tables in the library to display the students' final projects. In these cases, I have the students supply sheets of paper with their name and project title at the top, and I invite visitors to write comments about the individual projects. For example:

> Really nice job—I found the information about the catching of dolphins interesting. I promise I'll only buy dolphin safe tuna.
> Mrs. Ryan

The children get to keep these comment sheets when the exhibit is finished. Students need to know that what they have worked so hard on is valuable information to share. And they need to receive positive feedback on their work.

It's hard to capture in written form the excitement and satisfaction of this final stage of the theme, but Figures 6–6, 6–7, and 6–8 illustrate some examples of the finished products.

EVALUATION

Assessment for the whale unit was a four-stage research project grade. I use a teacher-created grade sheet that assesses students in four areas (preresearch, research, first draft, and final report/presentation), and that computes a final grade based on these four areas.

Preresearch

During initial conferencing I check students' work for questions raised. I look at how well they have broken their larger questions into topics. I watch to see if they are beginning to narrow down their information to one specific question. I check to see how organized they are keeping their initial notes. I check to see if they are making efforts to view and review general information to broaden their background knowledge so as to find the topic they will continue to research.

FIGURE 6–6.
Script of
Michael's
Video Report
on Dolphins.

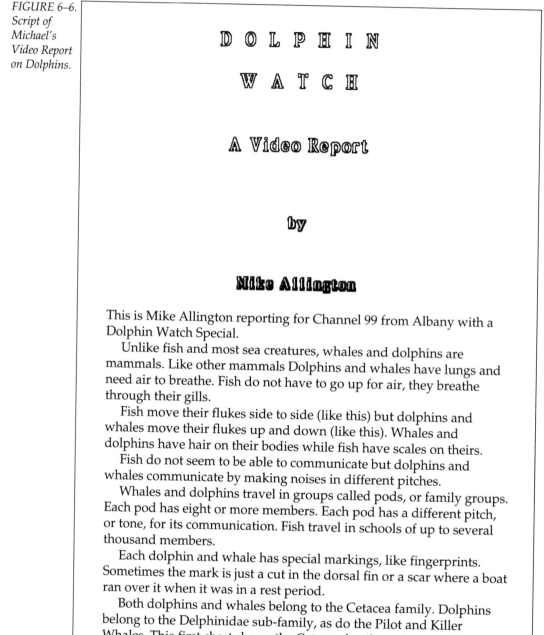

DOLPHIN

WATCH

A Video Report

by

Mike Allington

This is Mike Allington reporting for Channel 99 from Albany with a Dolphin Watch Special.

Unlike fish and most sea creatures, whales and dolphins are mammals. Like other mammals Dolphins and whales have lungs and need air to breathe. Fish do not have to go up for air, they breathe through their gills.

Fish move their flukes side to side (like this) but dolphins and whales move their flukes up and down (like this). Whales and dolphins have hair on their bodies while fish have scales on theirs.

Fish do not seem to be able to communicate but dolphins and whales communicate by making noises in different pitches.

Whales and dolphins travel in groups called pods, or family groups. Each pod has eight or more members. Each pod has a different pitch, or tone, for its communication. Fish travel in schools of up to several thousand members.

Each dolphin and whale has special markings, like fingerprints. Sometimes the mark is just a cut in the dorsal fin or a scar where a boat ran over it when it was in a rest period.

Both dolphins and whales belong to the Cetacea family. Dolphins belong to the Delphinidae sub-family, as do the Pilot and Killer Whales. This first chart shows the Cetacea family and some of its sub-families. (Pause).

These same families are illustrated on this next chart from National geographic magazine. While the names are hard to read it does show

FIGURE 6–6.
Cont'd

the different sizes of the different members of the Cetacea family. (Pause).

Dolphins mostly eat fish. A dolphin's eyesight is not the best but it has better hearing.

Dolphins and whales usually migrate during different seasons going to warm places, for instance, during the winter and returning to cooler areas in the summer (point to map of Pacific Ocean near California).

Dolphins seem to be smart. They can talk to each other and they are easy to train. Dolphins perform in place like SeaWorld and have been trained to work for the Navy. Dolphins seem friendly to humans, often approaching boats and jumping out of the water and talking dolphin talk.

But every year hundreds of thousand dolphins are killed by Tuna fishermen. What happens is that Tuna fishermen put out nets which stay near the surface of the water but which keep dolphins from going up for air. The dolphins get caught in the nets and drown because they cannot get up to breathe.

In other cases the dolphins get caught in the nets and pulled up on the boats with the fish. The Tuna fishermen find they have caught a dolphin and they say, "If we kill the dolphin and mix it with the Tuna nobody will notice the difference.." So they crush the dolphin and sell it for the same price as the Tuna.

Striped, Spinner, Common and Pacific dolphins are the ones most often caught in Tuna nets. These dolphins are often found near schools of Tuna. They follow the Tuna and feed on the same fish.

In the 1980s people started to notice the loss of dolphins and began to take action.

People argued that Tuna fishermen could avoid trapping the dolphins and some fishermen tried. They put escape hatches in the nets and the dolphins would find their way out, but so would some of the Tuna. So many fishermen did not use nets with escape hatches.

Some fishermen played recordings of Killer Whale noises to scare the dolphins, but not many.

Then many people said they wouldn't buy Tuna if dolphins were being killed. So some companies began to use dolphin safe nets and fishing methods. These companies put special labels on their cans. The label shows a dolphin going into the water. But not all companies agreed to do this.

So, if you are shopping for Tuna be sure to look for the Dolphin Safe label on the can (hold up and show cans). Buy the cans like this with the dolphin safe label and do not buy cans like these with no labels.

This has been Mike Allington with Dolphin Watch for Channel 99.

E is for Extinction. When Something is Extinct it has died out. The whales are almost Extinct.

Fluke

F is for Fluke. A Fluke is a tail that helps the whale Swim by moving up and down.

FIGURE 6–8.
*Excerpt From
Laurie's
Fictional
Book, "A
Little Attack."*

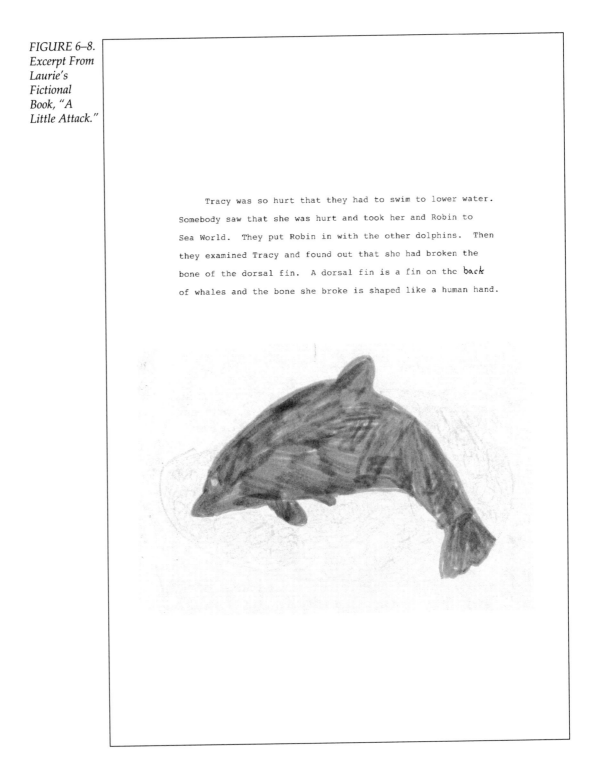

Tracy was so hurt that they had to swim to lower water. Somebody saw that she was hurt and took her and Robin to Sea World. They put Robin in with the other dolphins. Then they examined Tracy and found out that she had broken the bone of the dorsal fin. A dorsal fin is a fin on the back of whales and the bone she broke is shaped like a human hand.

Research

During conference time, I check to see that students' notes are organized. I look for clearly written information that they will be able to use in their report later on. I check that they are keeping records of materials used. I help them rephrase wording copied from texts. I check that the information they are copying is pertinent to the topic they have picked. This is clearly an assessment of how well they are learning to research. Each child is graded according to my estimation of their ability. I would expect more information and sources from a higher-level student. It is really how well they have mastered what has been taught as being important tools for gathering information.

First Draft

This is the progress the student is making in organizing the information they have gathered into a presentation form. It is important that the information gathered will lend itself to the type of presentation that the student has chosen, whatever it may be—a written report, a crossword puzzle, video tape, and so on. I look to see that they have enough information to support their points and answer their questions. I am not so much concerned with spelling or mechanics as I am concerned with content and form.

Final Report/Presentation

Here I look to see how well they have developed from first draft to final copy. I look for effort and quality. I want to be sure that the work of the first draft worked on in class meets the finished product. Too often, this is the stage parents take over and "redo." I also look at the pride and sense of accomplishment with which the student presents the material. I want the child to be able to defend his/her work and present it with knowledge and confidence. The student should not have to read word-for-word since by this stage the student should be familiar with the material and only need to review it just before presenting.

Grading

I used to give twenty points for the preresearch, twenty points for research, twenty points for first draft, and forty points for final copy (with consideration given to the oral presentation). I have recently reconsidered the idea of twenty points for research and forty for final copy. I now believe that forty points is more appropriate for the research phase since that is my true goal. I want to stress the way they read and write for information and then communicate that information to others. That would give twenty points to final copy. However, some parents are reluctant to accept this because they want a final paper (over which they have more control) given more points than the in-class, parent-free research!

I had not used the curriculum material prepared by the district science committee for the whale theme, and so to confirm that the students in my class did master sufficiently the information on the topic of whales, I allowed them to take the district created science test that accompanied the curriculum. Even though I did not use the district material, I wanted to see how well the students would do on the test. Twenty-five students took the test. The lowest grade (received by the one Resource Room student) was eighty-eight percent. The class average was ninety-seven percent.

Finally, I like to receive feedback from the students on their theme experiences, so I asked them to write about their views. Here's a sample of the responses:

> "I loved the whale unit. I think I might even grow up to be a cetologist."
>
> "I think the whale unit was fun and exciting. I learned many things I never knew before."
>
> "I loved the whale unit! I thought it was great !!!"
>
> "Yes, I did like this unit. It has gotten me interested in whales. In the summer, we're going to go whale watching. I really liked this unit because of the interesting wonders of the whale and magnificent wonders of these beautiful beasts."
>
> "I liked the whale unit a lot. I think that it was a lot of fun and you should do it next year."
>
> "I loved the whale unit because it was fun and not boring."

There were no negative responses. I guess that says it all!

REFERENCES

Books/Articles

Andrews, R. C. (1954). *All about whales.* New York: Random House.
[*This book is an account of Roy Andrews' own explorations in remote parts of the world, studying different species of whales.*]

Bunting, E. (1980). *The Sea World book of whales.* New York: Harcourt Brace Jovanovich.
[*Eve Bunting describes the evolution and habits of whales, as well as the problems of their survival.*]

Carrick, C. (1993). *Whaling days.* New York: Clarion Books.
[*This book is about the whaling industry from colonial days to current efforts to save whales. Beautifully illustrated with woodcuts by David Frampton.*]

Carwardine, M. (1992). *Whales, dolphins and porpoises.* New York: Dorling Kindersley.
[*Describes the physical characteristics, behavior, habitat, and feeding habits of whales.*]

Cook, J. J., & Wisner, W. L. (1973). *Blue whale: Vanishing leviathan.* New York: Dodd.
[*Discusses the evolution of food, anatomy, behavior, and conservation of the blue whale. Illustrated with photographs.*]

Ford, J., & Ford, D. (1986). Narwhal: Unicorn of the Arctic seas. *National Geographic, 169*(3), 354–363.
[*A description of the narwhal, with its characteristic unicorn horn. Superb photographs accompany the article.*]

Gale Research, Inc. (1987). *Encyclopedia of associations.* Detroit, MI: Gale Research, Inc.
[*An excellent reference source, available in public libraries, for locating local, state, and national organizations.*]

Gambell, R. (1991). *The concise illustrated book of whales and dolphins.* New York: Smithmark.
[*A good reference book on all the different species of whales.*]

Gardner, R. (1984). *The whale watcher's guide.* New York: Messner.
[*This is an excellent guide to the spectator sport of whale watching, but it also deals with whales and their behavior.*]

Giddings, A. (1984). An incredible feasting of whales. *National Geographic, 165*(1), 88–93.
[*A photographic essay on whales off southeast Alaska by one of the world's leading underwater sea photographers. (See also the January 1979 issue of National Geographic Magazine for a related article on whales.)*]

Goldner, K. A., & Vogel, C. G. (1987). *Humphrey the wrong-way whale.* New York: Dillon.
[*The story of a whale that swam into San Francisco Bay in 1985.*]

Hendrick, R. M. (1985). *The voyage of the Mimi.* Scotts Valley, CA: Wings for Learning.
[*This book chronicles the voyage of the Mimi, a boat that sets out on a whalewatch. It's a delightful combination of fact and fiction.*]

Hoyt, E. (1984). The whales called "Killer." *National Geographic, 166*(2), 220–237.
[*Describes the habitat, behavior, and myths about killer whales.*]

Hoyt, E. (1991). *Meeting the whales: The Equinox guide to giants of the deep.* Ontario: Camden House.
[*A detailed book about the different kinds of whales, their behavior, and relationship with humans. There's an enormous amount of information in this densely packed book.*]

Kalman, B., & Faris, K. (1988). *Arctic whales and whaling,* New York: Crabtree Publishing.
[*Superbly illustrated book about the Arctic whales. This book is a must for children doing projects on whales.*]

Katona, S. K. (1990). *Finbacks and friends: Adopt-a-whale program.* Bar Harbor, ME: Allied Whale at the College of the Atlantic.
[*Pamphlet that describes the adopt-a-whale project and gives details about the different kinds of whales.*]

Lauber, P. (1991). *Great whales: The gentle giants.* New York: Henry Holt and Company.
[*A simply written book about the different kinds of whales. The information is detailed but easy to access. Suitable for less able readers at this grade level.*]

McClung, R. M. (1978). *Hunted mammals of the sea.* New York: Morrow.
[*McClung describes the life cycle of the great whales and discusses the history and current dangers of whale hunting.*]

McCoy, J. J. (1989). *The plight of the whales.* New York: Watts.
[*This book is mostly about the threats to the existence of whales. Illustrated with black-and-white photographs, it is an excellent resource for the topic of endangered species.*]

McGowen, T. (1980). *Album of whales.* New York: Macmillan.
[*An introduction to the history of whales, their habits, and species. A good reference book for projects.*]

McMillan, B. (1992). *Going on a whale watch.* New York: Scholastic.
[*Although written for younger students, this book is useful as a resource for whale watching.*]

McNulty, F. (1975). *Whales: Their life in the sea.* New York: Harper & Row.
[*Comprehensive book about whales, including their eating habits, where they live, how they communicate, and how they care for their young. Good resource for projects.*]

Milton, J. (1989). *Whales: The gentle giants.* New York: Random House.
[*Discusses the different kinds of whales and their feeding, mating, and migratory*

habits. Written for younger readers, this book would be especially appropriate for less able readers at this level.]

Mizumura, K. (1971). *The blue whale.* New York: Thomas Crowell.
[*A well illustrated book. It's written for younger readers, and therefore would be useful only for its illustrations and for less able readers at this level.*]

Nicklin, F. (1982). New light on the singing whales. *National Geographic, 161*(4), 463–476.
[*Superbly illustrated with photographs, this article describes the remarkable behavior of humpback whales.*]

Palmer, S. (1988). *Humpback whales.* Vero Beach, FL: Rourke Enterprises.
[*Small book that introduces students to humpback whales—what they look like, their habits, diet, and habitat.*]

Papastavrou, V. (1993). *Eyewitness books: Whale.* New York: Alfred A. Knopf.
[*Superbly illustrated book about all aspects of whales, from evolution to myths and legends.*]

Patent, D. H. (1984). *Whales: Giants of the deep.* New York: Holiday House.
[*Informative book about whales, well illustrated with black-and-white photographs. Excellent source for student projects.*]

Patent, D. H. (1987). *All about whales.* New York: Holiday House.
[*A beginner's book about whales, well illustrated with black-and-white photographs, simply written text.*]

Patent, D. H. (1989). *Humpback whales.* New York: Holiday House.
[*This book focuses on the humpback whale and is superbly illustrated with color photographs. The text is quite easy, making it suitable for less able readers.*]

Rinard, J. E. (1986). *Dolphins: Our friends of the sea; dolphins and other toothed whales.* Washington, DC: National Geographic Society.
[*An interesting book that looks at killer whales and dolphins in the oceans and in captivity. It also discusses the scientists who study whales and dolphins.*]

Robinson, J. W. (1992). *The whale in Lowell's Cove.* Camden, ME: Down East Books.
[*True story of a young humpback whale that swam into Lowell's Cove in Maine. Interspersed within the story are a number of interesting facts about whales. Beautifully illustrated.*]

Royston, A. (1989). *The whale.* New York: Warwick Press.
[*A book about the different kinds of whales, their behavior, and their habitats. It's a good introduction to this topic.*]

Sattler, H. R. (1987). *Whales: The nomads of the sea.* New York: Lothrop, Lee & Shepard.
[*This book is full of information about whales and includes Helen Sattler's own accounts of whale watching. It's an excellent reference for projects.*]

Silis, I. (1984). Narwhal hunters of Greenland. *National Geographic, 165*(4), 520–539.
[*Describes how the polar Eskimos hunt the narwhal whale.*]

Simon, S. (1989). *Whales.* New York: Thomas Y. Crowell.
[*This book comprises twenty color photographs with simple accompanying text that presents Seymour Simon's explanation of how whales have survived.*]

Smyth, K. C. (1986). *Crystal: The story of a real baby whale.* Camden, ME: Down East Books.
[*Story about the first year of a humpback whale's life. Superbly illustrated.*]

Stonehouse, B. (1978). *A closer look at whales and dolphins.* London: Gloucester Press.
[*This book, intended for children in grades four to six, presents detailed illustrations of whales with minimal text. Great as a resource for projects.*]

Swartz, S. L., & Jones, M. L. (1987). Gray whales at play in Baja's San Ignacio Lagoon. *National Geographic, 171*(6), 754–771.
[*Description of a research study on gray whales in Mexico's Baja California.*]

Waters, J. F. (1991). *Watching whales.* New York: Cobblehill Books.
[*Describes the natural life of whales and the fascination that humans have for watching them. Well illustrated with color photographs.*]

Van Bramer, J., & Scott, J. (1992). *Whale rap.* Crystal Lake, IL: Rigby.
[*Fascinating book, written partially as a "rap" song, and partially as a factual book about whales. Great idea for a student project on whales.*]

Videotapes/Films

National Geographic Society. (n. d.). *All whales are mammals.* [videocassette]. Washington, DC: National Geographic Society.

[This videotape is no longer available. We recommend using the other National Geographic videotapes listed below.]

National Geographic Society. (1976). *The right whale: An endangered species.* [videocassette]. Washington, DC: National Geographic Society.

National Geographic Society. (1978). *The great whale.* [videocassette]. Washington, DC: National Geographic Society.

National Geographic Society. (1979). *Whales.* [filmstrip]. Washington, DC: National Geographic Society.

National Geographic Society. (1993). *Killer Whale.* [videocassette]. Washington, DC: National Geographic Society.

Smithsonian Institute. (1988). *Magnificent whales and other marine mammals.* [videocassette]. Washington, DC: Smithsonian Institute.

Groups Associated with Whales

Center for Coastal Studies
59 Commercial Street
Provincetown, MA 02657

Center for Marine Conservation
1725 DeSales St., NW
Washington, DC 20036

Ocean Alliance
Ft. Mason Center, Bldg. E
San Francisco, CA 94123

Pacific Whale Foundation
Kealia Beach Plaza, Suite 25
101 N. Kihei Road
Kihei, HI 96753

Save the Whales
P. O. Box 3650
Washington, DC 20007

Whaling Museum Society
P. O. Box 25
Cold Spring Harbor, NY 11724

Chapter 7

Westward Movement: A Fifth Grade Theme

Joanne Kelly Paulson

In the spring of 1990, my fifth grade performed the Westward Movement Readers' Theater. In this performance, each student read aloud his or her own piece of writing, which was the culmination of several weeks of interdisciplinary study involving reading, writing, and social studies.

I was particularly satisfied with the writing component of this project. At its end, I felt that the students' writing reflected a knowledge and a sense of the 1800s, and exhibited more style than was evident in other writing projects we had attempted. It seemed to be a project that came together effectively.

In 1985, North Warren Central Schools reformed its language arts philosophy, setting aside traditional basal instruction as the primary language arts program. We integrated reading and writing, utilizing themes to make connections between literature and composition. Two kinds of themes are explored: themes that examine *concepts* such as survival or family, and themes drawn from *content areas* such as science (e.g., light and photography, endangered species), and social studies (e.g., immigration, Civil War), which use literature as the primary source for reading, writing, and discussion. In particular, content-area themes allow the class to follow a science or social studies concept through, from instruction in the basic facts to the deeper connections inherent in a topic. In a content-area theme, we encourage the students to read literature from a variety of genres in order to expand their knowledge of a subject. Historical fiction, primary source materials (diaries, logs, letters), standard reference materials, periodicals, and other sources provide a wealth of rich information that students rarely find in their social studies textbooks.

In the fifth grade, themes may run from a week (e.g., a mini-theme on mammals) to ten weeks (e.g., a major theme such as westward movement). During a major content area theme, we devote language arts and subject area periods exclusively to the theme. On some days, we rearrange the class schedule so that these periods run consecutively, yielding lengthy blocks of time for the theme.

What I'm really trying to accomplish through a content theme is to have students become more knowledgeable about what I think are important scientific or historical topics. This is the primary goal. Students can't become

217

more knowledgeable unless they read widely, read deeply, and enjoy their reading; unless they write widely and enjoy their writing; and unless they engage in a variety of language activities (e.g., performing and sharing). Learning about content and improving one's reading and writing skills are interwoven; reading and writing are essential to learning content, and knowledge of content immeasurably improves reading and writing.

I start each theme by trying to lay down a core of information about the theme. I do this with guided readings of full-length pieces and other materials that I've chosen. Once the core has been established—this takes about two to three weeks—I then shift the focus of instruction to the students themselves, inviting them to select aspects of the topic that they want to explore on their own. In this phase of the theme, each student gathers materials from the classroom, school, and public libraries, and then settles into a period of extensive independent reading, taking notes on what has been read. In the next phase, students will draft a written narrative that explores an aspect of their topic, and they will take this draft through revision and editing stages. In the final phase, these narratives are used as the basis for a dramatic presentation. I readily concede that themes start off being highly teacher-directed. I know of no other way to delve into an historical theme in which students have such meager prior knowledge or interest, yet I know from experience that once they get into the topic, they will become very enthusiastic, and the momentum will grow. Once they are hooked on the topic through activities I have chosen, the project takes on a life of its own, and the students take ownership of it. It's very hard to take ownership of something you know very little about or have little prior interest in.

Thus, I start each theme with guided reading. To do this, I have to find books and other materials that present worthwhile and useful information about topics, are neither too hard nor too easy for them to read, and are enjoyable and satisfying for students to read. Guided reading of a full-length work, as well as shorter pieces, occupies most of the allotted reading time in the first weeks of a theme. As the students become more familiar with the topic, they make the transition from guided reading to independent reading. Multiple copies of books, articles, and other materials related to the theme are made available to students for reading on their own; they are also encouraged to explore other sources available to them in local libraries, museums, and personal collections. Independent reading then becomes the major reading activity. (An annotated list of some of these sources is provided in the References section at the end of this chapter.)

Students write every day in our program. During a theme, the writing is focused on various aspects of the theme; students will normally write several shorter pieces and one major written narrative. The guided reading, classroom discussions, role-playing, and content area textbook all serve as stimuli for the shorter written pieces; the longer piece is generally drawn from the student's own research.

In addition to the reading and writing, students will be engaged in a number of other language related activities such as reader's theater, role-playing, map making, creating time lines, and building bulletin boards.

When I joined the staff as reading teacher in 1986, the fifth grade had just begun reforming its language arts program, and the staff had already developed the kernel of a theme, "The Westward Movement." As the reading teacher, I was assigned to work with the fifth grade; the classroom teacher and I collaborated on implementing the theme. It was a broad theme, and it included the many events and trends of the 1800s leading to the development of the American West (e.g., the Pony Express, the Oregon Trail, the Transcontinental Railroad, homesteaders, pioneers). For three years, the classroom teacher and I worked together on this theme, learning what worked and what didn't, adding new books, creating new activities. In 1987, my husband and I took a trip west during the summer vacation. Originally, our plan was simply to travel west, but having spent so many hours with the fifth grade students reading about the Oregon trail, we decided to add a wagon train experience to our journey. We spent three days on a wagon train, another three days at a mountain man rendezvous, and viewed and photographed the remains of the Oregon Trail. It was an unforgettable experience, and I was able to bring back many personal observations for the students. In 1990, the fifth grade classroom teacher moved away to New Jersey, and I moved into her classroom position. I have done the westward movement theme twice since becoming the fifth grade teacher, once in 1990, and again in 1993. In the intervening years, I did a Civil War theme, following the same basic format.

TEACHING THE WESTWARD MOVEMENT THEME

The district had purchased multiple copies of four books that could be used for whole-class guided reading for the westward movement theme. They each offered a different perspective on the broad theme of the development of the west, and each were valuable in stimulating interest in the history of the time. *Save Queen of Sheba* (Moeri, 1981) relates the tragedy that sometimes befell wagon trains. *Caddie Woodlawn* (Brink, 1935) is a pioneer story much like the *Little House* series; the family is forging a life in a new territory, facing all the rigors and adventures of such an endeavor. *Moccasin Trail* (McGraw, 1952) interrelates the experiences of mountain men, Indians, and the early pioneers in a saga of the old west. *Sing Down the Moon* (O'Dell, 1970) explores the plight of the Navajo who were forced from their homeland in what came to be known as the Long Walk.

In our class I selected the novel *Sing Down the Moon* to be read together as guided reading. As we read each chapter, we noted that although the book was fiction, many facts and names were drawn from history. This added a human perspective to the facts and figures of our textbook. Tall Boy was a person to be cared about, not a fact to be memorized.

On alternate days, students were encouraged to read independently from other full-length selections relating to the theme. They could choose from a bank of books, including the books described above, as well as other full-length books. Our program encourages different modes of reading, including directed reading of full-length and shorter works, independent reading, and selections that are read aloud.

We often read related shorter selections; for example, if Monday's lesson plan in social studies called for a discussion of the Lewis and Clark expedition through the Rockies, then during Monday's reading class, the class could share a short account of the expedition, or perhaps have a read aloud from the journals of Lewis and Clark. One might follow the reading lesson with a short writing assignment, for example, "From what you read this morning, what do you think was the scariest part of the expedition?" In this way reading, writing, and social studies are truly integrated.

Once I began to teach in this way, I noticed the wealth of resources that exist to illustrate subtopics of this theme. *Cobblestone*, a children's history magazine, has been an outstanding source for this and many other themes we have developed. The July 1989 issue is exclusively devoted to the Navajo Indians, with one article entitled "The Long Walk." The December 1981 issue deals with the Oregon Trail: The Whitman's Mission, Wagons on the Oregon Trail, The Great Desert Register, and so on. Each of the articles in the issue have an appropriate length and readability for fifth grade and are ideal for directed or independent reading or to be read aloud.

I like to seek out fictional works, in print or film, that have literary and/or entertainment value but that also depict accurately some historical aspect of the theme. We read a whimsical excerpt from the novel *By the Great Horn Spoon!* (Fleischman, 1963) that relates the antics of two gold-seekers in San Francisco in 1849. At first we read it for the enjoyment of a well-told tale. But later we went through it again, page by page, searching for any details that may have actually been true for the 49ers. We compiled this list during Social Studies class, once again integrating the disciplines. Here are the historical facts we learned from our short reading:

1. They used picks and shovels.
2. Miners came by boats.
3. San Francisco—the fastest growing city in the world—new buildings, crowded—peddlers selling supplies.
4. Very few supplies—all have to be shipped.
5. Prices were very high.
6. Get to the mines by mule, foot, stagecoach.
7. San Francisco—on the bay; gold—on the mountain.
8. Collect gold dust in a pan.
9. Gold is very heavy—sinks to the bottom of the pan.

10. "Color" means gold—yellow.

11. $14 an ounce.

As we all know well, these facts simply memorized from a textbook would be soon forgotten. By using a humorous piece of literature, the students internalized these facts quickly, as demonstrated by later class discussions and written essays.

This guided reading phase usually takes about three weeks.

Individual Student Exploration

Soon the stage was set for a meaty research/writing project. The class as a whole had acquired a general knowledge base on the broader theme of the westward movement. It was now time to brainstorm individual research topics. I asked the students if there were topics we had touched upon that they would like to know more about. The students generated close to fifty topics that I listed on the chalkboard as they were suggested. (Topics included Thomas Jefferson and the Louisiana Purchase, construction of wagons, San Francisco during the gold rush, Kit Carson's role in the Navajo removal, Santa Anna vs. Sam Houston, pioneers, homesteaders, Chief Joseph, and many, many others.)

Then we talked a bit about "what we know now" and "what we would like to know." I suggested that they chat in groups so they could sound out their ideas. For example, a student knew the "textbook" facts on the railroad, but was there more to the story? How long did it take to build? Who actually constructed it? Our textbook had no information on the Pony Express (and coincidentally, the television series "The Young Riders" had just run its first episodes), so we talked about this. What information do we have right now on the Pony Express? What would we like to know about it?

Because the culminating activity for this project was to perform a series of narratives as a readers' theater, I wanted to avoid repetition of topics. (The students did not know about the performance; they simply were selecting topics they wanted to know more about.) I made the rule that no two students could share the same topic, but they could research different aspects of a given topic. To facilitate this selection, as each student chose a topic for his or her own, I erased that choice from the chalkboard. The remaining choices were then visually apparent.

Time spent on topic selection was time well spent. If the student had no genuine interest in researching, then the entire project would fall flat for that student. I wanted to try to engage every student in meaningful reading right from the very beginning of the research.

I have an unproved theory of research motivation, which is somewhat akin to the carrot and the stick theory. Create the desire for resource material, but don't let the resources be available too easily or too soon! In our fifth grade, we selected topics. Eyes were lighting up, our hearts were happy as we marched to the school library to find the perfect references. But alas, our efforts were in vain; there just didn't seem to be enough books on our topics. (I was well aware that this would happen.)

About forty-five minutes away by school bus exists the most wonderful solution for our kids: Crandall Library in Glens Falls, New York. Mr. Jim Karge, children's librarian, has been an invaluable friend and mentor, and his library has a well stocked supply of fiction and nonfiction.

When these crestfallen fifth graders bemoaned the lack of resources in our school library, that was the moment to suggest, "Maybe we could schedule a trip to Crandall Library. Would you like to go there?"

Perhaps it was manipulative, but I have found that it works every time! Mr. Karge greeted twenty-five kids ravenous for literature on their topics. A quick lesson on the new-and-improved computerized card catalog prepared the students to scour the library. They found dozens of books—biographies, historical fiction, geography texts, journals of pioneers—and each was a treasure to be cherished later in the classroom.

The next morning, we spread out our treasures, our books from Crandall Library. For twenty-five students, we had borrowed close to one hundred books. Never were my kids more intense than they were that morning. Free reading meant just that. There was no note taking, no "work" in their minds. They were absorbed in the joy of reading these wonderful books that we had to wait for. And this was not a short-lived joy. They continued to treat their silent reading time as something special, and groaned when we had to return to "work."

It was interesting (and very rewarding!) to watch students begin to "own" their topics. Before we started the research, each student listed what he or she knew about the topic and what he/she would like to know. All twenty-five students shared these ideas aloud; often during the course of the project we would share aloud the status of our work. Ownership developed very quickly. During silent reading time, one could often hear stage whispers: "Psst! I found two pages on Sutter's Mill. Do you want me to save this book for you?" or "Hey, I found a great map of the railroad. Do you want to trace it?"

At this point, the students did not know what the final outcome of this project (i.e., the Readers' Theater) was going to be. They were simply reading to acquire information on their chosen topic, and after all, isn't that the purpose of reading in the real world?

Note taking is the most difficult task of all. Fifth graders do not find it easy to paraphrase, nor do they easily identify the most important idea from prose filled with examples and illustrations. We spent a bit of time talking about informal outline style, using abbreviations and headings. I told them they shouldn't write in paragraphs in their note taking. Even complete sentences were to be avoided—just the opposite of the writing teacher's usual warnings! We talked about trying to put notes "in our own words," but for some this is almost an impossible task. However, if students are not allowed to copy out paragraphs, they have to search for some little bit of information that might be the most important. Brevity was praised; copying sentences was not.

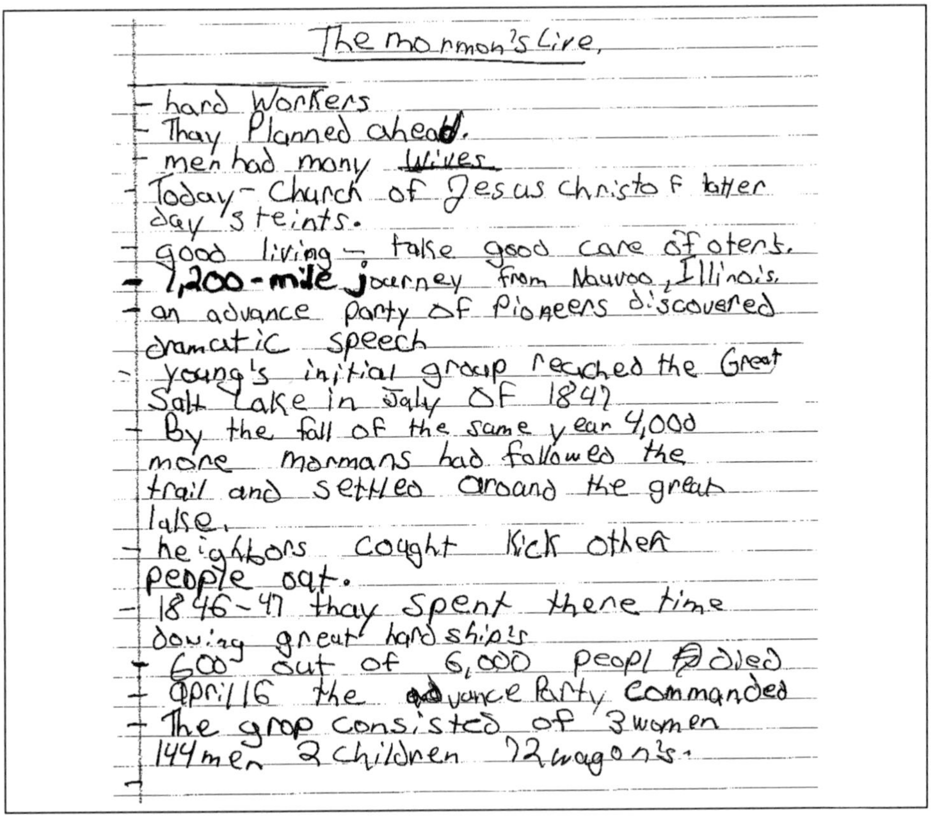

The mormon's Live,

- hard workers
- Thay Planned ahead.
- men had many wives
- Today - Church of Jesus christo F later day's teints.
- good living — take good care of otent.
- 1,200-mile journey from Nauvoo, Illinois.
- an advance party of pioneers discovered dramatic speech
- young's initial group reached the Great Salt lake in July of 1847
- By the fall of the same year 4,000 more mormans had followed the trail and settled around the great lake.
- heighbors cought Kick other people out.
- 1846-47 thay spent there time douing great hard ships
- 600 out of 6,000 peopl died
- April 16 the advance Party commanded
- The grop consisted of 3 women 144 men 2 children 72 wagons.

FIGURE 7–1. Ray's Notes on the Mormon Trail.

I first practiced this task early in the theme by having the whole class silently read a short selection on the Navajo. Then, before discussing or writing anything, they reread the entire selection silently. Again with no discussion of the text, I collected the readings from them, and asked them to make notes grouping facts with headings and abbreviating wherever possible. I admit that the first attempts were not as thorough as they might be, but much more importantly, the notes were in the kids' own words. For the first time, they were paraphrasing! We used this technique a few more times with other related readings, and students' note-taking skills improved measurably. Figure 7–1 is an example of one student's notes on the Mormon Trail.

Sharing the students' notes on the short class readings, either orally or on an overhead projector, had two benefits in terms of the overall project. First, it continued the instruction and practice in good note-taking techniques. Second, it reinforced another "westward" topic in their shared bank of information, which proved to be invaluable in later class discussions. Had we run the usual outline lesson from a more traditional English grammar text, we would have lost that opportunity for real reading and extending their knowledge of the broader theme.

I believe we should allow ample time for free reading and note taking before the actual rough draft writing begins. I allot as much time as I can possibly justify for the reading/note-taking component of the project. It seems to me that the quality and style of the students' writing is directly proportional to the amount of time allotted for resource reading. We are talking weeks, not hours! This time allotment is not wasted time by any means, as long as the students are genuinely reading for information and not losing momentum.

We spend four weeks in this independent work, with an occasional guided reading or writing activity added as needed. I also like to show topical videos in this phase as a supplement to the reading/writing experience. I always enjoy the students' enthusiasm as they jump up and say, "I'm reading about this! I know all about this!"

During the independent reading/note-taking phase of the project, I've had to be flexible in allowing the students the freedom to work at their own pace, and in their own manner. One girl read novels almost exclusively to learn information about life in the plains. Her knowledge was thorough, and she read with an uninterrupted intensity that surpassed the others. Yet, her written notes were not as voluminous as some. Another girl was much more involved in searching through nonfiction for all the details on her topic; she took copious notes.

I am often asked how differently-abled students fare in a project like this. Two of my students currently in the Chapter I remedial reading program collaborated on their research, reading sources aloud together, and sharing their notes. Following their collaboration, they were able to compose well written, individual pieces on their topic. Sometimes it is hard for a traditionally-trained teacher to allow for that simultaneous variety of activity—some reading silently, some writing notes, some reading aloud in the corner or out in the corridor, some browsing through the collection of resources. I have found that by allowing each child to shape the independent reading/note-taking according to his or her own needs, more learning takes place.

At a certain point, I knew my students had become experts on their topics. Everyone in class knew if they had a question on the Pony Express, they should consult Christian. Kate had the facts on the Santa Fe Trail; Fletcher had mastered the Gold Rush. But what now? Write encyclopedia-like reports based upon their notes? What a mundane task for these "experts"!

We talked about point of view. We talked about the difference between the Indians' and the pioneers' point of view on the Homestead Act. We discussed Kit Carson's point of view vs. the Navajo in reference to the Long Walk. I prepared and handed out a set of guidelines for writing up the research project (see Figure 7–2). I encouraged each student to tell the story of his or her research from the point of view of someone—be it positive or negative—from the 1800s.

"This is my point of view."

There are many different ways of looking at the same event. For example,

The Long Walk < the Indians' point of view
                Kit Carson's point of view

The Oregon Migration < the pioneers
                       the mountain men
                       the Indians
                       the US government

Write an essay from the point of view of someone in the 1800s. Tell the story of your topic through their eyes.

You, yourself, do _not_ have to agree with that person! For example, you may relate Kit Carson's point of view, and you may not agree with him.

① What is your topic? _____

② From whose point of view will you tell your story? _____

③ Briefly — what is your point of view?
_____

FIGURE 7–2. Teacher's Guidelines for Research Project.

Again, we chatted in small groups. We discussed the intriguing possibilities of the task. "Well, we know how the railroad men felt about the railroad. But how did the Indians feel?" And so on.

The students did not need to copy their notes into the usual social studies report. As a matter of fact, I asked them to leave their notes in their desks and just write their stories, their personal, well researched narratives, with just a clean sheet of paper on their desks (see Figures 7–3, 7–4, and 7–5).

Steven researched the natural monuments that existed along the Oregon Trail in Nebraska and Wyoming. He described them from the point of view of a wagon master on the 1800s.

Kate researched the Santa Fe Trail; she called herself Cactus Needles, and she spoke of the foolish white man on her family's land.

Kristin had researched the life of Buffalo Bill Cody. She did not choose to speak as Buffalo Bill. Instead, she wrote in the voice of Annie Oakley, looking back on the contributions of her boss.

The students wrote with personality and with flair. Their stories conveyed the excitement, the pathos, the human experience they had found in their

FIGURE 7–3.
Excerpt From
Kate's
Research on
the Santa Fe
Trail.

The Santa Fe Trail.
By: Kate Chalosch

I am Nocturs Needles. My father says there are too many white men coming from the north. He says they talk of building a trail to a place they call Santa Fe, and Albequerque.

Already, many people come and try to steal Pawnee water. My father says they are bad medicine for the land. White men do not look for snakes and get bit. They try to trade animal fur for bow and arrows. They carry big guns and try to shoot us Pawnee.

They talk of great riches we have. We tell them nothing. William Becknell goes to Santa Fe many times. Father says we must embush them soon. He talks of precious stones there.

Father says there are people called mountain men who come to trade. He says they make places called saloons in a place called Taos. Other white men try to steal trader man's horses. →

White men talk of a place called "New Mexico." Father says other kind of white men hurt the Anasazi long ago. He says that is why we do not trust the white man.

FIGURE 7–4.
Excerpt from
Christian's
Research
on the Pony
Express.

I am Bill cody I ride for the
Pony Express. I earn $25 a week and
ride an average of ten miles in one
hour. I carry 2 colt revolvers but I
have the option of 1 light rifel and 1
colt revolver.

The Pony Express is a system to
carry mail from st. josiph mossouri to
Sacramento california, it consists of stations
ten miles apart and relays where men go
from one horse to another. The Pony Express
is owned by Russell Majors and crandell.
It has 190 relay stations 165 swing statio
ns, and used 500 select horses worth
$200 each.

A rider would come into sight
He rounded the house, I got ready, The
rider was here. He jumped off with
the mochila and gave it to me. I
flung it over my horse, got on and
was off. I moch

A mochila is a piece of leath
er that has two pockets on each side
It has a hole in it so I can slide i

FIGURE 7–5.
*Excerpt from
Jerry's
Research on
Chief Crazy
Horse.*

Jerry Van Wilder   Writing
April 22.   Mrs. Paulson

How! my name is chief Crazy Horse,
Chief of the Sioux. I live out here in this
great land that belongs to all. I am a fast
rider on horse and can kill any raging buffalo.
In my tipi, I have the finest buffalo
hides in the whole Sioux nation. My
people say I have the finest feathers, which
I put in my hair. I wear the finest buffalo
skin pants with red, yellow, and blue beads on
them.
     The whole Sioux nation agrees with
me, we should get rid of the white man
before he gets rid of us with his Iron Horse."
     "We must, we must," said Chief Sitting Bull.
He was the head of all the chiefs of the Sioux.
     "I know we should, but if we do they'll only
attack us." I said. But inside I really wanted
to get the white man and stop his Iron Horse
from slaughtering our buffalo before the people of
our tribes weren't able to survive. Then it
came upon me thats what the white man
wanted, if he killed all our buffalo then we

readings. Their writings expressed a sense of reality based upon their knowledge, rather than cartoon caricatures that might have been written by less sophisticated authors.

I feel that the fascinating aspect of these pieces of writing, and the significance for a book such as this collection for teachers, is that none of the writings resembled the owner's notes. No piece was copied from any source. Every single writing was truly generated creatively, and from the student's knowledge base that almost entirely came from research.

A second factor, which I feel is significant, is that these pieces were drafted incredibly fast. Most of the authors listened to the discussion about point of view, chatted briefly in groups to establish their focus, and then in fifteen or twenty minutes of actual writing created the essence of superior essays. A project that consisted of several weeks of prewriting experiences wrapped up the rough draft in a class or two!

From this point, the writing class was probably similar to any process writing class. Students shared their rough drafts with teacher or peers. We held conferences for content, then for editing, and then students wrote their final copies.

It might be interesting to take a look at two students working their way through the process just described. These two students are representative of the typical students in our fifth grades.

When selecting topics, Brandi expressed a desire to learn about the Oregon Trail. Billy said he was interested in the Gold Rush in California. They had each learned a basic core of information about their general area of interest from the directed reading phase of the project.

We can see from Brandi's reading log that her first full-length selections, *Frontier Dream* (Chambers, 1984b), and *Sarah, Plain and Tall* (MacLachlan, 1985), related generally to the pioneer experience. (The reading log is a record of full-length works read during independent reading time.) Then she chose to read a short biography of Narcissa Whitman (Sabin, 1982). It was at this point that she narrowed her focus. She no longer read about pioneers in general, but now she read for more information on the first woman to travel the Oregon Trail. Her reading log then cited two additional books, which were both collections of stories about famous people, and the pages listed refer to chapters on her newly refined topic, Narcissa Whitman (see Figure 7–6).

Similarly, Billy's topic was a bit general at first. In February, before our topic selection activities began, he had been reading books from our collection of theme titles, *Frontier Dream* (Chambers, 1984b), *Pioneer Cat* (Hooks, 1988), and *Sarah, Plain and Tall* (MacLachlan, 1985). In early March, Billy started skimming through many sources we had borrowed on the Gold Rush from Crandall Library, but because he was not reading full chapters, he didn't record them in his log. During this time, he alternated between research, (e.g., perusing the charts, maps, and illustrations about the Gold Rush) and reading, (e.g., finishing *Sarah, Plain and Tall*). I didn't worry that some pages were not recorded in the

FIGURE 7–6.
Excerpt from
Brandi's
Reading Log.

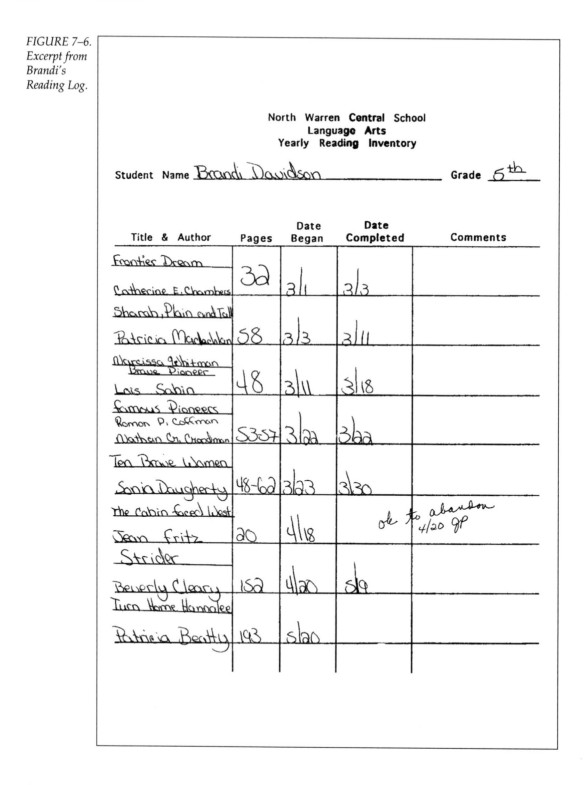

North Warren **Central** School
Language Arts
Yearly Reading Inventory

Student Name Brandi Davidson   Grade 5th

Title & Author	Pages	Date Began	Date Completed	Comments
Frontier Dream Catherine E. Chambers	32	3/1	3/3	
Sharah, Plain and Tall Patricia MacLachlan	58	3/3	3/11	
Narcissa Whitman Brave Pioneer Lois Sabin	48	3/11	3/18	
Famous Pioneers Ramon P. Coffman Nathan G. Goodman	5357	3/22	3/22	
Ten Brave Women Sonia Daugherty	48-62	3/23	3/30	
The Cabin Faced West Jean Fritz	20	4/18		ok to abandon 4/20 JP
Strider Beverly Cleary	152	4/20	5/9	
Turn Home Hannalee Patricia Beatty	193	5/20		

log since it was apparent that he was truly engaged in the research, poring over books beyond his reading level, and gleaning many facts that he shared regularly at my desk. "Mrs. Paulson, did you know that the miners used...?" By mid-March he was reading books on his topic, and he, too, began to focus more on the miners themselves, fascinated by their techniques and lifestyle (see Figure 7–7).

Brandi took notes from *Famous Pioneers for Young People* (Coffman, 1945) in a manner that I encourage. Her notes are not paragraphs copied from a text, but they are short bits of information she considered important. She did a fine job of identifying critical facts and paring them down into brief statements. I really like Billy's notes from *The Great American Gold Rush* (Blumberg, 1989); they get right to the point. His outline style may not come straight out of an English grammar book, but he certainly was able to record his notes accurately with appropriate groupings and headings, and his notes were very useful to him in writing his piece about gold miners. Both students were able to handle the difficult task of note taking, avoiding the plagiarizing tendency of most fifth graders (see Figures 7–8 and 7–9).

Once we began the "point of view" discussions, Billy and Brandi were well prepared to write a piece filled with factual information gleaned from their research. They had internalized their topics enough that writing the essay was an easy and enjoyable task. Fun-loving Billy, and Brandi, sensitive to the cares of others, show us much of their own personalities in the final products (see Figures 7–10 and 7–11).

Presenting the Projects

In 1990, one of our objectives was to provide narratives for a Westward Movement Readers' Theater to be performed for the parents. Throughout the year, we had been learning a few tunes that related to our stories. And we had rather long narratives, which taken all together were quite impressive. Most of the narratives needed to be edited in the interest of time since we had twenty-five speakers. We went into rehearsal during language arts class time, reciting our stories and practicing in small groups to save time. We grouped the speakers according to topic and chronological history. Everyone was a performer and a coach! When our Home and Careers teacher heard of our project, she offered to teach the children to make sourdough biscuits, and the enthusiasm began to grow.

Finally we were ready. A narrator introduced the presentation. The first speakers were Thomas Jefferson discussing the Louisiana Purchase, followed by members of the Lewis and Clark Expedition. Of course, all students were in costume, but we performed with no props in a rather formal, stylized format. All students were on stage throughout, and at their given times, stood to address the audience in their groupings. A few lively tunes provided segues

FIGURE 7–7.
Excerpt from
Billy's
Reading Log.

North Warren Central School
Language Arts
Yearly Reading Inventory

Student Name BillyTrudsoe   Grade 5

Title & Author	Pages	Date Began	Date Completed	Comments
frontier Dream Catherine E. Chambers	32	feb 26	feb 26	
Pioneercat William Hooks	62	feb 26 ~~Feb 6~~	March 4	
Sarah plain and tall patriciamclachlan	58	March 4	march 8	
The Great American gold Rush	133	march 10	March 15	
Dame shirley and the gold Rush Jim rawls	55	march 17	March 25	
SacaJawea Kate Jassem	48	march 30	March 30	
Stone fox John Gardiner	81	march 30	~~April~~ april 29	
michHnEL JorDan Devra Newberger	44	may 3	May 5	
Patrich Ewing Bruce weber	44	may 5	MAY 14	

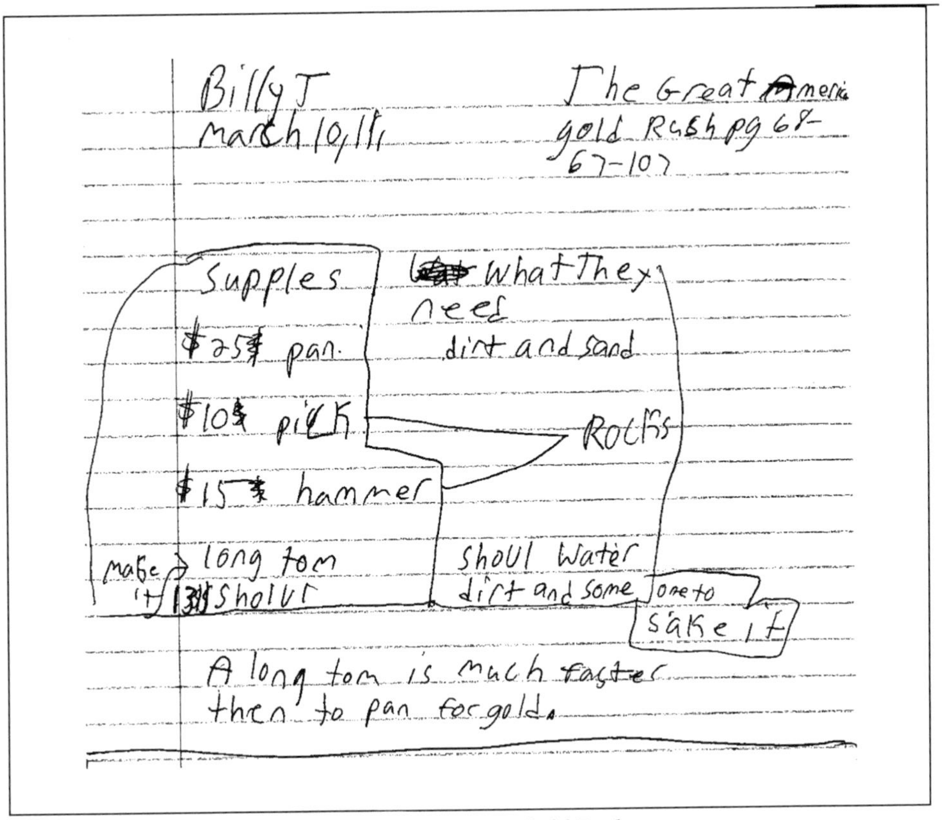

Billy T
March 10, 11

The Great Americ
gold Rush pg 6?-
67-107

Supples   What They
                 need
25 pan.   dirt and sand

10 pick   Rocks

15 hammer

make→ long tom   shoul water
if 3 sholvl   dirt and some one to
                            sake it

A long tom is much faster
then to pan for gold.

FIGURE 7–8. *Billy's Notes on* The Great American Gold Rush.

between groups of characters. We sang "Fifty Nifty United States" as a finale, and then invited our audience to share in the sourdough biscuits we had made.

Needless to say, the students enjoyed this kind of activity. The parents were also happy with the performance. Personally I felt it provided a satisfying closure to a lengthy and educationally stimulating project.

In 1993, we followed essentially the same reading/writing format, but the end product was slightly different. The whole-class directed reading, note taking, and individual research was pretty much the same as the project just described. However, rather than a scripted Readers' Theater, we performed what we called the Western Jamboree. We began with a short presentation introducing each child, not by his or her own name, but instead, "We would like to introduce Narcissa Whitman. She was the first white woman to travel west in a wagon. With her today is a Mormon girl...." This presentation also included a few tunes such as cowboy and railroad songs easily found in most standard elementary music textbooks.

Since our middle school stage was unavailable to us at that time, we borrowed another classroom; it was quite large and had little furniture. We set

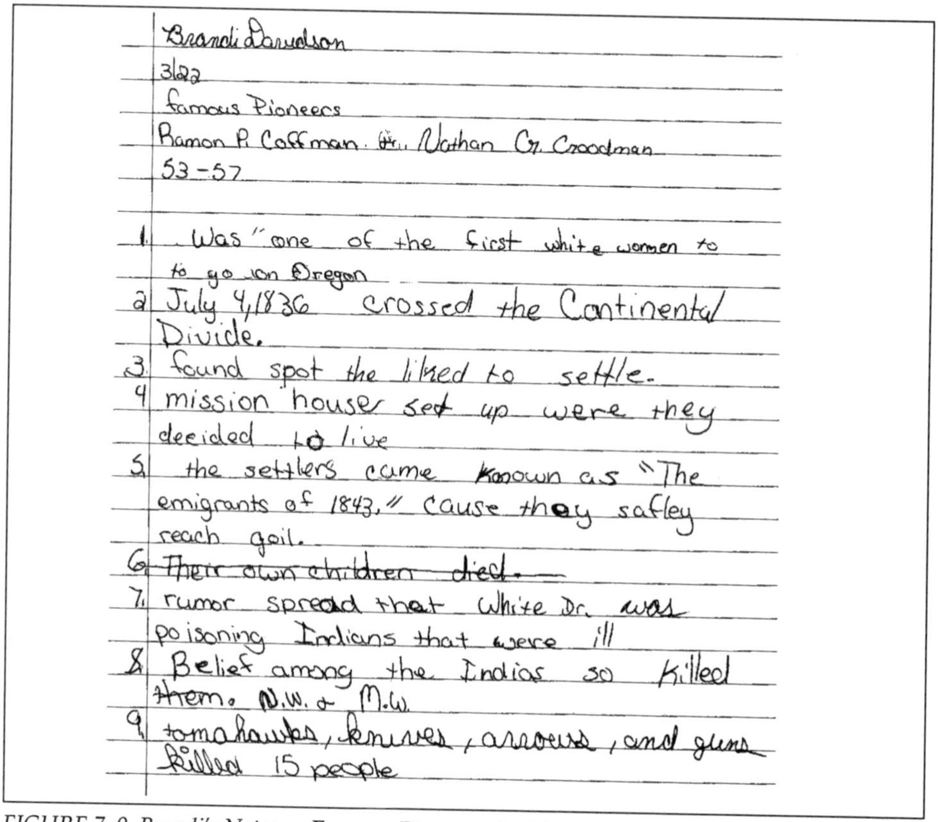

Brandi Danielson
3/22
Famous Pioneers
Ramon P. Coffman. &. Nathan G. Goodman
53–57

1. Was "one of the first white women to to go on Oregon
2. July 4, 1836 crossed the Continental Divide.
3. found spot the liked to settle.
4. mission house set up were they decided to live
5. the settlers came known as "The emigrants of 1843." cause they safley reach goil.
6. ~~Their own children died.~~
7. rumor spread that White Dr. was poisoning Indians that were ill
8. Belief among the Indias so killed them. N.W. & M.W.
9. tomahawks, knives, arrows, and guns killed 15 people

FIGURE 7–9. Brandi's Notes on Famous Pioneers for Young People.

up folding chairs in rows facing one wall where the short opening presentation took place. Following that, the audience chairs were removed from the room, and the parents were invited to browse around. The students had created eight stations along the walls and corners, complete with props, paraphernalia, and costumes to physically represent the characters they were portraying. For example, four students investigated various aspects of the Sioux Indians during the 1800s. They set up a small teepee, a Styrofoam buffalo, and a map of the Great Plains. They each chose an Indian name and responded to visitors in the character of the Sioux.

Meriwether Lewis, Sacajawea, and Thomas Jefferson chose to meet in front of the White House. The pioneer girls created a very effective covered wagon from a child's red wagon and painted "Oregon or bust" on its side.

Each student was prepared to answer a variety of questions about his or her role in the development of western United States. The students were very knowledgeable about their own topics. They enjoyed role-playing, and they performed exceptionally well, incorporating all sorts of props and western drawls, and colorfully portraying the knowledge they had acquired. It was

FIGURE 7–10.
*Excerpt from
Billy's Final
Copy of his
Report.*

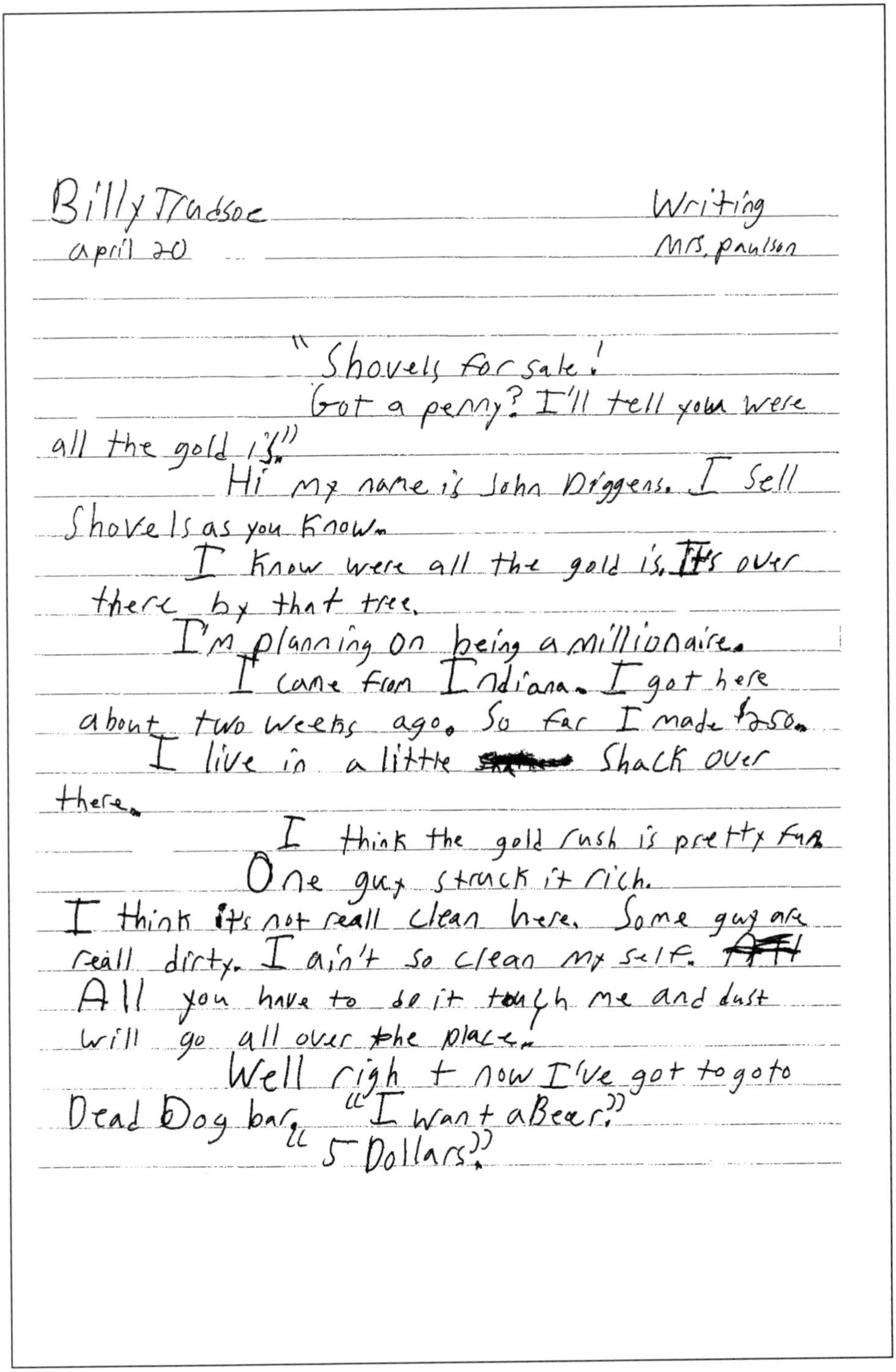

Billy Tradsoc   Writing
april 20   Mrs. paulson

            " Shovels for sale.'
        Got a penny? I'll tell you were
all the gold is.''
            Hi my name is John Diggens. I sell
Shovels as you know.
            I know were all the gold is. It's over
there by that tree.
            I'm planning on being a millionaire.
            I came from Indiana. I got here
about two weeks ago. So far I made $250.
            I live in a little ~~shack~~ Shack over
there.
                    I think the gold rush is pretty fun.
            One guy struck it rich.
I think it's not reall clean here. Some guy are
reall dirty. I ain't so clean my self. ~~All~~
All you have to do it touch me and dust
will go all over the place.
            Well righ t now I've got to go to
Dead Dog bar. "I want a Bear.''
            " 5 Dollars.''

FIGURE 7–11.
Excerpt from
Brandi's Final
Copy of her
Report.

Brandi Davidson   Writing
April 21   Mrs. Paulson

I'm Narcissa Whitman. When I was a little girl
we had missionaries over for dinner one night. They told
my two brothers and me the lots of adventures they had
on their trips. It really sounded fun so I decided I wanted
to be a missionary when I grew up. My parents didn't think
I could do it but I proved them wrong.

The year 1835 I was married to Dr. Marcus Whitman.
I wanted to marry him because he tells about God too.
The night we were married we left to go westward
for our honeymoon. At first I had my doubts and I
really was really nervous nervous nervous to but Marcus
calmed me down.

July 4, 1836 Marcus and I crossed the Continental
Divide. Continental Divide is in the Rocky Mountains and
a ridge divides divided rivers or streams that flow to opposite
sides of a continent.

Marcus and I found a spot that we could settle. It was a
nice place and cozy. A mission house was set up where we
decided to live. The house was really warm inside inside
and kind of crowded. After we settled there we were called
"The emigrants of 1843." because we safely reached
our goal.

The year 1847 all the missionaries brought measles and an
epidemic suddenly broke out. One after the other, the Indians
broke out with them and died.

When Marcus was fixing up people and I was teaching,
a rumor was spread that my husband was
poisoning Indians. The Indians believed the rumor
so the Indians reached the mission house and killed
15 of us. We were killed with tomahawks, knives, arrows,
and guns. We were also killed November 29, 1847.

exciting to see the characters come alive. (By the way, this was a low-budget project; there was no cost to the school. For costumes, most students got by with their parents' flannel shirts or long skirts. Props were very easy to obtain. Billy used a Chinese wok to demonstrate panning!)

ASSESSMENT

In 1990, I assigned a letter grade to each component part of the project; these letter grades were used in part to determine the reading, writing, and social studies grades on the report card. I wasn't very happy with this procedure, however. Should ten pages of written notes earn more credit than one or two pages? Does a list of fifteen shorter books read earn more credit than one really lengthy book? Luckily, since then our school district made the shift from numerical or letter grades to a narrative report card. Now at report card time, I ask myself this question of each child: Has this child's knowledge truly grown as a result of focused and careful independent research? I look at several factors for measurement, including the quality and quantity of notes, the quality and quantity of actual pages read, the actual usage of the notes in the final piece of writing, and also the ability of the student to verbally share that new knowledge with others in preparing for the presentation.

Throughout the project I meet with the students formally in conferences to discuss what they have read recently, and I informally meet with them numerous times for short chats, especially by the classroom library shelves when they are looking for another book on their topic. I try to assess the project holistically, rather than assign each component a certain amount of credit. Therefore, the child who reads so many novels on her topic would not be penalized for having a different kind of note-taking style than the child who devoured the nonfiction shelf, recording reams of facts. I look at each child individually and describe their growth in all these areas in a narrative report.

To assess the theme as a whole, I turn to the students themselves. Prior to the rehearsal phase of this project, I asked my students to verbalize their evaluation of our study so far. (Had I waited, they would have written about nothing but music and props!) One remedial student wrote, "The part that made me learn more was doing work with my friends and not just working out of the textbook. I think the textbook is hard and confusing. The part I enjoyed the most was probably the group work because you're not afraid to ask questions to your friends."

He went on to say something that appeared in many of the students' responses. "The writing part was easy because we went over everything and so it made it really easy. I studied about it a lot." I would not have predicted that given the large amount of reading, note taking, and writing, nearly all of the students would characterize the project as "easy."

Billy was much more succinct. "We did it the fun way. We did not have to use the textbook."

And there you have it. If you can release the curriculum from the traditional basal approach, from the usual reading, language, and content-area textbooks, then the students are liberated to learn, and, more importantly, they retain ever so much more knowledge. I suspect these students will remember for a long time the information they stored in their minds for the presentation. Amanda wrote, "I think you learn more because everybody has different topics and we share them with everybody. So we get to learn about different people at the same time."

One might wonder if the students grew in language arts as well as in their knowledge of history. Here is Jenny's response. "I like my writing that I wrote from the notes. That was fun because we got to change our name, voice, clothing and house. I liked living in Oregon. My last writing was better than the notes." And she was absolutely right!

REFLECTIONS

I feel that this basic framework could work quite well for many areas of student research. Admittedly I have researched the westward theme quite thoroughly through travel and reading. Yet a teacher who wanted to begin such a project would not have to invest months and years of research. I would suggest that he or she must have some basic knowledge through reading beforehand, and have a genuine interest in the theme and its subtopics. For example, I have used the same format to implement a similar project on the topic of the Civil War. In order to prepare, I needed to do some reading over the summer and acquire multiple copies of a few appropriate paperbacks, many of which came from book clubs. Once I had that, all the techniques described here—the library trip, note-taking lessons, reading, discussion of point of view—transferred very easily.

As I look back, I think there are several things that contribute to the success of this theme. First of all, whenever possible, I believe we should allow the students to make choices. However, we must create an environment in which the students acquire a broad knowledge base *before* they select specific topics to research. The reason the students thoughtfully selected each topic for research was because they truly wanted to learn more about that topic. (In my past experience, pulling teacher-written topics from a hat has been a dismal failure!)

Second, students need access to grade-appropriate and interesting materials. These materials will have to include real literature, not just textbooks. One of the things I've learned by doing this theme is the wealth of fiction and nonfiction literature available on this topic. It takes a little work to find it, but it's well worth the effort.

Most important of all, the students need the time to read, absorb, digest, and internalize the materials. Students need to have their own bank of knowledge in order to write and present their projects with assurance. Once that happens, even the most reluctant writers will find that they have quite a bit to say!

REFERENCES

Abell, E. (1958). *Westward, westward, westward.* New York: Franklin Watts. [*One chapter, "Ordeal by Handcart," provides information on the Mormon experience walking from the East to Salt Lake City.*]

Blumberg, R. (1989). *The great American gold rush.* New York: Bradbury Press. [*An informative book about the gold seekers in California in the mid 1800s.*]

Brink, C. R. (1935). *Caddie Woodlawn.* New York: Macmillan. [*A true story related by Caddie's granddaughter. It depicts the adventures of a pioneer family learning to survive with the land, the Indians, and their neighbors. Caddie's escapades appeal to fifth graders.*]

Buehr, W. (1963). *Westward with American explorers.* New York: Putnam's. [*This book has several chapters relevant to the theme (e.g., Lewis and Clark expedition, pushing westward, westward tide), which could be read aloud or used as the basis for a history lesson.*]

Chambers, C. E. (1984a). *Flatboats on the Ohio: Westward bound.* Mahwah, NJ: Troll Associates. [*This and the other Chambers books listed here comprise a series of 32-page illustrated stories called "Adventures in Frontier America."*]

Chambers, C. E. (1984b). *Frontier dream: Life on the great plains.* Mahwah, NJ: Troll Associates.

Chambers, C. E. (1984c). *Frontier farmer: Kansas adventures.* Mahwah, NJ: Troll Associates.

Chambers, C. E. (1984d). *Frontier village: A town is born.* Mahwah, NJ: Troll Associates.

Chambers, C. E. (1984e). *Wagons west: Off to Oregon.* Mahwah, NJ: Troll Associates.

Cobblestone. (1981), 2(12), 4–48.
[*The entire issue is worthwhile, as several articles illustrate different aspects of the Oregon Trail.*]

Coffman, R. P. (1945). *Famous pioneers for young people.* New York: Dodd, Mead & Co.
[*Biographical accounts of a number of early pioneers, written in a fairly simple style.*]

Conrad, P. (1985). *Prairie songs.* New York: Harper & Row.
[*Louisa's life in a loving pioneer family on the Nebraska prairie is altered by the arrival of a new doctor and his beautiful, tragically frail wife.*]

Conrad, P. (1991). *Prairie visions: The life and times of Solomon Butcher.* New York: Scholastic, Inc.
[*A nonfiction account of one of the earliest photographers to document life on the prairie. Its anecdotes show much of the character of the frontiersmen and women.*]

Eisenberg, L. (1991). *Sitting Bull, Great Sioux Chief.* New York: Dell.
[*Depicts the Sioux way of life in the 1800s. An enjoyable and easy read for fifth grade.*]

Erdoes, R. (1978). *The Native Americans: Navajos.* New York: Sterling.
[*A colorful and informative resource describing the history and land of the Navajo, including traditional and modern life.*]

Fleischman, S. (1963). *By the great horn spoon!* Boston: Little, Brown.
[*This book recounts the antics of two gold seekers in San Francisco in 1849.*]

Freedman, R. (1983). *Children of the wild West.* New York: Scholastic.
[*A rich reference filled with black-and-white photographs, describing the skills, activities, schools, homes, etc. of nineteenth century children.*]

Freedman, R. (1988). *Buffalo hunt.* New York: Holiday House.
[*Examines the importance of buffaloes in the day-to-day life of the Indian tribes of the Great Plains.*]

Grant, B. (1971). *Famous American trails.* Chicago: Rand McNally.
[*This book offers insights and factual information on the well known trails such as the Oregon Trail, the Mormon Trail, the Santa Fe Trail, and the Pony Express Route.*]

Hafen, M. A. (1983). *Recollections of a handcart pioneer of 1860.* Lincoln, NE: University of Nebraska Press.
[*An autobiography. Part 1, "From Switzerland to Utah," shows the roots of a Mormon family and relates their experiences in traveling west*].

Hooks, W. H. (1988). *Pioneer cat.* New York: Random House.
[*The wagon train experience told through the eyes of nine-year-old Kate. An easy read for fifth graders.*]

Jassem, K. (1979). *Sacajawea: Wilderness guide.* Mahwah, NJ: Troll Associates.
[*This book is perfect for a read-aloud. It can be read in one session, and is enjoyable and informative.*]

Lavender, D. S. (1980). *The overland migrations.* Washington, DC: U.S. Government Printing Office.
[*A National Park Service handbook, it contains beautiful color photography of Oregon Trail landmarks, as well as an extensive history of the migrations.*]

Lawlor, L. (1986). *Addie across the prairie.* New York: Minstrel Books.
[*A fictional account of life in the Dakota territory.*]

Levenson, D. (1971). *Homesteaders and Indians.* New York: Franklin Watts.
[*An overview of the general theme highlighting many subtopics: Native Americans, homesteaders, railroad, women's roles, U.S. army, etc. This book features many pen and ink illustrations as well as original nineteenth century photographs.*]

Levine, E. (1989). *Ready, aim, fire! The real adventures of Annie Oakley.* New York: Scholastic.
[*A favorite in fifth grade. It's a biography with illustrations and photographs.*]

MacLachlan, P. (1985). *Sarah, plain and tall.* New York: Harper.
[*A beautifully written story of a pioneer family and their mail-order bride and mother.*]

McGraw, E. J. (1952). *Moccasin trail.* New York: Puffin Books.
[*This book is recommended for more able readers because of its dialect and vocabulary. It ties together pioneers, mountain men, and the Native American culture in a wonderful saga of family relationships.*]

Moeri, L. (1981). *Save Queen of Sheba.* New York: Avon Books.
[*A courageous twelve-year-old boy and his younger sister survive an Indian attack on their wagon train.*]

Murphy, D. (1984). *Lewis and Clark: Voyage of discovery.* Las Vegas, NV: KC Publications.
[*Rich landscape and nature photography, together with many excerpts from actual journal entries, make this a valuable reference.*]

O'Dell, S. (1970). *Sing down the moon.* Boston: Houghton Mifflin.
[*This Newbery Award winning book brings a very human perspective to the forced*

migration of Native Americans. Fifth graders begin to care for Tall Boy and his people, and they develop an empathy for the victims described in the story.]

Rounds, G. (1968). *Prairie schooners.* New York: Holiday House.
[*One chapter, "Prairie Port," is particularly helpful in building knowledge of pioneers.*]

Sabin, L. (1982). *Narcissa Whitman: Brave pioneer.* Mahwah, NJ: Troll Associates.
[*A short but informative biography, easy to read for fifth graders.*]

Stewart, G. R. (1954/1987). *The pioneers go west.* New York: Random House.
[*Relates the hardships encountered by a group of pioneers traveling by covered wagon from Iowa to California in 1844.*]

Tunis, E. (1961). *Frontier living.* New York: Thomas Crowell.
[*Life on the American frontier is vividly brought to life in text and illustrations including all aspects of pioneer cultures.*]

Chapter 8

Egyptian Mummies: A Sixth Grade Theme

Tanya Willcox-Schnabl

My roommate put her fork down and asked me to please stop. I was in the middle of explaining how the Egyptians removed the brains of their dead while mummifying them. They believed that feeling and thinking were in the heart and that the brain was useless, so they didn't preserve the brain. Instead they used long metal hooks to pull the brain, piece by piece, through the nose. Before I started my research, this really would have disgusted me, but because I now knew the reasons and the philosophy behind the ritual, I found myself intrigued. Apparently my roommate wasn't as intrigued.

This project had its beginning in a reading and writing class I was taking with Sean Walmsley in the summer of 1989. My assignment was to develop a theme of my own choice, suitable for the grade I taught. Choosing a topic was a difficult task for me because I had so many new units to teach in social studies the following year. I started out thinking that I would research Greece, Rome, or perhaps mythology. When I began my research I found so much information that I couldn't narrow down my topic. Also, nothing really got me very excited—so excited that I couldn't wait to find out more. In class one day another student brought me some information on the Ramses II collection she has seen while it was on display at Brigham Young University in 1986. I read the information and was fascinated by the mystique of the pyramids and the mummies. After class that day, I went to the university library to research mummies and pyramids. I really didn't know where to begin because I didn't know anything about either of the two topics.

I typed *Egyptology, Pyramids,* and *Mummies* into the computer catalog, and added *Ramses II,* since I had information on him already. Most of the call numbers were in the Ds so I went to the third floor of the library to begin my research. I was amazed by the amount of information that I found—six shelves full of books on Egypt, its history, pyramids, and mummies. As I began to read more about Egypt, I became curious about why the Egyptians mummified people. What was the purpose of this ritual? I started to make a list of questions that I wanted answers to. This list of questions helped to guide my research.

The next book I opened was strictly about mummies. As I read it, I found out that mummification was how the Egyptians preserved their bodies to go on to their next life. Mummification was critical to their religious beliefs. The Egyptians believed in life after death, and their afterlife was based entirely on the individual's life on earth and was thought of as a continuation of that life. The Egyptians believed there were spirits in the body, and in order for the spirits to recognize the body after death it needed to remain intact.

I had so many questions that I didn't know where to go next. I was sitting in the middle of the aisle with twenty books around me, frantically searching for the explanation behind the Egyptian religious beliefs. While I read, I began to learn about the Nile, the flooding of the Nile, and the pyramids. Finally, I made a connection—the great pyramids were built as tombs to safely (they thought) keep and preserve the mummies. So much information and I still needed to get a focused theme or topic! I decided to take out about fifteen books ranging from the history of Egyptian life to pyramids to, finally, mummies. My real interest was in mummies and the mummification process, but I found that I couldn't concentrate on this without knowing about the Egyptian people, their beliefs, and their ceremonies. I left the library feeling overwhelmed but extremely excited. One fact that stuck in my mind all the way home was the fact that it took seventy days to complete the mummification process.

That night I couldn't help but tell my roommate everything I had learned. She's a nurse, so I kept asking her what certain medical words meant, such as *natron*. (I found out later that it was a salt that the Egyptians used to cleanse and preserve the dead bodies.) Initially, she was disgusted by my description of removing the brains, but soon she became just as interested as I was in the mummification process. In fact, she was very helpful to me later when I needed to know how a CAT-scan was used to examine the insides of a mummy without unwrapping it.

The next day I went to our public library to find information geared to children. I found two fantastic books. *Pyramid*, written by David Macaulay, is an informational book on pyramids. The pictures give the perspective of being at a pyramid, and the reader can see a pyramid from the ground up. The illustrations are precise and beautifully constructed—just like the pyramids. The information is accurate and not boring; the combination of the printed word and the illustrations helps to create an interesting account of the pyramids, their construction, and their purpose. This book was much more informative than many of the "adult" books on pyramids.

The other book, *Mummies Made in Egypt*, written and illustrated by Aliki was also fascinating. This book gives accurate information on mummies and the mummification process. The pictures or drawings are engaging: Aliki says that many of her illustrations came from Egyptian paintings and sculptures found in ancient tombs. This book is anything but morbid, and it gives background information intertwined with the actual process of mummification. In order to describe the mummies, it was important to give a little information on the pyramids because they are the burial chambers for mummies. As I read this book, I thought it would be great as an introduction to mummies, perhaps as a read-aloud. The book raises many questions on mummies and the mummification process. It is packed full of information, too much to absorb all at one sitting, but it would be an excellent jumping-off point. It would spark interest in not only mummies, but also gods, pyramids, and the religious beliefs of the Egyptians. This book is an excellent reference tool for classroom use.

Bubbling over with information, I began to list the questions that I wanted to research. I knew I should look at some *National Geographic* magazines and maybe contact someone in the archaeology department at the State University at Albany. The next day during our class, a fellow student happened to mention an exhibit at the Albany Institute of History and Art; she said that there were mummies there. I impatiently made it through the rest of the class and then rushed to my car to go to the museum. When I got there they told me the Egyptian room was in the basement. I hurried down the stairs and saw the sign: EGYPTIAN ROOM. My heart was beating pretty fast—I'm not sure if it was from the excitement or from running to the museum from my car in the pouring rain. I entered the room, and right before me in glass cases were two mummies. I walked up to them and stared in awe. The bodies were relatively small, probably less than five feet tall. One body was completely wrapped. I recognized the linen wrapping from one of the books I had read earlier. The other body had been unwrapped from the waist up. It looked black but you could see that it was a body because it had not deteriorated. You could see the hands, arms, and head clearly; the features on the face were amazing. I could even see the shape of the eyes. It was an eerie feeling looking at a body that had been buried between 1085–945 B.C. I felt like an expert standing in that room because I had recently read so much about Egypt, its people, and their customs—especially about mummies. Here they were, real mummies right in front of me. There were plaques on the walls with information of all kinds from background of Egyptian history to their jewelry to their communication. Between the printed information there were glass cases holding ancient Egyptian relics of whatever the plaques were describing. There was also a time line on the wall with the important dates and events in Egyptian history. While I looked around, notebook out, frantically writing, I realized it was pretty cold in the room. I later found out it had to be cold for preservation of the mummies.

While I was writing, a family came into the room. I was eavesdropping on their discussion as I was curious to know what younger children found interesting. After about fifteen minutes, I decided to ask the younger girl what she found the most exciting in the room. I introduced myself and explained what I was doing. I found out the girl, Amy, was going to be in fifth grade. I talked with her for twenty-five minutes. She was fascinated by the mummies. She had a lot of questions and I found I could answer most of them. She liked being able to actually look at a real mummy. She told me that was better than any picture in a book. I agreed with her. She also found the plaque on the wall—

Technology Aids and Scholarly Research—fascinating. We talked about this for quite awhile. The plaque shows x-rays of the mummies in the museum that were done in November of 1988 at the Albany Medical Center. She was fascinated by the actual pictures of the skeletons. You could see the organs of the mummies wrapped up inside of their bodies. I explained to her how Egyptians took the organs out of the body when they started the mummification process and then put them back into the body wrapped before they wrapped the entire body. A moment or two later she left. After about five minutes, she came back into the room, tapped me on the shoulder and said, "I forgot. I think the jewelry is really neat too!" Now I had some ideas of what my students might like. I finished my note-taking, talked to the Educational Programs Director about bringing my students to the museum, and found out that there was a series of lectures on Egypt offered in the fall. One of these lectures was to be given by the doctor who did the x-rays on the two mummies at the museum. It was an unforgettable afternoon. Not only did I discover a museum I'd never heard of before, but I'd also found two real Egyptian mummies within ten miles of my school that local doctors had x-rayed. I left the museum with more information than I could immediately digest.

Since the Albany Public Library is located almost next door to the museum, I thought I'd see if they had children's books on mummies and Egyptian life that weren't in my local library. Up until this point, I wasn't sure if there would be enough books on Egyptology that sixth graders could read independently, and searching my local library only yielded a handful of useful titles. In the Albany Public Library, there was an entire section devoted to nonfiction books about Egypt, and I left with twelve of them from which students could obtain interesting and accurate information on mummies and Egyptian life. One of the books I found was *Mummies in Fact and Fiction* (Madison, 1980), which led me to think about fiction in relation to mummies (for example, the use of mummies in horror movies and ghost tales). It occurred to me later that I would never have found this source (which led directly to a fiction-writing project in the classroom) had I limited my search to one public library.

When I got home that afternoon, I called Albany Medical Center to try to reach the doctor who had x-rayed the mummies. He wasn't immediately available, but eventually I did reach him, talked to him about the project, and discussed the possibility of his coming to the class to explain his findings to the students. As it turned out, we weren't able to coordinate our respective schedules, so the students never did meet him. But when I do this theme again, I will do my best to build in a visit from this expert.

There were also two scientists from the General Electric Research and Development Center (in Schenectady, New York) who did three-dimensional reconstructions of the mummies at the museum. I was anxious to get in touch with these local experts, so they could share with the students the techniques they used to make the reconstructions. Again, it didn't work out, and for various reasons it hasn't since then, but they are a valuable source I am still trying to tap.

PLANNING THE THEME

As I began planning for this theme, I knew I had to find a way to entice my students into wanting to learn more about Egypt without simply dumping out everything I had learned. I wanted to get them as engrossed in their research as I had become in mine. I wanted them to work on the process of researching and writing questions, searching for answers, note-taking, and citing sources.

I decided to organize the theme around four major activities. In the first activity, students would research a personal topic related to Egypt; in the second, we would work together on mummies as a shared research experience (a topic I had chosen); the third would be a visit to the museum; and in the fourth, we would create fiction stories incorporating Egyptian facts. In this way, I hoped to balance teacher-chosen with student-chosen topics, to balance reading, writing, and hands-on activities, and to balance fiction and nonfiction sources and activities. Students would have two opportunities to practice researching techniques: once with their own topic and again in the shared research experience.

I expected the entire theme would take between seven to eight weeks. I don't have a self-contained classroom, so there are several constraints I have to work around. I have one class of twenty-six students that comes to me for both language arts (one hour a day) and social studies (forty-five minutes a day). I also teach language arts to fifty-six other students (forty-five minutes a day). Thus, I planned to do the entire project with the students I had for social studies and language arts, using both the social studies and language arts class periods; with the others, I planned to do just the fiction-writing activity in their language arts classes. I expected to use only the social studies periods during the first part of the project, then to use both social studies and language arts while doing the mummies project, and then only language arts time during the fiction-writing activity.

THEME ACTIVITIES

Initial Discussions

I began the personal research topic with a general discussion about Egypt. I started by asking students to list individually on sheets of paper all of the things that they knew or thought they knew about Egypt. Most students seemed to have good working knowledge about mummies, pyramids, hieroglyphics, King Tut, and sphinxes; some students had detailed information (for example, one student knew all about the treasures that were buried with the kings; another wrote that boats were buried with the pharaohs; a third knew that Egyptians worshipped cats). Then we shared the information orally, separating relevant (e.g., plagues, River Nile) from irrelevant (e.g., Zeus) subtopics, and I summarized the major categories on the board, and from this list we constructed a web of Egypt.

Instead of having them copy the web while we were constructing it on the board—this would have distracted them from the discussion—I made copies afterwards of the web for each of the students (see Figure 8–1).

Personal Research Topics

Students were now asked to choose their personal research topics. The first year I did this project, I let students create their own list from our initial discussion. The problem was that some topics didn't have sufficient resources available, so students would become frustrated and quickly find themselves at a dead end. In the second year I changed the approach. I created the topic choice list, using my knowledge of the resources available, and the topics that students had found stimulating and challenging.

- The architecture of pyramids
- Pharaohs
- The Great Pyramid
- Architecture (obelisk)
- Sphinx
- Valley of the Kings
- Food and drink
- Scribes
- Hieroglyphics
- Hunting and fishing
- Mummies from other cultures
- Education and schooling
- Battle
- Weapons
- Tombs
- Carpenters
- Gods and goddesses
- Recreation, toys, and games
- Magic and medicine
- Currency
- King Tut
- Geography (flooding of the Nile)
- Clothing, jewelry
- Customs
- Daily life (farming, living quarters, everyday activities)
- Egyptian queens—Cleopatra, Hatsheput
- Tools
- Priests and temples

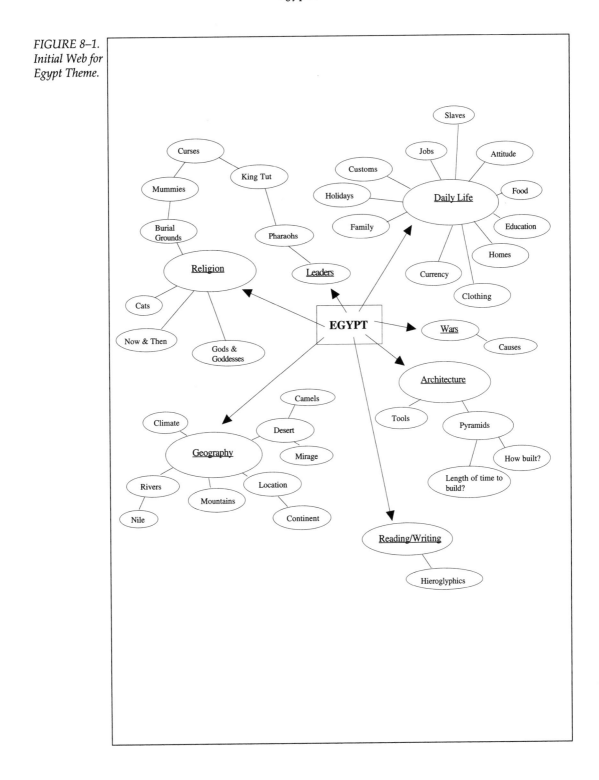

FIGURE 8–1.
Initial Web for
Egypt Theme.

I ruled out Egyptian mummies as a topic explaining that we would be doing a shared research experience with mummies. (I told them that we would be learning everything there is to know about mummies, including all the "gory stuff.")

Because I wanted the students to explore a variety of topics, and I was concerned that if given complete freedom of choice most students would choose pyramids, I asked them to list three topics from the list that they'd like to explore, and I promised them one of their choices as a personal research topic. (As feared, most students did pick pyramids as their first choice, but as promised, they all were given a topic from their list.) I selected four students "out of a hat" to explore their first choice of pyramids; most of the remaining students got their second choice.

After choosing their topics, we spent the next eight social studies class periods in the Learning Center (our Library/Media Center). On the first day, the students wrote down the questions they had about their topic (for example, "How did they build pyramids?" or "When did King Tut rule?"). From there they went to the computer catalog to find sources. Students have a hard time with library catalogs because they assume that if their topic is on Egyptian daily life, all they need to enter is "Daily Life" and lo and behold, all the relevant books will be listed. I showed them how to narrow down a search by starting with more general key words, and then I left them to their own devices to do their searches. For example, to find books about Egyptian daily life, I suggested starting with Egypt as a key word, then look at the titles of the books to see which ones are likely to cover daily life, then call up the title of a specific book and examine its summary. If the summary mentions daily life, write down the call number (and availability) and then go to the shelves and take the book out. With book in hand, students may still need help locating relevant information, and they may need to be shown how to use an index or how to scan to locate what they are looking for.

Any books they had gathered during this period were placed on a reserve cart so that they would be available at the beginning of the next class period. On the second day, the students took their books off the cart, but before they started using them to answer their questions, I modeled some note-taking strategies. I picked a book from the cart and showed how I would find information relevant to my topic and how I might represent this information in my own words. First, I found the section that covered the topic. I read the first paragraph of this section out aloud, paraphrased it orally myself, then read another paragraph and asked each student to paraphrase it orally. We then discussed the students' paraphrases. Next, I asked the students to pick a partner, and take turns reading, paraphrasing, and discussing passages from their chosen books. This exercise took the whole of the second class period, and by the time we were finished, I felt more confident about the students taking notes from the books.

For the remaining six class periods, the students worked on their personal research projects, using the note-taking sheets designed by the Learning Center. These sheets are color-coded according to the different kinds of sources (green

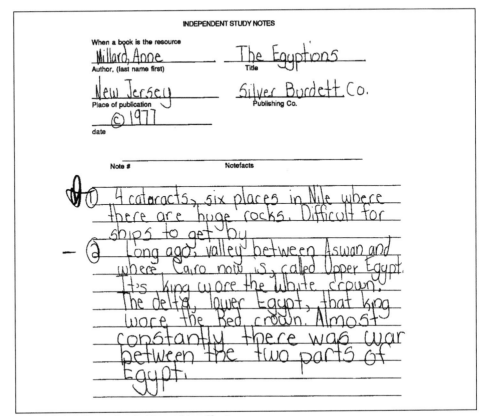

INDEPENDENT STUDY NOTES

When a book is the resource

Millard, Anne
Author. (last name first)

The Egyptians
Title

New Jersey
Place of publication

Silver Burdett Co.
Publishing Co.

© 1977
date

Note #   Notefacts

① 4 cataracts, six places in Nile where there are huge rocks. Difficult for ships to get by

② Long ago, valley between Aswan and where Cairo now is, called Upper Egypt. It's king wore the white crown. The delta, lower Egypt, that king wore the Red crown. Almost constantly there was war between the two parts of Egypt.

FIGURE 8–2 Example of a Note-taking Sheet.

for books, blue for magazines, yellow for encyclopedia, etc.). Each sheet has the appropriate bibliographic format at the top of the page, with blank lines underneath for taking notes (see Figure 8–2).

While the students were busy taking notes, I circulated giving assistance to individual students. Erin, who had chosen Egyptian clothing as her topic, was having a hard time finding a book with enough information about clothing. Since I had read all the books before the project began, I was able to steer her in the right direction without simply giving her the information. Brandon and Chris picked "Battles," and they were stuck on a specific battle. I suggested they think about the weapons used in Egyptian battles, and that got them thinking about weapons as the link between different battles. After reading one or two passages, some students would declare they had exhausted the subject ("I learned it all, now what do you want me to do?"), and I would take this opportunity to introduce a source that either they hadn't consulted or one that explored their topic from a different point of view. I also noticed that students were picking up a lot of information from their sources that didn't relate to their topic but that did enlarge their knowledge of Egypt, including mummies (which they put to good use later in the theme).

For me, being familiar with the books is extremely important during this student research time. For instance, if students are having a hard time finding the information they need, I need to be able to locate sources that they can use quickly. If students struggle too much during the beginning stages, they give up easily and it's hard to gain their interest again. This is when researching the topic myself and copying a representative page of each book comes in handy. I can quickly locate a book for the student and set them on their way, wasting no time.

After they return to the classroom from the Learning Center, most students can't control their desire to share what they have learned, making things a little chaotic for a while. So I gave them fifteen minutes at the beginning of class to share with someone else in the class what they had learned. They like being able to talk and also this gives them the chance to broaden their knowledge. I asked the students to organize their notes at home and to prepare a three- to five-minute oral presentation on their personal research topic for the following Monday.

Shared Research Experience

By now we were ready to start our shared research experience on mummies. The students were practically begging to begin. I made a list of their questions about mummies, and I told them that we were going to answer as many of these questions as possible during the rest of the week.

As they entered the room the following day, I knew that I had them eager to know everything they could find out about mummies, especially since they had some information from their prior research. I began reading *Mummies Made in Egypt* (Aliki, 1985) to them right away. Initially, you could hear a pin drop, but by the time I got to the part about pulling the brains through the nose, most of the girls were getting pretty disgusted, and the boys acted as if I were reading them a Stephen King novel: "This is cool. Awesome!" This soon changed as the class became more accustomed to the rituals and beliefs of the Egyptians. Talk of brains being pulled through the nose became old hat in our classroom, while it remained a "hot" dinner topic in many of my students' homes.

Mummies Made in Egypt is too full of information to absorb in one reading, but it gave students the general knowledge they needed to get started. I have since done this theme again, and instead of reading *Mummies Made in Egypt* myself, I used the PBS Reading Rainbow videotape of Lavar Burton reading it. The tape begins with a reading of the text, while showing all the illustrations. Then it moves to the Museum of Fine Arts in Boston, where the curator takes the viewer through the Egyptian exhibits, and then into the basement, where the artifacts are cleaned and prepared for display. The tape also shows how three-dimensional reproductions of the mummies' heads are created. These are the things that really interest sixth graders, and the videotape is superbly done. From now on, I'll use the tape to introduce the shared research experience, but I'll always have the book available for students to read.

My students sit in clusters, with about five students to each table. I assigned each table a few questions from the list we generated the previous day. I had already taken out a number of books on mummies from the Learning Center and now distributed them to each table. Since I'm very familiar with the topics covered in these books, I'm able to distribute the appropriate ones to each of the groups. We followed the same process we had used previously with the personal research topics. The students wrote questions, scanned the sources for relevant information, and took notes using the paraphrasing strategies they had learned. This took a couple of class periods.

Our next three to four class discussions focused on the information they had acquired from the sources and questions that arose from their reading. One class was particularly interesting and enlightening, as I learned that it's impossible to explore Egyptian mummies without discussing death. On this day a student asked me if I was scared to die. At first I was a little apprehensive; in order for me to answer her question I would have to discuss my religious beliefs, something I didn't want to get into. On the other hand, I felt they needed the opportunity to express themselves, so I answered her. It ended up being a very open discussion. In trying to understand the Egyptians' belief in the afterlife, they began questioning their own beliefs and asking some serious questions. Most of my sixth graders were afraid to die and they couldn't relate to the Egyptians preparation and celebration of death. Making these connections between the Egyptians' beliefs and concerns about death and our own fears of dying really brought it all home to the students. To this day I'm glad I answered the student's question.

Oral Reports

During the following week my students gave oral reports on their personal research topics. I asked them to take notes on each other's reports, thinking that they would learn more about other students' topics. I probably should have modeled this activity, because it didn't work as well as I thought it would, but the oral reports were truly amazing. Students' topics ranged from how to read and write hieroglyphs to the long and complicated process of building pyramids. It was obvious from their presentations that students had taken ownership of their topics, knew what they were talking about, and enthusiastically communicated what they had learned. There is no way that this could have been accomplished through reading a textbook and answering questions on a test.

Writing Fiction Stories

While the students continued working on the shared research experience in social studies, I decided to use our Egyptian knowledge in language arts class. My idea was to have my students write a fiction story of their own, weaving in some of the facts they had learned in their research. In order to make this work I thought they should first be introduced to how authors do this.

I found several fiction books that included or were based on Egyptian facts: *The Mummy, the Will, and the Crypt* (Bellairs, 1983), and *The Curse of the Blue Figurine* (Bellairs, 1984). I also used *The Egypt Game* (Snyder, 1982). All three of these authors do an excellent job of weaving Egyptian facts into their storylines to add suspense as well as mystique.

I used these books for two main activities. The first was simply a read-aloud. I read a few representative pages to the students and we talked about the facts and how the author wove these facts into the story. Next, I copied a chapter for each student to read silently and to underline the facts. After they finished reading, we brainstormed why the author may have included certain facts and not others, as well as how the author used the facts to enhance the storyline. Now I felt my students were ready to write their own stories. They asked if they could work in pairs. I knew it would be a difficult assignment, so it made sense to have the students work together.

As they wrote their stories, they referred back to the books for models. They imitated the authors' styles, some successfully, others less so. Although they all didn't come up with "great" pieces of writing, they tried a new technique and enjoyed doing it (see Figures 8–3 and 8–4). I plan on using this activity again next year.

Constructing a Mummy

During the week in which the students were completing their stories, I was busy preparing the culminating activity for the shared research experience, namely constructing a life-size model of a mummy. I knew I wanted the class to make a mummy the second I read *Ancient Egypt* (Purdy & Sandak, 1982). This project book shows students how to reproduce ancient Egyptian relics, and includes instructions on making a mummy. I was convinced that constructing a mummy would be the perfect way to pull all the threads of this theme together.

With twenty-six students in my class, I could picture sheer chaos in my classroom if everyone were to be working on the same project at the same time. Therefore, I split the project into several smaller tasks. I began with the mummy itself, an appropriately-sized reproduction made from papier-mâché over a chicken-wire frame. (I made the frame ahead of time, not wishing to risk almost certain injury if students themselves handled the razor-sharp edges during the cutting process.) Approximately five students could work on this at a time. Some students would be cutting paper strips, others dipping them, while others smoothed them on the wire frame. The layering is a very important aspect of this project as the Egyptians wrapped as many as twenty layers of linen around the bodies of their dead (see Figure 8–5).

Since royalty usually had four canopic jars to hold their vital organs, I decided that a second task could involve four to eight students making canopic

Operation: TUT
by Keith Watts and Chris Lupo

It was a Saturday night and Clark was staying over at Wendal's house because his parents were going to a funeral. They just finished watching a special on the discovery of King Tut's tomb.

They shut their eyes and drifted off to sleep. They both awoke to a roar of thunder as a flash of lightning filled the room with light. They looked over on the dresser and there was a coffin!

Clark grabbed a flashlight and they both went over timidly. They noticed on the side of the coffin was ancient hieroglyphics. They opened the coffin and there was another coffin. They opened that one and there were all these jewels. They both said a faint "wow!" Then they opened the third and final coffin. A shiver went down their spine as they saw the remains of what was a man!

"Help me," the thing moaned. "Help me," it repeated.

"Who are you and what do you want?" said Clark. A long bony hand reached out and grabbed Wendal by the neck and pulled him into the coffin and all three doors quickly shut. Three minutes later the doors opened. Wendal and the Mummy popped up and the Mummy said:

"I am King Tut. I once was the ruler of Egypt. I wasn't a very good king, I was only ruler for nine years. Anyway, they didn't mummify me very well and my face is all dried up and I need you to break into the museum and get back my mask so the ba and the ka will find me."

"What are the ba and the ka?" asked Clark.

"The ba is my soul and the ka is my invisible twin and they have to recognize me so they can take me to the afterlife."

"We're going on a field trip to the museum on Monday!" said Wendal excitedly.

"Wait a minute, we could get into some major trouble!" Clark said.

"If you do not, I will put a curse on you!" Tut said.

"Okay, okay, we will do it."

The weekend passed quickly and Monday morning was soon here. Wendal and Clark both arose to the sound of blasting sounds from Wendal's stereo. Tut was dancing around the room singing the words

FIGURE 8–3.
Continued

to the song on an off-pitch note. Tut described his mask to them. He said it was pure gold with blue stripes and at the top of it was a cobra and a vulture which stood for upper and lower Egypt.

They got to school and boarded the bus for the museum. They got there in no time. Wendal looked at a map and found where King Tut's mask was. They quickly split from their group unnoticed and found their way to the mask. It was encased in a glass show case. They broke the showcase with Clark's binder. An alarm went off. They reached in and got the mask and slid it into Clark's book bag and rejoined their group. A policeman ran behind them and chills went down their backs.

They came home after a long and tiring day. They raced up to Wendal's room where the sarcophagus was still laying on the dresser. They placed the mask on Tut's head and he was the happiest person dead. He reached into his gold pile and gave them both a handful of gold. King Tut said," Thank you. You will be rewarded in the afterlife."

All three doors shut in a flash and lightning struck the sarcophagus and it was gone forever.

They awoke to Wendal's mother's voice. They asked what day it was and Wendal's mother said it was Saturday morning. They quickly ate breakfast and went out to hit the tennis ball around. While they were throwing it, Clark shook it and it rattled. He told Wendal and they both sent into the house and sliced it open with a knife. Inside they found two little pieces of gold carved into two cobras and a note which said, "Thanks...Love, Tut."

FIGURE 8–4.
Patrick's
Egypt
Composition.

Patrick Correia
Egypt Composition

I was not in a good mood. After half of a day's work carrying water in buckets from the Nile to fill the animals' water trough, I had looked forward to relaxing a little. But that was not the way it worked around here, my newly adopted father explained. So I worked the rest of the day in the fields, planting wheat and grain.

It was for that reason that when the vision came, it did not excite me the way it usually had in the past—even so, it still took my breath away. A gleaming white figurine, its legs and waist embedded in rock. As fast as the vision had come, it was gone. Suddenly, I was overcome with fatigue. Still my father urged me to work on.

This was the reason no one had adopted me for so long—my case worker did not understand my sudden bursts of fatigue any more than my stepfather did. Only I knew that the reason I was not suited for work in the fields was not because I am physically weak, for I'm as strong as any farm worker, but because every time the vision comes, I have to sit and rest before I can work again.

Although I'm a fairly good worker, my real strength lies in intelligence. "I know that I could be a scribe, or get into a governmental job, if it wasn't for this stupid class system!" I exclaimed, thinking aloud. But it was no use. I might have just as well have been dumb as a box of rocks. I'm now the son of a farmer, so I'm destined to grow up and become a farmer—that's how a class system works.

But then the vision came again. Never before had it come more than once in a day, much less twice in five minutes! This time the vision was different, though. The statue was being pulled from the rock. There was an air of dampness, as if this were underground. The roar of the ocean filled my ears. Suddenly, the figurine was gone, and all I could see was water. I was filled with a sense of urgency, as if there was something I had to do. Never before had my vision encompassed more than my sense of sight. I knew there was something I was supposed to do, something the vision was trying to tell me.

The vision came again and again, haunting me all day. I lay awake all night, thinking, trying to figure out what I needed to do.

As the morning light was just beginning to make its ascent into the sky, I jumped out of bed and headed for the old sage's house. It was rumored he was over one hundred years old, and had once held the position of vizer, or king's assistant. He was said to be able to answer any question asked of him, no matter what it was about.

Even though it was the middle of the night, the old man opened the door before I could even knock. "Come in, come in," he said in his feeble voice.

FIGURE 8–4.
Continued

Stepping inside and sitting where he indicated, I told him everything,starting with how my mother and father were sentenced to death after a cat died by eating some rat poison they had left out.

"Yes, I agree that there is something you must do," he remarked after I had finished. "I've seen this only once before..." Trailing off, he paused, thought for a moment, and with a confused look on his face, asked, "What were we talking about? I've plumb forgotten."

"You were saying something about seeing this once before?" I prompted.

"Ah, yes. Khe-tu was a good friend of mine. He had visions not unlike your own—the same tiredness, the same feelings of urgency. I believe it was even a similar vision..." He sat back, trailing off again. Then he jumped up. "Yes! It was the same vision! He died before he figured out what it meant. He mentioned something about it just before he died, something about caves, the Nile..." His look of excitement turned to one of sadness. "That is all I remember," he said abruptly.

"Are you sure there's nothing more?" I asked, stupidly not seeing that this was a touchy subject.

"NO! Now you must leave," he demanded. He stood up and led me to the door. I even thought I saw a tear forming in the corner of his eye.

Stepping out the door, I turned to thank him for his help, but he shut the door before I could say a word.

Walking home in the mid-morning light, an idea hit me. Maybe the water I kept seeing was the Nile! And a cave would explain the dampness! A cave filled with the water of the Nile—that meant a cave underwater. That was no good. I couldn't do anything about an underwater cave. There must be some other explanation.

By this time I was home. In the several hours since I had left, my family had awakened and were now frantically searching for me. When my mother saw me making my way across the fields, she let out a yelp and ran over to me.

"Where have you been?" my mother exclaimed. "I was worried sick!" Grasping my head between her hands, she kissed my forehead.

"You had your mother and I scared silly," my father reprimanded. "You should never run off like that! I would have thought you would know that by now! I would send you to your room if there wasn't work to be done, work that I could have done if I wasn't looking for you. Now get the tools and go to it."

With the punishment my father established, I had plenty of time to think about the message I was supposed to receive through the visions. On the third straight day of going straight to my room after my chores I realized I could get inside a cave that would be underwater soon—the caves in the bluffs along the Nile would fill with water when the Nile flooded! If I was going to do some exploring, though, I would have to do it soon. The Nile

FIGURE 8–4.
Continued

was due to flood in two weeks! But my punishment lasted for almost another month now. I would have to employ a little "stretching" of the rules. The next morning before dawn I climbed out the window with four sandwiches, two candles, and my tinderbox. Setting out in the direction of the bluffs, I tried to justify my actions at every step.

I reached the bluffs and randomly picked a cave to start exploring. I didn't even have time to light my candle before I reached the end of the cave. The next three caves were the same story. But the fifth cave was different. It stretched so far back, twisting and winding, that it took the rest of the day to explore. But at the end I was rewarded with a plain blank wall.

I explored this way for four more days, budgeting myself to one sandwich a day. The afternoon of the fourth day found me far back in a cave and so ravenously hungry I was ready to give up and go back home when the corridor I was in opened into a splendid cavern! Right at the center of the cavern was a giant boulder. Embedded in that boulder was a gleaming white, gem-encrusted figurine! It was at that point that I collapsed.

I awoke laying in an inch of water. It took me a moment to gather my thoughts and realize what had happened—the Nile was beginning to flood! Figuring this out took incredibly long because my head was throbbing from hitting the ground when I fainted, I had had only four sandwiches in the past four days, and I had only had a few hours of sleep each night since I came out exploring. When I finally did collect my thoughts, I got up and made my way out into the morning sun. I must have slept for over twelve hours, I thought to myself. Joy overcoming my exhaustion and fear of my father, I sprinted all the way home.

The scene before me in the kitchen shocked me. My mother had her head on my father's shoulder, sobbing and wailing. When my father saw me enter the room, his look of intense sorrow changed to one of surprise, to one of joy to one of anger, all in a matter of seconds.

"Where have you been, you- you-" my father was cut off by my mother's scream.

"OH MY LORD!" she exclaimed. "YOU'RE ALIVE! We thought you were dead! Don't you ever, EVER do that again! Where were you?" She had been walking towards me as she said this, but her approach was blocked by my father, who had unslipped his belt and was advancing on me with it held menacingly.

"Wait!" I held up my left hand and with my right, pulled the figurine out of my pocket. When I showed it to my parents, their jaws both fell.

A number of celebrations followed, along with a visit from the Pharaoh himself! My figurine was taken to the Pharaoh's palace where it still stands today. My popularity was unbounded. The press had a field day, but I won't go into that. Let it just suffice to say that this little period of my life had a happy ending.

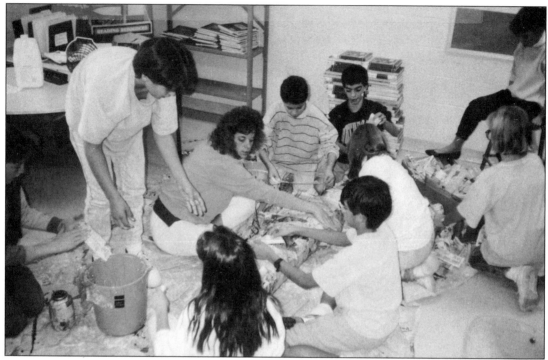

FIGURE 8–5. Wrapping the "Mummy."

jars. The closest thing I could find to that shape was a spaghetti jar, so that's what we used as the underlying structure. Each jar was first covered with papier-mâché, then painted to match the color and texture of a clay jar. The lids were formed from modeling clay and were molded into various shapes, such as human heads and animals.

The students and I had already decided that a large cardboard box would make a perfect sarcophagus. Finding a suitably-sized box turned out to be quite difficult (refrigerator and other large appliance boxes were generally too wide), but as luck would have it, a student brought in a box approximately 8' x 2' x 2' that a water tank came in, and this proved to be the ideal container. We could have converted a refrigerator box if we'd had to by cutting it apart and gluing it. The task here would be to design and decorate the box.

I had ordered a generic papier-mâché face from an art catalogue earlier in the year, so I decided to use this as the basis for our mummy's mask. Using a perfectly formed set of facial features underneath the finished mask helped create an image that was hard to distinguish from a genuine mummy. The task here was to build the full mask (it needed a beard and the ornamental pieces on either side of the face, as well as enlarging the forehead to create a fully three-dimensional head), and paint it in an authentic color (see Figures 8–6 and 8–7).

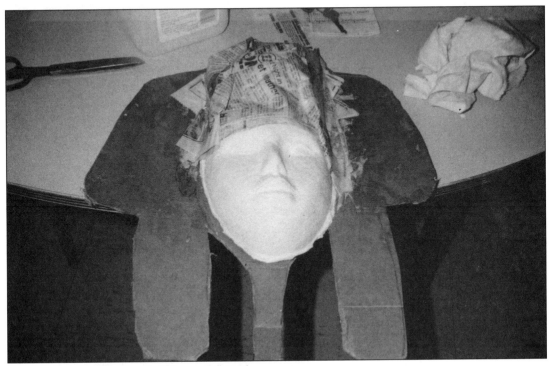

FIGURE 8–6. *Constructing the "Mummy's" Mask.*

I came up with three other less elaborate activities: Making cards describing the process (ours and the Egyptians'); making amulets, shabtis, and jewels to be placed inside the sarcophagus with the mummy; and designing Egyptian mosaics on cellophane to be taped to the windows. This last activity might involve one student standing outside the window holding up an illustration, while another traces the design on the cellophane that is taped to the window.

The materials needed for these activities include: chicken wire, wire cutters, newspaper, glue, wallpaper paste, a drop cloth (to protect the classroom floor against the ravages of student "slave-workers"), linen (muslin cut into strips), a papier-mâché face, paint, a cardboard box, spaghetti sauce jars, clay (to form canopic jar heads), markers, *Ancient Egyptian Design: Coloring Book* (Sibett, 1978), and cellophane. This sounds like an expensive and difficult project to gather materials for, but I'm always amazed at what I can pick up from students, parents, colleagues, and friends. I usually type up a brief description of my project with a list of supplies, and before I know it I have everything I need.

The last thing was to schedule students for certain activities each day. Most students wanted to work on the mummy so I tried to give them all a chance. I rotated them through the activities on a daily basis. I found, however, that the mask needed to be done by the same two students as it required real artistic talent. The hieroglyphs and mosaic scenes on the sarcophagus could be done by

FIGURE 8–7.
The Finished
Mask.

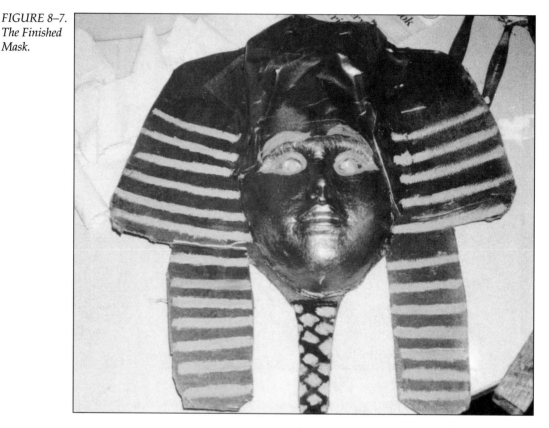

anyone if they used the *Ancient Egyptian Design: Coloring Book* (Sibett, 1978). I thermofaxed several of the drawings so they could be projected on to the cardboard sarcophagus. Students then could trace the designs and color them in, resulting in authentic Egyptian mosaics. My hieroglyph specialist, Keith, took the job of overseeing the hieroglyphs on the sarcophagus.

To accomplish the tasks, I used a two-hour block of time every day for one week. If I had more time available, I could easily have used it. I would spend about fifteen minutes before class preparing for the activities (mixing paste, setting up the overheads, putting the drop cloth down, and arranging the paints and markers); the other hour and three-quarters was spent actually doing the tasks. We all dressed in old clothes—mummification is an indescribably messy business.

As the class entered the room, you could feel the energy. We were all on a common mission. I have to admit that on the first day my palms were sweaty and my heart was racing. I was nervous for two reasons. First, I had never worked with papier-mâché before and I wasn't sure how this project was going to turn out. Second, I wasn't convinced that my students could handle so much activity at once, especially when I knew I'd be on the floor covered with wallpaper paste.

After I explained the responsibilities involved in each task, I began working with the group making the mummy. We covered our hands with paste and began wrapping. After experiencing the difficulty of keeping the surface smooth, the students appreciated the effort it took to complete the mummification process. We discussed how hard it must have been for the Egyptians to wrap a body. We also talked about Egyptian traditions, growing up in ancient Egypt, and the Nile River. As we worked together on the floor, all covered in wallpaper paste, our conversations strayed from Egyptian history to our daily lives; after a while, we weren't teacher and students in a sixth grade classroom but more like friends on a playground, swapping stories. It was as though the barriers between teacher and student were taken down; a camaraderie took its place in those sessions that permanently changed our relationship. From that point onwards, we formed a trust between us that carried through the entire year. Even today, students from that project, now in eighth grade, routinely come back and share new information about Egypt and reminisce about our experience.

I think Susan put it best when she said, "What I liked about making the mummy was making the mummy itself. It was fun to wrap the layers of newspaper around it. It was fun to dip your hands in the glue to paste the strips of newspaper around the mummy. I especially liked talking to you, Miss Willcox, and working at the same time."

The rest of the week proved to be quite exciting. Each day we could see things really taking shape. The wire began to look like a body and the blank mask became King Tut. The refrigerator box soon became an ancient stone coffin used by Egyptians to protect their dead. My students became artisans, skillfully carrying out the steps of the mummification process. You could see their pride as they invited their parents and friends in to our classroom and explained what we were doing and why. After we completed our project we transported it to the Learning Center to be displayed for the entire school. One week later at our special area open house, two of my students gave a presentation on the Egyptian mummification process and our process to several groups of parents. My students had learned more than I could have ever taught them alone or from their social studies textbook. They were truly experts on Egyptian history, especially mummies.

This learning was even more apparent as we traveled to the Albany Institute of History and Art that same week to visit their mummies. The tour guide was amazed by my students' knowledge. In many cases they knew more than the guide. Keith had the class surrounding him as he knelt next to the glass to read the hieroglyphics on the side of the coffin. At first I think the tour guide thought he was simply telling a story, but as he began pointing to each picture and explaining what it meant, she didn't know quite what to say. My students were awed by the real mummies. In a letter to me later, Randy wrote, "The mummies in the museum brought back to life the mummy we made in the unit." All of my hard work and theirs had definitely paid off.

REFLECTIONS

Every year, near the end of September, some of my former students drop by the classroom and look around. They're looking for evidence of this year's mummy, and the one they worked on last year. Casually, they'll ask, "Started the Egypt project yet?" and they'll add, "Won't be as good as ours." Clearly, this project has not been forgotten. These comments remind me just how important this project is to all of us. I do the project early in the year, knowing that a couple of things are going to happen. One is that the students quickly see that I treat them as responsible learners and that I will not be the sole provider of information in the classroom. What I've noticed is that when I give them responsibility, they give me respect in return. Another is that the project establishes a special kind of classroom atmosphere. The shared research experience seems to bond the class together as a group, while the personal research experience enables each student to shine as an individual learner. Through both of these activities, students build respect for each other in an atmosphere where everyone can succeed.

It still surprises me that without a lot of effort on my part, I've managed to become an "expert" on Egyptian mummies, and I continue to build on that knowledge. Throughout the year—not just during the project—I continue to find new books, new materials, and new information on the topic. I have also noticed that people who know my interest in this topic continually bring me materials or tell me about what they've learned that I might want to use. In fact, former students are always stopping by my room to tell me about things they've seen or read and to bring me articles or artifacts relating to Egypt. Sometimes parents of former students stop me in the grocery store and talk about something their son or daughter recently discovered about Egypt. It's gratifying to know that some students develop an interest in this topic, an interest that doesn't end when the year ends.

Doing this project has had effects on other projects, too. I've transferred the process to a theme on the Middle Ages (an eight-week project) and to a shorter one on Greek and Roman mythology.

The process of putting this project together might at first seem overwhelming, but the benefits more than outweigh the legwork, and the legwork itself isn't as daunting as it appears. It would be wonderful if a teacher could simply follow someone else's project. Unfortunately, in order to make it work, the teacher has to have gone through the process, which includes reading the source materials, exploring the topic, and adapting the project to local conditions. For example, I was lucky enough to have found actual mummies in the Albany Institute of History and Art, but I'm still looking for an Egyptologist to visit my classroom.

One project leads to another, and each succeeding project is easier than the last. For me, taking the first plunge was the hardest part. Once I was in, I found project work to be the most effective way of organizing the curriculum for both myself and my students.

REFERENCES

Nonfiction

Aliki. (1985). *Mummies made in Egypt*. New York: Harper & Row.
[*An absolute necessity for this theme. A beautiful picture book that explains the Egyptian mummification process and beliefs behind it. A wonderful read-aloud and a handy resource.*]

Allan, T. (1977). *The time traveler book of Pharaohs and pyramids*. Tulsa: EDC Publishing.
[*This book explains in simple language what it was like to live during the New Kingdom. It covers topics such as war, agriculture, religion, pyramids, and hieroglyphics. The illustrations are based on actual research.*]

Bendick, J. (1989). *Egyptian tombs*. New York: Franklin Watts.
[*Straightforward research facts accompanied by actual photographs. All of the major topics are covered (e.g., skeleton of King Tut, Rosetta Stone, Sphinx).*]

David, A. R. (1988). *The Egyptian kingdoms*. New York: Peter Bedrick Books.
[*A perfect reference for the student who needs to be challenged. It covers most of the major research topics in depth. Superb photographs.*]

David, A. R. (1993). *The giant book of the mummy*. New York: Lodestar Books.
[*A "big" book focusing on the life and tomb of King Tut. The illustrations are wonderful. As you turn each page, you follow the uncovering of King Tut's mummy, beginning with a sarcophagus that contained a nest of three gold coffins, and ending with the mummy itself. A real eye catcher for students of all ages.*]

David, A. R., & David, A. E. (1984). *History as evidence, ancient Egypt*. New York: Warwick Press.
[*Beautiful illustrations of actual places accompanied by photographs. General references. Useful as source for projects*]

Defrates, J. (1991). *What do we know about Egyptians?* New York: Peter Bedrick Books.
[*An illustrated survey of ancient Egypt's history. This book is filled with bits of*

interesting information not found elsewhere (e.g., Egyptian songs, prayers, and poems). A great source for general research.]

El-Baz, F. (1988). Finding a pharaoh's funeral bark. *National Geographic, 173*(4), 513–533.
[*Story of an international team of scientists who unveil a 4,600-year-old ship in the underground chambers near the Great Pyramid of Khufu in Giza, Egypt.]*

Gold, S. D. (1990). *The pharaoh's curse.* New York: Macmillan Putnam.
[*Great information for those students fascinated by curses.]*

Gore, R. (1991). Ramses the Great. *National Geographic, 179*(4), 2–31.
[*A superbly illustrated article about the life and remains of Ramses II.]*

Hart, G. (1988). *Exploring the past: Ancient Egypt.* New York: Harcourt Brace Jovanovich.
[*A fantastic source for student personal research topics. A good overview of life in Ancient Egypt, including topics such as Pharaohs, religion, mummification and the afterlife, the role of scribes and craftsmen, home and family, and common occupants. Wonderful illustrations!]*

Hart, G. (1990). *Eyewitness Books: Ancient Egypt.* New York: Alfred A. Knopf.
[*A photo essay on ancient Egypt and the people who lived there, documented through the mummies, pottery, weapons, and other objects they left behind. Fantastic, accurate source.]*

Kendall, T. (1990). Kingdom of Kush. *National Geographic, 178*(5), 96–125.
[*Archaeologist Timothy Kendall describes some remarkable finds at the Kushite capital of Nepata located in the south of Egypt.]*

Lauber, P. (1985). *Tales mummies tell.* New York: Thomas Y. Crowell.
[*This book ties the study of mummies with their scientific significance. What can mummies tell us about the past? Excellent photographs and research.]*

Lehner, M. (1991). Computer rebuilds the ancient Sphinx. *National Geographic, 179*(4), 32–39.
[*Mark Lehner describes how computer generated models are helping visualize how the great Sphinx at Giza appeared in the time of Ramses II.]*

Macaulay, D. (1975). *Pyramid.* Boston: Houghton Mifflin.
[*This author is an architect, which gives this book true authenticity. The drawings are to scale and amazingly real. Macaulay weaves a historical fiction story into the book, enabling students to become involved in the entire process of building a pyramid.]*

Madison, A. (1980). *Mummies in fact and fiction*. New York: Franklin Watts.
[*Fantastic source for discussion of the use of facts in fiction from movies to literature. Photographs of mummies from several cultures as well as mummies used in movies.*]

McHargue, G. (1972). *Mummies*. New York: Lippincott.
[*Excellent reference for mummies from other cultures as well as Egyptian. This book deals with the concept of death very well. Actual photographs.*]

Millard, A. (1977). *The Egyptians*. Morristown, NJ: Silver Burdett Co.
[*Excellent general reference book. This book covers in depth all of the possible research topics from daily life to maps and general historical facts. The information is clear and straightforward.*]

Millard, A. (1979). *Ancient Egypt*. New York: Warwick Press.
[*A detailed reference book covering all of the major research topics. Actual photographs coupled with drawings emphasize the largeness of Egyptian history. Excellent for the students who want all the facts or want to go one step further.*]

Millard, A. (1987). *Great civilizations, Egypt 3118BC–AD642*. New York: Franklin Watts.
[*Excellent overview of Ancient Egyptian history. The book is broken up into the different periods of Egyptian history and the major events of each.*]

Miller, P. (1988). Riddle of the pyramid boats. *National Geographic, 173*(4), 534–550.
[*Peter Miller explores the mystery of the royal ships of Khufu. Was Khufu taken to his pyramid in one of his ships?*]

Pace, M. (1974). *Wrapped for eternity*. New York: McGraw Hill Book Co.
[*Although a little more advanced than other books cited, it is a must for the details of the mummification process. The illustrations help to make the reading accessible for readers of varying levels.*]

Perl, L. (1987). *Mummies, tombs, and treasure: Secrets of ancient Egypt*. New York: Ticknor & Fields.
[*Excellent research information with real photographs of mummies and tombs that are bound to engage any reader.*]

Purdy, S., & Sandak, C. R. (1982). *Ancient Egypt*. New York: Franklin Watts.
[*This book is a must in organizing the making of a mummy. Not only does it explain how to make a mummy, but it includes nine different projects that students may want to work on. The directions are straightforward and easy to follow. The accompanying illustrations help in visualizing the final project.*]

Putnam, J. (1993). *Eyewitness books: Mummy.* New York: Alfred A. Knopf.
[*A must for accurate and detailed information about mummies. This book covers mummies, both natural and man-made. It also covers the principles and ceremonies associated with them. Fantastic photographs. This is a book that students will want to pore over for hours at a time.*]

Robinson, C. (1984). *Ancient Egypt.* New York: Franklin Press.
[*Nice map of ancient Egypt. Useful chapter on religion.*]

Roehrig, C. (1990). *Fun with hieroglyphs.* New York: Viking.
[*This is a kit made up of the hieroglyph alphabet, a stamp pad, and a book, produced by the Metropolitan Museum of Art. The book is a fantastic resource.*]

Sibett, E. (1978). *Ancient Egyptian design: Coloring book.* New York: Dover Publications, Inc.
[*The pictures in this book are based on actual Egyptian designs. It is a fantastic source for use in decorating the sarcophagus or in designing mosaics on cellophane. This book makes art accessible to the nonartistic student.*]

Stead, M. (1985). *Ancient Egypt.* New York: Gloucester Press.
[*This is a great book to use for personal research topic choices. It has bigger print and not too much detail.*]

Unstead, R. J. (1986). *An Egyptian town.* London: Grisewood & Dempsey.
[*Excellent information on life in an Egyptian town. Actual names and places cited.*]

Wilcox, C. (1993). *Mummies and their mysteries.* Minneapolis: Carolrhoda Books.
[*A great book for teaching about mummies. It discusses mummies found around the world, including in Peru, Denmark, and the Italian Alps. This book has the best explanation of the importance of studying mummies to provide clues about past ways of life.*]

Wright, K. (1991). Tales from the crypt. *Discover, 12*(7), 54–58.
[*Explanation of the use of CAT scans in researching mummies.*]

Fiction

Bellairs, J. (1983). *The mummy, the will, and the crypt.* New York: Bantam Skylark.
[*Another adventure involving Johnny and Professor Childermass. This time Johnny wants to solve the puzzle left by an old man in order to find the old man's will and collect the $10,000 reward. An important part of the plot involves several people being mummified.*]

Bellairs, J. (1984). *The curse of the blue figurine*. New York: Bantam Skylark.
[*Johnny likes reading about ancient Egypt and the terrible curses of the Pharaoh's tombs. He never actually believes in evil spirits until he finds an old blue figurine with a message scrawled inside. This book distorts the time sequence of preparing a mummy, but it makes a nice contrast to nonfiction sources.*]

Climo, S. (1992). *The Egyptian Cinderella*. New York: Harper Trophy.
[*An Egyptian version of Cinderella set in the sixth century, B.C. A good real-aloud about a slave girl who eventually is chosen by the pharaoh to be his queen.*]

Dexter, C. (1992). *The gilded cat*. New York: Morrow Junior Books.
[*Twelve-year-old Maggie buys a mummified cat at a yard sale and is drawn into a frightening world of ancient Egyptian magic.*]

Masterman-Smith, V. (1982). *The great Egyptian heist*. New York: Four Winds Press.
[*This is a story of the adventures of Angel Wilson and Billy Beak. It all begins when they find that an Egyptian coffin in Angel's attic (her father is an archaeologist) has a false bottom with a fortune of diamonds beneath it. Fantastic source for Egyptian facts in fiction.*]

Mike, J. (1993). *Gift of the Nile: An Egyptian legend*. Mahwah, NJ: Troll Associates.
[*An interesting legend about a magical boat ride on the Nile in which a girl proves her love for a pharaoh doesn't need to be held in her heart.*]

Nixon, J. L. (1985). *The house on Hackman's Hill*. New York: Scholastic.
[*Wonderful read-aloud for uses of fact in writing fiction. Extremely engaging read-aloud.*]

Peck, R. (1986). *Blossum Culp and the sleep of death*. New York: Dell.
[*It is thought that Blossum Culp has psychic powers, so she is the natural contact for the spirit of an ancient Egyptian princess. Enraged that her tomb has been rifled and her mummy stolen, the princess Sat-Hathor threatens poor Blossum with a certain curse—unless Blossum and Alexander can locate the missing mummy.*]

Schlein, M. (1979). *I Tut, the boy who became Pharaoh*. New York: Four Winds Press.
[*A fascinating personal story of the boy who became Egypt's Pharaoh. This book is a biography based on research.*]

Snyder, Z. K. (1982). *The Egypt Game*. New York: Dell.
[*A wonderful book about two girls who become friends when they realize they both love anything to do with ancient Egypt, so they begin the Egypt Game. Is it really a*

game? Everyone begins to wonder when strange things happen. This book is great for chapter read-alouds. Otherwise, it would be better for a more advanced reader.]

Voigt, C. (1991). *The Vandermark mummy.* New York: Atheneum.
[When their father is made responsible for a collection of ancient Egyptian artifacts, twelve-year-old Phineas and his older sister, Althea, try to find out why the collection is the target of thieves, especially when the mummy disappears.]

Videos

Macaulay, D. (1988). *Pyramid.* [videocassette]. Alexandria, VA: PBS Video.

Mummies made in Egypt. (n. d.). [videocassette]. Lincoln, NE: GPN.

The curse of the Pharaoh's tomb. (1989). [videocassette]. Bethesda, MD: Terra X Series, Discovery Channel.

Index